Indiana Birds
and Their Haunts

Indiana Birds and Their Haunts

A Checklist and Finding Guide

by Charles E. Keller
Shirley A. Keller
and Timothy C. Keller

Indiana University Press   *Bloomington & London*

To Bernadette,
the non-birdwatching member of the family,
with deep affection.

Manufactured in the United States of America

Library of Congress Cataloging in Publication Data
   Keller, Charles E   1929–
      Indiana birds and their haunts.
      Bibliography: p.
      Includes index.
      1. Birds—Indiana.   2. Bird watching—Indiana.
   I. Keller, Shirley A., 1930–   joint author.
   II. Keller, Timothy C., 1954–   joint author.
   III. Title.
   QL684.I5K44   598.2'9772   78-20406
   ISBN 0-253-15437-5   1 2 3 4 5 83 82 81 80 79
   ISBN 0-253-20233-7 pbk

Contents

Part I – The Haunts

Part II – The Birds

List of Maps

Preface

It has been said that the study of science can be likened to ascending a flight of stairs, one step at a time. Each succeeding step is built upon the efforts and the work of countless others, some prominent, some obscure. All any of us can really hope for is that our endeavors might provide a portion of at least one of those steps.–Mitchell Steinberg, 1972.

While he was serving as a sectional editor for *American Birds*, the senior author was asked, "Why doesn't someone publish a finding guide to Indiana birds, with an annotated list for the southern and northern portions of the State?" The suggestion came from a resident of southern Indiana who evidently felt that the birding information then in print was inadequate for his area. Not long after that query, a northern Indiana birder made a similar request. It seemed clear that a workable yet concise finding guide and annotated list of the birds found in Indiana was needed. Because we have been "knocking around" Indiana observing birds for some time—the senior author for almost thirty-five years, the second author, in defense of home and sanity, for twenty years, and the junior author, a victim of circumstance, for twenty years as well (the fourth family member having steadfastly refused to buckle under this pressure)—we thought it possible that a collaboration, by pooling our individual talents and/or cancelling out our individual faults, might produce a book to fulfill the needs of active birders within the State, one that would serve as a handy guide to some of the "hot spots" around Indiana and to the birds that are found here.

If we have been successful, it is due to the host of talented observers —some of the leading birders in the State—who generously supplied us with notes and advice, supplemented by published results primarily from the *Indiana Audubon Quarterly*. These birders include: Tom Alexander, Delano Arvin, Kenneth Brock, Michael Brown, Alan Bruner, Harold Bruner, Dorthy Buck, William Buskirk, Larry Carter, Lee Casebere, James B. Cope, Neil Cutright, Jo Davidson, Bobbi Diehl, Steve Dierker, Jackie and Diane Elmore, Ruth Erickson, Max Forsyth, Steve Glass, Ray Grow, James Haw, Dick Heller, Edward Hopkins, Virgil Inman, Robert Krol, Lynn Lightfoot, Gene Muench, Tim Manolis, James and Amy Mason, Charles Mills, Russell Mumford, Fritz Neal, Donald Parker, Jerome Parrot, Larry Peavler, Amy Perry, Tom and Sallie Potter, Nancy Rea, Marietta Smith, Litha Smith, Anne Stamm, Alfred Starling, Nathalee Stocks, Mr. and Mrs. Francis (Frenchy) Van Huffel, Helen Weber,

Mark Weldon, Henry C. West, and Bret Whitney. We thank each of them and hope we have omitted no one. Special thanks are due to Franklin Norris, who helped with the reproduction of the maps, and to the staff of the Indiana University Press for valuable assistance and suggestions.

Based primarily on contemporary data, this guide makes no claim to being a "definitive work." But it can easily be updated and further annotated with a minimum of time and effort should you, the reader, desire to do so. We feel quite confident that you will note the important gaps in our knowledge of Indiana birdlife and hope that at least some of you will be motivated to concentrate on these "missing links" as you engage in birding around the State, thereby perhaps making some important new discoveries about the birds of Indiana.

Charles, Shirley,
and Timothy Keller
December, 1978

Introduction

This book is divided into two sections: Part I (The Haunts) is a finding guide; Part II is an expanded annotated checklist, which we have given the title, The Birds. There is a fair amount of latitudinal difference in species distribution, as noted by Cope et al. in 1952; we have incorporated their area approach in dividing the State into three areas—North, Central, and South—for the convenience of those using this book. Both sections reflect this approach. The county breakdown is as follows:

NORTH

Adams	DeKalb	Jay	Newton	Tippecanoe
Allen	Elkhart	Kosciusko	Noble	Tipton
Benton	Fulton	Lagrange	Porter	Wabash
Blackford	Grant	Lake	Pulaski	Warren
Carroll	Howard	LaPorte	St. Joseph	Wells
Cass	Huntington	Marshall	Starke	White
Clinton	Jasper	Miami	Steuben	Whitley

CENTRAL

Bartholomew	Fountain	Jackson	Morgan	Rush
Boone	Franklin	Jennings	Ohio	Shelby
Brown	Greene	Johnson	Owen	Sullivan
Clay	Hamilton	Madison	Parke	Union
Dearborn	Hancock	Marion	Putnam	Vermillion
Decatur	Hendricks	Monroe	Randolph	Vigo
Delaware	Henry	Montgomery	Ripley	Wayne
Fayette				

1

SOUTH

Clark*	Gibson	Lawrence	Pike	Switzerland
Crawford	Harrison	Martin	Posey	Vanderburgh
Daviess	Jefferson	Orange	Scott	Warrick
Dubois	Knox	Perry	Spencer	Washington
Floyd				

Part I presents birding areas numbered sequentially from north to south, and the numbered map on the facing page roughly indicates their locations. However, it is best to use the Guide in conjunction with an Indiana road map. Although not all birding areas have been included, we have tried not to miss any of the important ones. In some areas where there has been intensive observation, we have included maps that provide specific locations in which certain species are known to have been seen. In others, where extensive literature exists, we have added references for further study. For the convenience of the overnight traveler, accommodations, where known, are included, either within the area described or in the nearest city or town.

A note on birding etiquette: Two busloads of avid birders recently encroached on private property in southeastern Arizona. Not having had the courtesy to seek prior permission from the owner, they were asked to leave. Since then, all birders have been refused entrance to that particular property—another case of the inconsiderate few spoiling things for the responsible majority. We feel sure that most of you share our concern about some birders' trespassing on private property. Areas described in this book are not always automatically accessible to birders. They are sometimes on private property, and if entry is desired permission should be obtained in advance from the owners. In most fish and wildlife areas there are well-marked, off-limits portions during certain seasons or years. These areas are reserved for hunting and fishing enthusiasts who pay for the upkeep and use of the land, but birders reap the benefits during off-season periods. Your respect for private property laws and for the rules regarding fish and wildlife preserves will ensure continued use of these areas for future generations of birders.

In Part II we have followed the sequence and nomenclature used in the American Birding Association Checklist for 1975 and its supplements. We realize that there are some discrepancies between it and the current A.O.U. Check-List and its supplements, but feel that the former is more realistic and therefore preferable.

* Data from the Falls of the Ohio have not been used in Part II, since that area was thoroughly covered by Mengel (1965).

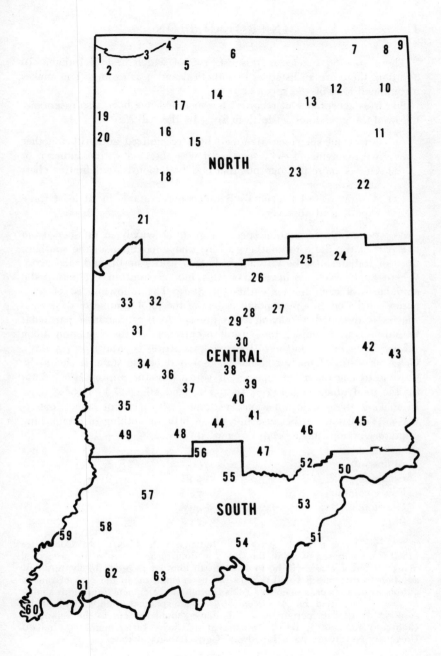

There are 363 species in this list, 166 of which nest in Indiana. In addition, there are 16 listed as hypothetical and 3 as exotics. This makes a combined total of 382 species.

So far as acceptance of records° is concerned, we have also essentially followed the guidelines set forth in 1975 by the A.B.A.:

(1) An extant specimen identified by a recognized authority together with convincing evidence that it was obtained within Indiana; or

(2) One or more photographs that clearly demonstrate definitive characteristics; or

(3) A sight record backed by detailed observations by at least three experienced observers.

As we said above, certain species can differ widely in numbers from one part of the State to another; a bird that is common in the southern third of Indiana may be virtually unknown in the north, and vice versa. Where applicable, we have taken this into account in evaluating the abundance of each species within the State. The following list of categories was based on a percentage system of the total number of days each species is recorded as having been present in the area in a particular season. As an example, the spring occurrence of the Common Loon (*Gavia immer*) in northern Indiana (10 April–15 May) is 35 days. Given its status of fairly common in that part of the state, it should be possible to encounter this species, if you are in the appropriate habitat for the total time, on between 18 (51%) and 26 (74%) of these days. In making these determinations, extreme dates (except some "out-of-season" occurrences), because they mean little or nothing in establishing migratory periods, have been disregarded.

Abundant	100%
Common	75–99%
Fairly common	50–74%
Uncommon	25–49%
Rare	5–24%

° As we were going to press, the Indiana State Check List Committee (ISCLC), composed of six of the state's leading birders, was in the process of being formed. Its task will be to evaluate all unusual records. Briefly, any new addition to the state list will require full agreement, or, in the case of rare or out-of-season records, a majority of this committee. Documentation forms similar to those being used for *American Birds*, but expanded slightly, will be incorporated. All data pertaining to the above should be sent to the committee chairman: Kenneth J. Brock, Indiana State Check List Committee, Indiana University Northwest, 3400 Broadway, Gary, Indiana 46408.

Very rare (absent some years)   1–4%
Casual (absent most years)   1%
Accidental   Out of normal range
Hypothetical   Insufficient evidence for admission to the main list
Extirpated   Species may occur in other states but no longer occurs in Indiana
Extinct   Species believed to be extinct
Exotic   Species believed to have escaped either from public or private collections and which have not established themselves over the past 20 years
§   before species' name denotes breeding in state within last 30 years
Migrant   Refers to species that arrive in the State during the spring and depart during the late summer/fall, either passing through the State or, in some cases, nesting, but so differentiated from true summer residents
Resident   Species that occur year-round
Summer Resident   Species that breed in the area
Summer Visitant   Species that occur primarily from post-breeding season incursions
Winter Visitant or Resident   Species that occur during the winter

In addition to the above, we used two modifiers: *local*, to indicate species with colonial nesting habits or limited distribution; and *irregular*, for cyclic eruptions.

We realize these criteria are rather complicated, but believe that the reader who keeps them in mind will benefit by having a more accurate guide than would be provided by a more simplistic system.

In all instances where it was available we have provided information on the former status of each species, much of it taken from Amos W. Butler's 1898 *Birds of Indiana*, so that the reader may easily visualize the changes that have taken place over the years. It is fascinating to conjecture about the reasons for these changes, and about the ones that are sure to occur in the future, undoubtedly rendering some of our estimates out of date, but more importantly, playing a major role in making birding the absorbing occupation that it is.

Part I
The Haunts

NORTH

1.
HAMMOND DUMP

DESCRIPTION AND BIRDING AREAS: The Hammond Dump can be reached by taking Interstate 94 to the Burr Street exit near the Gary—Hammond City Limit line. Turn north on Burr Street to 15th Street and then turn west for four blocks to Calhoun Street. Park at the dead end of Calhoun Street. As the name implies, this area is nothing more than a landfill. Despite the unnatural conditions, it is an excellent place for viewing gulls, particularly in the winter. Herring, Ring-billed, Glaucous, Iceland, and Greater Black-backed Gulls have all been observed here, and sightings of any of the other midwestern gulls are possible. On occasion as many as 5,000–6,000 gulls are present during December, January, and February.

ACCOMMODATIONS: Nearby Hammond and Gary have many motels and restaurants.

2.
WOLF LAKE
CEDAR LAKE
LAKE GEORGE

DESCRIPTION AND BIRDING AREAS: This highly industrialized northwest portion of Lake County is not as attractive to birds now as it was earlier in the century. Wilson's Phalarope, Yellow-headed Blackbird, and other unusual species nested at one time in this area.

Wolf Lake is now bisected by Interstate 90 and looks like a disaster area. Industrial refuse, raw sewage, and pollution have taken their toll. Southeast, near the Hobart area (Highway 51), Lake George has fared only slightly better but, while unattractive to birders, may still harbor a few unusual finds. Further south, and just off Highway 41, Cedar Lake has produced American Avocet and has been extensively birded by Chicago bird clubs.

Visiting and area birders should explore what remaining possibilities exist before complete destruction overtakes the region.

ACCOMMODATIONS: Many motels near Highway 41 and Interstate 65.

9

REFERENCES:
Baker, F. C. (1897) Collecting about Chicago. *Sports Afield* 19:112.
Bognar, A. J. (1951) Wilson's Phalarope and Yellow-headed Blackbird. *Indiana Audubon Quarterly* 29:11–12.
Butler, A. W. (1937) Common Tern and Wilson's Phalarope nesting in northern Indiana. *Auk* 54:390.
Eifrig, C. W. G. (1919) Notes on birds of the Chicago area and its immediate vicinity. *Auk* 36:513–524.
Ford, E. R. (1956) *Birds of the Chicago region.* Chicago Academy of Sciences Spec. Pub. No. 12, 117 pp.
Lewy, A. (1930) European Widgeon (*Mareca penelope*) on Wolf Lake, Chicago. *Auk* 47:552.
Woodruff, F. M. (1907) *The birds of the Chicago area.* Natural History Survey, Bull Nᴏ VI, Chicago Academy of Sciences. 221 pp.

3.
INDIANA DUNES NATIONAL LAKESHORE

DESCRIPTION: The area between Gary and Michigan City has long been a magnet for birders. The dunes were formed from uncovered quartz that was left exposed to the wind and waves when the water level receded after the Ice Age. Because of its diversity of environments, a wide variety of plants, some unique, is found in this region.

The National Lakeshore occupies four separate areas: (1) West Beach Area, characterized by interdunal ponds, forested dunes, prairie areas, and Long Lake. (2) Baily Area, containing the Joseph Baily homestead, a historic cemetery, the Chellburg Farm, and part of the Little Calumet River Basin. (3) Furnessville-Tremont Area with two historic dune ridges formed during early, higher stages of the Lake. (4) Mount Baldy Area, a huge, active dune that is moving slowly southward, in the process burying an oak woodlot.

Under development is Cowles Bog Area consisting of a quaking bog, a sedge prairie, and a wetland woods. The Indiana Dunes State Park is sandwiched in among these areas and offers extensive dunes, beach, and hiking trails.

The variety of habitat and location at the southern extremity of Lake Michigan have produced the following rarities: White-winged, Surf, and Black Scoters, Swallow-tailed Kite, Piping Plover (formerly nested), Pomarine, Parasitic, and Long-tailed Jaegers, Sabine's Gull, Roseate Tern, Burrowing Owl, Boreal Chickadee, and Hoary Redpoll. In addition, many

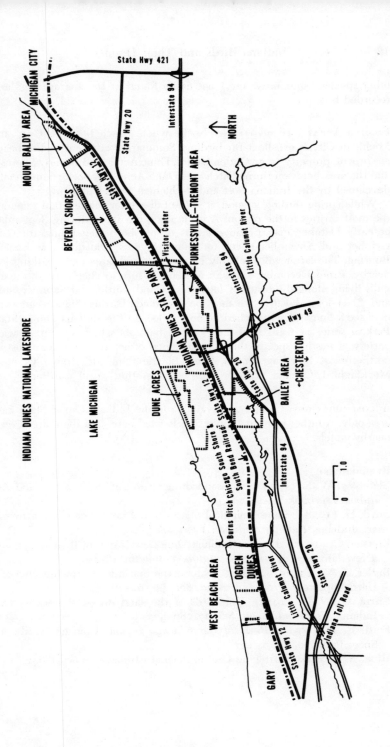

other species (shorebirds, etc.) not easily found in Indiana are regularly recorded here.

BIRDING AREAS (see map): Nearly the whole beach between Gary and Michigan City is excellent for birding. Some areas adjacent to the beach are private property (e.g., Ogden Dunes, Dune Acres, and Beverly Shores), and the area between Burns Ditch and Dune Acres has been commercially developed by the Indiana Port and Bethlehem Steel Company.

While spring birding is good, it is the fall–winter seasons that generate the most rarities in the region. A walk along the shore during September or early October may produce sights of off-shore jaeger migration. In October and November check for Brant, Scoters, Oldsquaw, and Snow Bunting. The latter will probably be on the beach area or in parking lots nearby. From December through March, be sure to check out the many gulls flying along the beach: Glaucous, Iceland, Little, and Sabine's Gulls and Black-legged Kittiwake may be observed. During flight years, you may see a Snowy Owl perched on an ice floe. In the Indiana Dunes State Park, a series of trails lead into various habitats which support a wide variety of nesting species that have reached either their southernmost or northernmost breeding ranges. Some of these include Brown Creeper, Mockingbird, Canada Warbler (suspected nesting), and Cardinal.

ACCOMMODATIONS: Camping is available in the Indiana Dunes State Park area only. A rather primitive inn is also located here, and there are several nearby motels.

REFERENCES:

Blatchley, W. S. (1934) The sand dune region of Indiana, *Indiana Audubon Yearbook* 10–16.

Boyd, D. (1938) Some ecological phases of the sand dunes of northwestern Indiana. *Indiana Audubon Yearbook* 9–20.

Bretsch, C. (1927) Birds of Indiana Dunes, extension of their range, and a few late records. *Indiana Audubon Bulletin* 18–19.

Butler, A. W. (1925) Strange visitors: the Starling, Burrowing Owl and Harris' Sparrow. *Proc. Ind. Acad. Sci.* 34:162–168.

Eifrig, C. W. G. (1918) The birds of the sand dunes of northwestern Indiana. *Proc. Ind. Acad. Sci.* 27:280–303.

Ford, E. R. (1956) *Birds of the Chicago region.* Chicago Acad. Sci. Spec. Pub. No. 12, 1–117.

Hine, A. (1924) Burrowing Owl in northern Indiana. *Auk* 41:602.

Landing, J. (1966) Jaeger migration in northwestern Indiana. *Indiana Audubon Quarterly* 44:32–37.

Pitcher, E. B. (1974a) Breeding bird survey; Indiana Dunes. *Indiana Audubon Quarterly* 52:32–33.

———— (1974b) Breeding bird survey; Indiana Dunes. *Indiana Audubon Quarterly* 52:120–127.

Russell, R. (1973) The extirpation of the Piping Plover as a breeding species in Illinois and Indiana. *The Audubon Bulletin* (Illinois), Summer 1973:46–48.

Schantz, O. M. (1932) Birds of the sand dunes. *Indiana Audubon Yearbook* 22–24.

Segal, S. (1960) Bird tragedy at the Dunes. *Indiana Audubon Quarterly* 38:23-25.

Smith, H. M. (1936) Notes on the birds of the Calumet and Dune regions. Mimeo, 40 pp.

———— (1950) Notes on the birds of the Chicago region. *Auk* 67:109–110.

Southern, W. E. (1974) Seasonal distribution of Great Lakes region Ring-billed Gulls. *The Jack Pine Warbler* 52(4) 155–179.

Stoddard, H. L. (1917) The Roseate Tern (*Sterna dougalli*) on Lake Michigan. *Auk* 34:86.

———— (1921) Rare birds in the Indiana sand dunes. *Auk* 39:124.

West, H. C. (1954) A wintering Sanderling in Lake County, Indiana. *Indiana Audubon Quarterly* 32:62.

Woodruff, F. M. (1907) *The birds of the Chicago area.* Natural History Survey, Bull. No. VI, Chicago Academy of Sciences. 221 pp.

4.
MICHIGAN CITY

DESCRIPTION AND BIRDING AREAS: Situated on Lake Michigan, Michigan City has long been considered one of Indiana's finest birding locales. A wide sand beach coupled with a long stone jetty and accompanying breakwater produce a habitat for many varieties of shorebirds as well as for the more lake-oriented species. To reach the jetty drive north on U.S. 421 to 9th Street. Take 9th Street east to Pine Street and then go north to Washington Park. The park borders the Lake and a parking lot is located only a short distance from the jetty, so very little actual walking is required. Dress warmly, for winter temperatures and the brisk north wind can become quite uncomfortable.

A walk out to the end of the jetty puts one in the area most advantageous for viewing. From here the lake harbor and the breakwater can readily be seen at the same time. A spotting scope is of great value from this point. Another short walk out on the nearby boat docks can be rewarding, for an occasional Old Squaw or Scoter may be hiding under them.

Trail Creek, which terminates into Lake Michigan just west of the jetty, is a great place for winter waterfowl. The water in the creek is warmed from use in the city sewage treatment plant and remains comparatively ice-free during severe weather. In the sheltered water large concentrations of waterfowl are sometimes recorded. To reach this area, drive south from Washington Park on U.S. 421 about three-fourths to one mile, then east on any available street that crosses the creek. Because most of the land bordering the creek is privately owned, most of the viewing must be done from one of the bridges that cross over it.

Over the years quite a number of Midwest rarities have been sighted from the harbor and in Trail Creek. Listed below are only a few of these: Western and Eared Grebe, Harlequin Duck, King Eider, Black Scoter, Purple Sandpiper, Red Phalarope, Little Gull, Iceland Gull, Glaucous Gull, at least two Jaegers, and a Magnificent Frigatebird. While the end of November and the beginning of December is the best time for rarities, any time between October and May can produce a good trip.

ACCOMMODATIONS: Hotels and motels, including a Holiday Inn, can be found quite readily in Michigan City, as can restaurants. Boat docking facilities are available at the harbor; and, for the information of fishermen, Michigan City is labeled "the Coho Capital of the World."

REFERENCES:

Brock, K. J. (1977) Thankgiving Day at "The Harbor," Michigan City. *Indiana Audubon Quarterly* 55:9–11.

———— (in press) Bird life of the Michigan City Harbor area. *Indiana Audubon Quarterly.*

Buskirk, W. (1962) List of birds—Michigan City—Dunes 1962. *Indiana Audubon Quarterly* 40:63–64.

Grow, R. (1952) Rare and semi-rare winter visitants in northern Indiana. *Indiana Audubon Quarterly* 30:31–34.

Heaton, G. (1951) Purple Sandpiper, *Erolia maritima. Indiana Audubon Quarterly* 29:22.

Landing, J. (1962) Exotic bird records for Michigan City, LaPorte County, Indiana. *Indiana Audubon Quarterly* 40:15–16.

———— (1963) The occurrence of Arctic species in Michigan City, Indiana. *Indiana Audubon Quarterly* 41:63–64.

———— (1966) Jaeger migration in northwestern Indiana. *Indiana Audubon Quarterly* 44:32–37.

Mumford, R. E. (1956) Little Gull taken in Indiana. *Wilson Bulletin* 68:321.

———— (1957) Specimen records for Indiana birds. *Indiana Audubon Quarterly* 35:18–19.

Segal, S. (1953) Michigan City harbor observations. *Indiana Audubon Quarterly* 31:37–38.

———— (1954) Additional notes from Michigan City. *Indiana Audubon Quarterly* 32:8–10.

5.
KINGSBURY STATE FISH AND WILDLIFE AREA

DESCRIPTION AND BIRDING AREAS: Two large marshes, extensive grasslands, and the wooded Kankakee River bottoms support many species of birds at Kingsbury Fish and Wildlife Area 6 miles southeast of LaPorte on County Road 500S. off Highway 35. Established during World War II as an ammunition assembly and supply depot, it still has "contaminated" portions where the possibility exists of finding active land mines and explosives. These areas are of course strictly off limits to birders and other visitors.

The marshes attract large numbers of waterfowl and herons during the spring. Occasionally, during late March or early April, the Greater White-fronted Goose can be observed. Late April and early May might turn up a Wilson's Phalarope. The adjoining grassland is good for Grasshopper Sparrow and Bobolink during the summer and for Common Redpoll and Short-eared Owl during the winter. It is also during the latter season that large numbers of Northern Harriers abound and a Shrike or Snowy Owl is possible. The hedgerows which border the fields attract large flocks of sparrows at all times of the year.

During "winter finch years" check the stand of pines near the campground for crossbills or, if you are lucky, the rare Pine Grosbeak. The pines also are a logical place to search for owls, accipiters, and small land birds, which utilize them for cover.

The wooded Kankakee River bottoms host large numbers of migrating warblers with various species of woodpeckers a sure bet. During the winter large flocks of icterids, including Rusty, Brewer's, and Red-winged Blackbirds, occur.

ACCOMMODATIONS: A campground (well-shaded by pine trees) is in the area. For those preferring motels, nearby LaPorte has several. Further information can be obtained by writing: Kingsbury State Fish and Wildlife Area, R.R. #4, Box 242, LaPorte, Indiana.

6.
SOUTH BEND AREA

DESCRIPTION AND BIRDING AREAS: The South Bend Area includes:

1. St. Joseph River: Take U.S. 31 to Riverside Drive. Follow the river north about 4 miles. This is an excellent area for ducks during the winter. Species recorded include: Common Goldeneye, Barrow's Goldeneye, Bufflehead, Common Merganser, Red-breasted Merganser; during the winter of 1976–77, five Mute Swans were seen.

2. South Bend Audubon Society Sanctuary: Located in adjacent Mishawaka at 59395 Clover Road just south of George Wilson Park. Here the local Audubon Chapter maintains an attractive sanctuary, with a small pond and a well-kept series of trails that permit splendid views of migratory species.

3. Izaak Walton League Sanctuary: Located about ½ mile east of where the four-mile bridge crosses the St. Joseph River. During the winter of 1976–77, John Buck observed a Varied Thrush that was also seen and photographed by a number of other observers.

4. Rum Village Park: Located west of U.S. 31 on Ewing Avenue. Has a small, attractive nature center and a variety of habitat. A nearby area along Bowman Creek is quite productive for American and Least Bitterns; occasionally, a rail is sighted.

ACCOMMODATIONS: Nearby motels and restaurants in South Bend.

REFERENCES:

Buck, J. (1977) A Varied Thrush in St. Joseph County, Indiana. *Indiana Audubon Quarterly* 55:3.

Dufendach, R., and Dufendach, M. (1973) A Green-tailed Towhee in Indiana. *Indiana Audubon Quarterly* 51:93.

Eckmans, E. (1926) My observation of birds at Notre Dame. *Indiana Audubon Bulletin* 17–21.

Inman, V., Inman, C., and Dierker, S. (1977) Mute Swans on St. Joseph
River, South Bend. *Indiana Audubon Quarterly* 55:44.

Meek, D. (1954) Rare winter visitors to St. Joseph's County. *Indiana Audubon Quarterly* 32:48–49.

7.
PIGEON RIVER FISH AND WILDLIFE AREA

DESCRIPTION AND BIRDING AREAS: Consisting of over 13,000 acres, Pigeon River Fish and Wildlife Area is considered one of Indiana's better birding spots. It is located in the northeast portion of Indiana between State Roads 3 and 327 and just north of State Road 20. A rich diversity of habitat—mixed farmland, scrubby pastureland, wetlands, and forests—attracts over 200 species, including 29 species of warblers and 26 species of waterfowl.

The established waterfowl resting area attracts most of the State's species of ducks as well as an occasional Whistling Swan and Greater White-fronted Goose. This marsh area is equally good for herons, Sandhill Crane, and several species of rails in season.

The fields adjoining the above area have produced many species of warblers, sparrows, and such rarities as Northern Shrike, Short-eared Owl, and Yellow Rail. It is here that the Alder Flycatcher can quite frequently be found.

The campground near the river should not be overlooked for good numbers of waterfowl. The area is also good for several shorebirds: Dunlin, Short-billed Dowitcher, and an assortment of "peeps," while the trees draw a large number of woodpeckers and nuthatches as well as many species of warblers in both spring and fall.

Check the numerous pine groves for owls and several species of hawks, including Northern Goshawk in the winter. The adjacent farmlands often produce large numbers of Lapland Longspur, Snow Bunting, and on at least one occasion a Snowy Owl.

ACCOMMODATIONS: Camping facilities are available within the area. For further information write: Pigeon River Fish and Wildlife Area, R.R. #2, Howe, Indiana.

REFERENCES:
Casebere, L., and Weldon, M. (1975) Birds of the Pigeon River State Fish and Game Area. Mimeo (unpublished).

Weldon, M. (1977) The Veery in northeastern Indiana. *Indiana Audubon Quarterly* 55:6–8.

8.
POKAGON STATE PARK

DESCRIPTION: Pokagon State Park is located on U.S. 27 near Angola. Bounded by Lake James and Snow Lake, amid the rolling hills of Indiana's lake country, it offers good birding year-round. The park takes its name from a famous chief of the Potawatomi tribe who transferred to the government approximately a million acres of land, including what is now Chicago, at a price of three cents an acre. Established in 1925, it contains some 1,173 acres of mixed hardwoods, marshes, and lake frontage. Some birds that are characteristic of this region are not easily found in any other part of the state. These include: American and Least Bitterns, King, Virginia, and Sora Rails, Black Tern, Marsh and Sedge Wrens, Blue-winged Warbler and the hybrid Brewster's Warbler.

The abundance of large, marshy areas provides excellent habitats for the above-named species. During the winter the erratic winter finch invasions are, at times, impressive.

BIRDING AREAS: A system of excellent trails offers the birder unusual opportunities to observe a wide variety of species. Trail 1 from the wildlife exhibit through a hardwood forest borders Lake James and is a good area to observe waterfowl. Trail 2 from the campground leads to Snow Lake where both species of bitterns, rails, and Black Tern are sometimes observed. Trails 3 and 6 meander through marshy areas where both Marsh and Sedge Wrens can be found. Trail 4 leads through hardwood forest and rolling land. Be sure to check the fringe areas for Blue-winged Warbler. Trail 5 begins near the campground and goes to the picnic area near the bathhouse. It passes through a deep woods and is a good trail to observe migratory warblers and spring flowers.

ACCOMMODATIONS: There are four campgrounds in the park and Potawatomi Inn has long been noted for its meals and service. Since it is an active winter resort, reservations are difficult to obtain during that season; however, there are numerous motels nearby. For information and reservations write: Reservations Clerk, Potawatomi Inn, Angola, Indiana 46703.

REFERENCE:
Spangler, I. (1948) Pokagon State Park. *Indiana Audubon Yearbook* 54.

9.
MARSH LAKE WETLANDS AREA

DESCRIPTION AND BIRDING AREAS: Located in Steuben County a short distance east of Pokagon State Park and Highway 27, the Marsh Lake Wetlands Area is owned by the State and is open to the public. Travel is best by canoe, and there are no marked trails. Breeding birds include: Veery, Least Flycatcher, Sedge (Short-billed Marsh) Wren, and Swamp Sparrow. The area has great potential and should be visited by knowledgable birders.

ACCOMMODATIONS: Nearby Pokagon State Park has an excellent Inn and campgrounds.

10.
CEDAR CREEK

DESCRIPTION AND BIRDING AREAS: Lee A. Casebere, who has birded in the area, writes: "The upper reaches of this stream run through DeKalb County, but the best of it dumps into the St. Joseph's River. The lower end of the DeKalb County segment and all of the Allen County segment are a part of the Indiana Wild, Scenic, and Recreational River System. Cedar Creek is canoeable in spring and early summer. The stream cuts deeply into the surrounding terrain and there is a steep dropoff of 50 feet or more from the general upland terrain down to the flood plain. The flood plain is very wet in places and all of it is moist woodland even in the driest situations.

"This area is probably the breeding place of some of the most unusual birds in our region, but nearly all of it is in private ownership and access is not easy. The Fort Wayne Chapter of the Izaak Walton League owns a nice chunk of land along the river and one can obtain permission from them to bird on this land.

"Some interesting birds noted, including a Great Blue Heron rookery along the river." Other birds include: Veery, Yellow-throated Warbler, Yellow-crowned Night Heron, Northern Parula Warbler, and Pileated Woodpecker.

ACCOMMODATIONS: Motels at nearby Fort Wayne.

11.
FORT WAYNE AREA

DESCRIPTION AND BIRDING AREAS: The Fort Wayne area includes the following regions:

1. Fox Island. A 381-acre tract located 6 miles southwest of the city at 7324 Yohne Road, approximately 3 miles south of the U.S. 24 and I-69 interchange. Habitat consists of a wind-deposited sand dune which is forested with oak and hickory that rises forty feet above a marsh. More than 10,000 years ago the fine sand of the dune was deposited to become an island in the Fort Wayne–Huntington sluiceway, the drainoff from the receding Wisconsin glacier. Organized as a natural area for outdoor education, with a Nature Center, it relies almost entirely on volunteer efforts. Fox Island is heavily birded and has produced an impressive list of over 170 species. Breeding birds include: Least Flycatcher, Veery, White-eyed Vireo, Yellow-throated Vireo, Blue-winged Warbler, Hooded Warbler, Kentucky Warbler, Yellow-breasted Chat. During the winter of 1975–76 3 species of Chickadees were recorded: Black-capped, Carolina, and Boreal. The latter bird remained for a considerable time. A borrow pit, just south of the park, has produced a Surf Scoter.

2. Franke Park. Located southeast of the U.S. 30 and I-69 interchange on Goshen Avenue, it contains a zoo and recreational facilities. A small lake occasionally attracts ducks during migration.

3. Foster Park. Located on Rudisill Boulevard approximately 2 miles west of Highway 1 (Lafayette Road), it borders the St. Mary's River. It attracts quite a few birds during migration.

4. Hurshtown Reservoir. Located southeast of Fort Wayne in Allen County, it is a backup water supply for Fort Wayne. Access is difficult because it is fenced in and permission must be obtained from the caretaker to enter. Good area for loons, grebes, diving ducks, gulls, and terns.

ACCOMMODATIONS: Many nearby motels and hotels in Fort Wayne.

REFERENCES:
Anonymous (1973) Fox Island bird study project. *Indiana Audubon Quarterly* 51:24–25.
Spangler, I., and Haw, J. (1975) Fox Island bird study project. *Indiana Audubon Quarterly* 53:15–16.

12.
NOBLE COUNTY AREA

DESCRIPTION AND BIRDING AREAS: The Noble County Area consists of the following regions:

1. Chain-O-Lakes State Park. Located 5 miles southeast of Albion on Highway 9, it contains 2,678 acres. Eleven small connecting lakes provide about 186 acres of water and 6½ miles of widely varying shoreline. A series of eight hiking trails covers a variety of habitat—wooded areas, swamps, and open fields. It has not been extensively birded.

2. Mallard Roost Wetlands Area. Stretching along the south branch of the Little Elkhart River between Ligonier and Albion, it is one of the largest remaining wetland areas in the state. Land access is difficult, so canoe travel is the best method of exploring this potentially highly productive region. Several county roads cross the river where canoe launching is permissible.

3. Merry Lea Environmental Center. It is located southwest of Wolf Lake, off Highway 109. Drive south of Wolf Lake to County Road 350S. Turn right (east) about one mile to County Road 500W., thence north to the Center (naturalist on duty every weekday from 8:00–5:00 and from 9:00–5:00 on Saturday). The Center's phone numbers are 799–5869 and 799–4151. This area includes some 900 acres of land around Bear Lake and High Lake which have been extensively birded but need more summer work. The Center offers numerous nature-related activities.

ACCOMMODATIONS: Campground available at Chain-O-Lakes State Park and motels in nearby Fort Wayne.

13.
TRI-COUNTY FISH AND WILDLIFE AREA

DESCRIPTION AND BIRDING AREAS: Located 6 miles southeast of Syracuse, bordered by State Road 13 on the west and State Road 5 on the east, Tri-County Fish and Wildlife Area contains about 3,000 acres of small ponds, marshes, and wet, boggy land. It has not received the attention birdwise that some of the nearby areas like Lake Wawasee or Winona Lake have, but should be a fertile field for ornithological exploration. Species that breed or are suspected to have bred there include: Pied-billed Grebe, American and Least Bitterns, Gadwall, Wood Duck, and Black Tern. The junior author spent part of a day in early April here and was impressed by the large number of migratory waterfowl, particularly dabbling ducks. The northern edge of the area borders Lake Wawasee. This, the largest natural lake in Indiana, is an excellent area for Common Loon and diving ducks. Two other rather large lakes in the same general vicinity are Tippecanoe Lake, near North Webster, and Winona Lake, near Warsaw. Both have been heavily birded in the past, but have not drawn much attention in recent years. It may well be that increased use by boaters et al. has made these areas less attractive to waterfowl than they once were.

ACCOMMODATIONS: Motels available in Warsaw and camping facilities are in the general area.

REFERENCES:
Test, L. A., and Esten, S. R. (1924) Observations on summer birds of Winona Lake, with a list of species. *Proc. Ind. Acad. Sci.* 33:403–408.
———— (1925) Further notes on summer birds of Winona Lake. *Proc. Ind. Acad. Sci.* 34:357–359.

14.
LAKE MAXINKUCKEE
BASS LAKE

DESCRIPTION AND BIRDING AREAS: Both areas can be reached by traveling west of U.S. 31 on State Highway 10 just west of Argos. Lake Maxinkuckee was extensively studied forty to fifty years ago, while Bass Lake has received only a few passing references in literature. The former lake is near the site of Culver Military Academy.

Before the impoundment of several large reservoirs, these lakes attracted large numbers of migratory waterfowl. It is assumed that they still offer some attraction to them and may provide fair birding during times of peak migratory passages.

ACCOMMODATIONS: Nearby motels available at Rochester.

REFERENCES:
Esten, S. R. (1936) Summer birds of Culver and vicinity. *Indiana Audubon Yearbook* 6–10.
Evermann, B. W., and Clark, J. (1920) *Lake Maxinkuckee. A physical and biological survey*, Vol. 1. (Indianapolis: Indiana Department of Conservation), pp. 481–579.

LeNeve, S. W. (1937) Ruddy Turnstones at Bass Lake. *Indiana Audubon Yearbook* 92.

Perkins, S. E. (1927) Notes on birds of Lake Maxinkuckee region. *Proc. Ind. Acad. Sci.* 36:461.

——— (1938) Additional notes on birds of Lake Maxinkuckee. *American Midland Naturalist* 20:(3)540–548.

Rossier, C. W. (1932) The Culver Bird Sanctuary. *Indiana Audubon Yearbook* 20–22.

15.
WINAMAC FISH AND WILDLIFE–TIPPECANOE RIVER AREAS

DESCRIPTION AND BIRDING AREAS: Consisting of over 6,000 acres, Tippecanoe River State Park lies east of U.S. 35. Winamac Fish and Wildlife Area lies immediately west of that same highway about 5 miles north of the town of Winamac. Neither area has been extensively birded.

The land in this region has a high sand content and offers a variety of habitats: oak forests, pine plantation, abandoned fields, marshes, and the river. Group Camp #1, also called Pottawattomie, is near the area where Amos W. Butler spent several days, almost fifty years ago, studying the bird life prior to its existence as a state park.

ACCOMMODATIONS: There are two group campgrounds and motels in nearby Winamac.

REFERENCE:
Butler, A. W. (1930) Pottawattomie Lodge. *Indiana Audubon Bulletin* 30–32.

16.
JASPER-PULASKI

DESCRIPTION: Jasper-Pulaski Game Preserve was established in 1929 and impounded in 1934. Since about 1945, local Audubon societies have made semiannual treks to this area during March and October to see one of Indiana's most outstanding spectacles, the migration of the Sandhill Cranes. During the early years a flock of 500 was considered unusual. Now they number in the thousands, and during the fall of 1976 an estimated 13,000 cranes visited the preserve. Cranes begin to arrive at

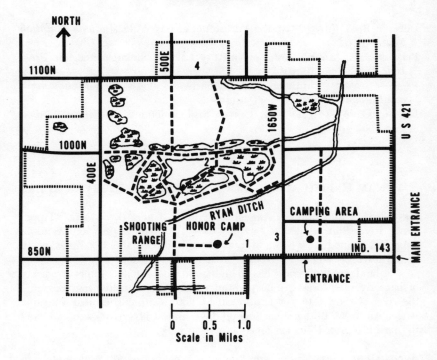

the refuge in the spring on about 10 March and depart usually by 15 April. During the fall, they appear about 15 September and depart about 5 December. It is during the peak periods of these migrations (around 1 April and 15 October) that the cranes are the easiest to see as they fly to and from their feeding grounds in the area. Visitors to the area may be required to register at the headquarters, particularly during the fall hunting season. Information concerning the cranes can usually be obtained there also.

The varied habitat of Jasper-Pulaski creates optimal conditions for many species, but it is the waterfowl and crane migrations that generate the most interest. Dabbling ducks are common during migratory periods in both spring and fall. Unusual birds recorded include Eurasian Wigeon and Fulvous Whistling Duck.

Interested birders may also enjoy a trip to the north portion of the 7,500-acre preserve for an excursion through a typical prairie—a remnant of original Indiana prairie land. Here a variety of prairie plants may be found that are unique to this region.

BIRDING AREAS (see map):
   1. Observation tower gives a good overview of surrounding areas. Sandhill Cranes can usually be seen flying to and from feeding grounds.
   2. Observation tower that overlooks the larger portion of one of the refuge's lakes. During peak migratory periods of March–April and again during September–November large flocks of waterfowl can be seen.
   3. Headquarters parking lot. In flight years large numbers of Pine Siskins inhabit the many hemlock trees that surround the parking lot. Not far from this area are a wildlife exhibit and a small pond where many captive waterfowl are displayed. Fringing the pond are Purple Martin houses that normally contain a good population of this species.
   4. Original prairie region. Good area for prairie-loving species.

ACCOMMODATIONS: Nearby motels are located at both Rensselaer and Winamac. Camping is permitted within designated areas.

REFERENCES:
Barnes, W. B. (1946) Bird refuges in Indiana. *Indiana Audubon Yearbook* 5–7.
Gorrell, P. H. (1945) Sandhill Cranes of Jasper-Pulaski Game Preserve. *Indiana Audubon Yearbook* 38–39.
Lindsey, A. A. et al. (1969) *Natural areas in Indiana and their preservation* (Lafayette: Indiana Natural Areas Survey), pp. 503–507.
Mumford, R. E. (1950) And the Sandhills dance. *Indiana Audubon Quarterly* 28:82–86.
Walkinshaw, L. H. (1950) Sizes of spring flocks of the Sandhill Cranes at Jasper-Pulaski Game Preserve, Indiana. *Indiana Audubon Quarterly* 28:78–82.
———— (1956) Sandhill Crane observations at Jasper-Pulaski Game Preserve. *Indiana Audubon Quarterly* 34:22–30.

17.
KANKAKEE AREA

DESCRIPTION AND BIRDING AREAS: Located about 10 miles north of North Judson, at the junction of State Road 10 and 39 near where the Kankakee River and the Yellow River converge, Kankakee Fish and Wildlife Area consists of a series of marshes and river habitat that are attractive to waterfowl and in particular to dabbling ducks. A good area to visit in the spring, it is heavily hunted during the fall-winter waterfowl season and at that time is closed to birdwatchers.

ACCOMMODATIONS: Camping areas at nearby Bass Lake. Motels available at Knox.

18.
LAKE SHAFER
LAKE FREEMAN

DESCRIPTION AND BIRDING AREAS: Located in White County about 20 miles northeast of Lafayette, the two lakes are separated by U.S. 24 at Monticello. Both areas are quite commercialized and heavily built up, with many cabins and homes, and neither has been heavily birded; consequently, little is known of their birdlife. The senior author visited here during the first week of April, at the height of the duck migration, many years ago, and found many Lesser Scaup and Ring-necked Ducks at both lakes.

ACCOMMODATIONS: There are several cabins for rent, and camping is available.

19.
LASALLE STATE FISH AND WILDLIFE AREA

DESCRIPTION AND BIRDING AREAS: Just north of Willow Slough and west of Highway 41 is the 3,244-acre LaSalle State Fish and Wildlife Area, a remnant of what was once the "Great Kankakee Swamp." Characterized by the same type of habitat as the slough, it is not as attractive to waterfowl. It does, however, host large numbers of Prothonotary Warblers and the surrounding fields often produce Smith's Longspur and impressive flocks of (Lesser) Golden Plover during early April.

ACCOMMODATIONS: Camping is permitted in designated areas. Motels are available near the State Road 110 interchange with Interstate 65.

20.
WILLOW SLOUGH

DESCRIPTION: Willow Slough State Fish and Wildlife Area is a mecca for birds. Perhaps more unique birds can be found within its 8,700 acres

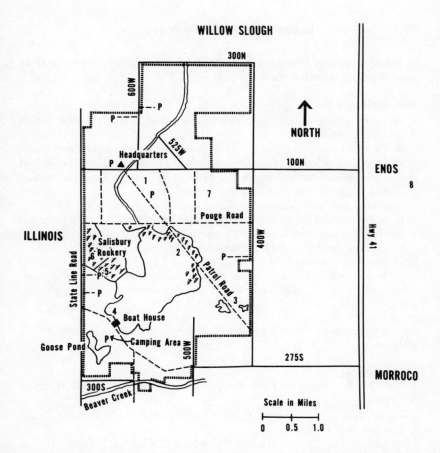

WILLOW SLOUGH

than in any other region in the state, with the exception of the Indiana Lakeshore. Established during the 1950s, it has produced such rarities as Great Egret (nesting), Ross' Goose, Greater White-fronted Goose, Black Rail, Lesser Black-backed Gull, Long-eared Owl (nesting), Veery (nesting), Yellow-headed Blackbird, and Canada Warbler (suspected nesting).

Originally part of the grand old marsh of the Kankakee, separated by a sandhill from the now-drained Beaver Lake which contained some 16,000 acres of open water, Willow Slough itself was for several years a wet marsh of varying depth, often used as pasture land. Now impounded, it produces habitat suitable for many species of migratory waterfowl and shorebirds.

In the area just east and north of the refuge Yellow Rail, large numbers of Lesser Golden Plover, and Smith's Longspur can be found regularly in the spring. This location is part of the original prairie region and an area of intense ornithological interest.

BIRDING AREAS (see map):

1. Good area for wintering falconiformes, e.g., Rough-legged Hawk, Bald Eagle, Merlin.
2. East of road, check marsh for herons, rails, marsh wrens and Brewer's Blackbirds. West of road, large numbers of migrating waterfowl and shorebirds. Whistling Swans often seen from this area during the spring.
3. Wood Ducks and Hooded Mergansers.
4. Picnic area and boat house. Good overview of west side of lake.
5. Excellent area for herons, dabbling ducks, rails, LeConte's and Sharp-tailed Sparrows. Marked 6A parking lot.
6. Herons, dabbling ducks, shorebirds.
7. Sandhill Cranes.
8. Yellow Rails, Lesser Golden Plovers, and Smith's Longspurs (late March–early April). Highway 14 east of Enos especially good for Longspurs.

ACCOMMODATIONS: Camping allowed in designated area. Nearby motels at Morocco.

REFERENCES:

Barnes, W. B. (1953) Willow Slough Game Preserve. *Indiana Audubon Quarterly* 31:42–43.
Ginn, W. E. (1954) American Egret nesting in Indiana. *Indiana Audubon Quarterly* 32:20.
Mumford, R. E. (1963) Lesser Black-backed Gull in Indiana. *Wilson Bulletin* 75:93.
———— (1966) A Ross's Goose in Indiana. *Indiana Audubon Quarterly* 44:116.
———— (1976) Nesting of Long-eared Owl in Indiana. *Indiana Audubon Quarterly* 54:95–97.
———— (1977) Summer record of the Black Rail in Indiana. *Indiana Audubon Quarterly* 55:1–2.

21.
PURDUE-BAKER WILDLIFE AREA

DESCRIPTION AND BIRDING AREAS: Located about 10 miles west of West Lafayette and north of State Road 26, the Purdue-Baker Wildlife Area consists of 250 acres of semi-marsh and lake habitat. Used for many years by Purdue University as a biological study area, it has been intensively studied by many of the students working toward advanced degrees. Herbst (1966) recorded Blue-winged Teal, King Rail, Tree Swallow, and Short-billed (Sedge) Marsh Wren as having nested there.

Over 150 other species have been recorded, including Common Loon, Double-crested Cormorant, Least Bittern, Whistling Swan, Sandhill Crane, King, Virginia, and Sora Rails, Purple Gallinule (once), Short-billed Dowitcher, Stilt Sandpiper, Wilson's Phalarope, Caspian Tern, Short-eared Owl, and Sharp-tailed Sparrow.

ACCOMMODATIONS: Numerous motels at nearby Lafayette.

REFERENCES:

Herbst, D. L. (1966) Ecological studies of the vertebrate populations of a northern Indiana marsh. M.S. Thesis, Purdue University.

Lindsey, A. A. et al. (1969) *Natural areas in Indiana and their preservation* (Lafayette: Indiana Natural Areas Survey), pp. 346–350.

22.

OUABACHE STATE RECREATION AREA

DESCRIPTION AND BIRDING AREAS: Ouabache State Recreation Area, formerly known as the Wells County State Game Preserve, is located on State Road 316 about 3 miles southeast of Bluffton. Four trails ranging from one to three miles in length traverse the area and offer the hiker or birder ample opportunity to observe wildlife.

Although it has not been extensively birded, an early- to mid-May trip here can produce good numbers of migrating warblers. Ruth Oswalt recorded eleven species of that group in 1971 (Carter, 1971).

A small 21-acre pond should be attractive to migrating waterfowl.

ACCOMMODATIONS: Several different classes of camping are permitted in the area. Some have electrical hookups. Motels are located in nearby Bluffton.

REFERENCE:

Carter, A. L. (1971) The season summary: 1971. *Indiana Audubon Quarterly* 49:134–154.

23.
SALAMONIE, HUNTINGTON, & MISSISSINEWA RESERVOIRS

DESCRIPTION AND BIRDING AREAS: As part of the upper Wabash River flood control project, the Army Corps of Engineers has constructed three rather large reservoirs in north-central Indiana. These are the Salamonie Reservoir located 8 miles east of Wabash, 12 miles north of Marion, and 6 miles southwest of Huntington; the Huntington Reservoir just southeast of Huntington; and the Mississinewa Reservoir southeast of Peru.

The 2,855-acre Salamonie Reservoir is joined on the north by the Salamonie State Forest. Both areas are productive birding spots, especially during migration when large numbers of waterfowl and/or warblers can be recorded. On the reservoir, prime areas include Herney's Bend, Lost Bridge Recreation Area, Majenica Creek, and Mt. Etna Recreation Area. Some of the birds recorded include Common Loon, Whistling Swan, Upland Sandpiper, Pileated Woodpecker (rare), Brewster's Warbler, Bobolink, and Savannah Sparrow.

The smaller 900-acre Huntington Reservoir has produced a documented Arctic Loon sighting; the large, 3,200-acre Mississinewa Reservoir has not been intensively birded, but is probably equally as good.

ACCOMMODATIONS: Camping is available at all three sites with motels in nearby Huntington, Peru, and Marion.

REFERENCES:
Anonymous (1974) Field notes—spring (Ft. Wayne Region). *Indiana Audubon Quarterly* 52:100–102.
Branham, J. F. (1974) Salamonie Reservoir and Salamonie State Forest Region, spring 1974. *Indiana Audubon Quarterly* 52:102–103.

CENTRAL

24.
PRAIRIE CREEK RESERVOIR

DESCRIPTION AND BIRDING AREAS: The 1,216-acre Prairie Creek Reservoir is located about one mile east of Highway 35, just southeast of Muncie. Local area observers have recorded several unusual birds: Western Grebe, Cattle Egret, Whistling Swan, Bald Eagle, Snowy Owl, and Snow Bunting. The area is attractive to migrating waterfowl during late fall and early spring.

ACCOMMODATIONS: Camping nearby and motels at Muncie.

REFERENCES:
Carter, L. (1976) Western Grebe at Prairie Creek Reservoir. *Indiana Audubon Quarterly* 54:35.
Cooper, R. (1963) The occurrence of the Whistling Swan (*Cygnus columbianus*) in Delaware County, Indiana. *Proc. Ind. Acad. Sci.* 72: 342–343.
───── (1971) Occurrence of Cattle Egrets in Delaware County, Indiana. *Indiana Audubon Quarterly* 49:168–169.
───── (1975) Adult Bald Eagle and Snowy Owl make December visit to Delaware County. *Indiana Audubon Quarterly* 53:14.
───── (1975) Snow Buntings in Delaware County. *Indiana Audubon Quarterly* 53:81.

25.
MOUNDS STATE PARK

DESCRIPTION AND BIRDING AREAS: Mounds State Park is located off State Road 67 near Anderson, and consists of some 254 acres. The mounds were formed by ancient Indians who used them as burial places for their tribe. Artifacts recovered from the so-called Great Mound revealed a crematorium, a stone pipe, deer-bone awls, arrow and spearheads, bone fragments, and potsherds. Archaeologists believe that the Great Mound was constructed somewhere between 10–50 A.D.

A series of four trails traverses the area, enabling the observer to visit the mound area and a variety of habitat. Trail 3 leads north through open woods to a ridge above White River, where you can scan the nearby treetops for migrating warblers; joining up with Trail 2, it leads along a beautiful small stream and then back through the picnic grounds.

ACCOMMODATIONS: Camping in the park and motels near Anderson.

26.
MORSE RESERVOIR

DESCRIPTION AND BIRDING AREAS: North of Noblesville and west of Highway 19 in Hamilton County, Morse Reservoir is a highly developed and commercial area, not as good for birding as it once was, but still with some possibilities. Best season is from late fall to early spring, before heavy usage by fishermen, boaters, et al. begins.

The spillway of the dam at the extreme southern end of the reservoir produced a Harlequin Duck several years ago. When the water level is low, shorebirding can be very productive. A small, wet, marshy area traversed by Highway 19 just north of Noblesville has been good for rails and herons, but is in the process of being destroyed by commercial peat production.

ACCOMMODATIONS: Motels at Noblesville or Indianapolis.

27.
GEIST RESERVOIR

DESCRIPTION: Since construction of Geist Reservoir in 1944, it has been the object of intense ornithological field work. Groups from local Indianapolis high schools and the Amos W. Butler Audubon Society regularly conduct field trips in the area. As many as 300 Common Loons in one flock were recorded by Val Nolan, and a list published by William Buskirk and Bruce Fall in 1961 recorded over 200 species, including such rarities as Eurasian Wigeon, Peregrine Falcon, Marbled Godwit, American Avocet, Pomarine Jaeger, Little Tern, and Bell's Vireo. Recent observations include the Western Grebe, Eared Grebe, Mississippi Kite, and Snowy Owl.

Adjacent to its 35-mile shoreline is sufficient habitat to attract many species which normally are quite rare. Water area comprises some 1,800 acres in its 7½-mile length. Although some development has been completed, it remains an attraction for hundreds of migratory waterfowl.

GEIST RESERVOIR

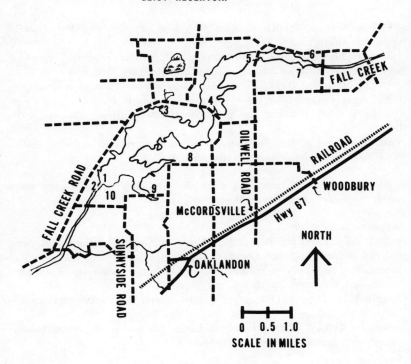

BIRDING AREAS (see map):

1. Dam (north side). Good area for overview of main portion of reservoir. Here good numbers of waterfowl can be observed during peak migratory passages in both spring and fall. Lining the parking area is a large planting of pine trees that provide sufficient foraging for migratory warblers and other species.

2. Below dam. A marshy region where wintering Common Snipe are often seen. Herons and Prothonotary Warblers can usually be found.

3. Lagoon crossover. Dabbling ducks can be seen on the lagoon portion while to the south an extensive open area of the reservoir proper provides excellent viewing of loons, grebes, and diving ducks.

4. Reservoir crossover. Check both sides of bridge for waterfowl, etc. Gulls and terns often seen; during drought years in the fall, extensive mudflats provide optimal habitat for shorebirds.

5. Reservoir crossover. Again, check both sides of bridge for waterfowl.

6. Iron bridge (north). Fishing path provides fair area for observation of marsh-inhabiting birds.

7. Iron bridge (south). Fishing path provides excellent area for viewing marsh birds as well as nesting Prothonotary Warblers.

8. Extensive fire trails. These lead back to overview of widest portion of reservoir and offer closer observation of waterfowl.

9. Long inlet. Provides shelter for waterfowl during inclement weather.

10. South end of dam. It can provide good observation of diving ducks, etc. Fire trails lead to dam area and vicinity.

ACCOMMODATIONS: No camping allowed on reservoir property but good motels available on nearby Highway 67.

REFERENCES:

Buskirk, W., and Fall, B. (1961) Birds of Geist Reservoir and their status. *Indiana Audubon Quarterly* 39:42–51.

Calvert, S. (1946) New records on the Oaklandon map—1946. *Indiana Audubon Yearbook* 24:38.

Campbell, M. (1945) Oaklandon Reservoir. *Indiana Audubon Yearbook* 23:32–36.

Nolan, V. (1949) Three hundred Loons in one flock at Oaklandon Reservoir. *Indiana Audubon Yearbook* 27:30–31.

28.
INDIANAPOLIS-NORTHWEST

DESCRIPTION AND BIRDING AREAS: Five separate areas constitute Indianapolis-Northwest:

1. Holliday Park: A small city park located immediately east of Spring Mill Road and south of 64th Street. This small, attractive area has several river bottom trails that annually harbor good numbers of migrating warblers. Yellow, Yellow-throated, Cerulean, and Kentucky Warblers and American Redstart are regulars during the summer.

2. Holcomb Gardens: Located near the junction of Sunset Avenue and 47th Street inside the Butler University grounds. The following rare species have been recorded: Northern Goshawk, Prairie Warbler, and Clay-colored Sparrow.

3. Butler Towpath: Adjacent to Holcomb Gardens, it follows the north side of the Indianapolis Water Company Canal south to 38th Street.

4. Indianapolis Art Museum: Located in the northwest corner of 38th Street and Northwestern Avenue. The area near the Indianapolis Horticultural Society Greenhouse is a winter feeding sanctuary maintained by the Amos W. Butler Chapter of the National Audubon Society. An active feeding program brings in a variety of species, among them Red-breasted Nuthatch, Evening Grosbeak, Purple Finch, House Finch (once), and an occasional Common Redpoll.

5. Crown Hill Cemetery: Located southeast of the Art Museum. Winter finches are sometimes abundant and Bachman's Sparrow has occurred.

ACCOMMODATIONS: Motels in the Indianapolis area.

29.
EAGLE CREEK RESERVOIR

DESCRIPTION: One of the newest birding attractions near the metropolitan Indianapolis area is Eagle Creek Park and Reservoir, just west of the 56th Street exit off I-465. Established in 1965, it consists of well over 4,000 acres of diversified habitat and is one of the best places to observe birds in the State. Of the more than 200 species recorded, at least 91 have nested, or been suspected of nesting, within the park boundaries. Some of these include Willow and Alder Flycatcher (suspected), Sedge Wren, Veery (suspected), Summer Tanager, Rose-breasted Grosbeak, and Savannah Sparrow. Periodic winter finch eruptions bring both species of Crossbill as well as Common Redpoll, Evening Grosbeak, and Pine Siskin. The reservoir itself has hosted such rarities as Red-necked Grebe, Oldsquaw, White-winged Scoter, American Avocet, and Northern Phalarope. Both Golden and American Bald Eagles have been recorded.

Sunday-morning bird hikes are conducted at 9:00 A.M. from the nature center by Alfred Starling and are both stimulating and informative. Other programs include periodic nature walks, lectures, and various outdoor recreational activities. The nature center contains wildlife exhibits, posters, and nature games. Admission to the park is $1.25 per car for residents of the county and $1.50 per car for nonresidents. Season passes are also available.

BIRDING AREAS (see map):
1. 38th Street overview. During migration large numbers of diving ducks, Common Loon, and both Horned and Pied-billed Grebe occur.

EAGLE CREEK RESERVOIR

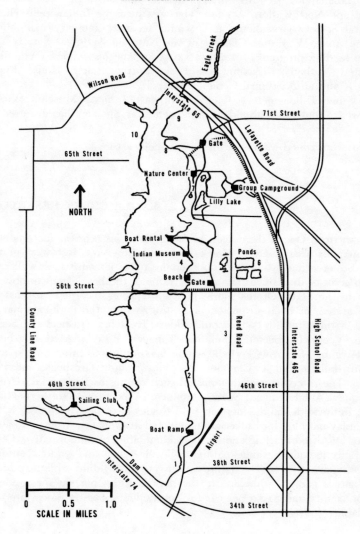

2. Dandy Trail. Gentle slopes (some private) overlook the reservoir and a small, wet, marshy area has produced Common Snipe and Sedge Wren.

3. Reed Road. East is farmland with migrating icterids and west is heavily-forested acreage with nesting Great Crested Flycatcher and Eastern Pewee.

4. Indian Museum. Behind museum is good overview of large inlet which can be very productive for close observation of waterfowl.

5. Boat Rental Area. Large peninsula juts into lake and gives the observer an excellent vantagepoint for gull and tern migration.

6. Ponds (Reed Road). The wet, marshy area west of the road has Common Snipe (March–April), Eastern Bluebird, and Swamp Sparrow. East of the road the ponds often have dabbling ducks, and an occasional heron or rail.

7. Nature Center. During winter finch years both Red and White-winged Crossbills are found in the hemlock trees surrounding the entrance and a small pond. During spring and fall the large Norway pines are sometimes spectacular for warblers.

8. Gravel Pits. Commercial development has left large gravel pits with steep slopes attractive to colonies of Bank Swallow. Both Killdeer and Spotted Sandpiper are common.

9. Marsh Area. Often produces Double-crested Cormorant, herons, and shorebirds (fall).

10. 65th Street Dead-end. A small road parallels the lake and provides good viewing of waterfowl.

ACCOMMODATIONS: A campground is planned and there are numerous motels in the surrounding area.

REFERENCES:

Starling, A. (1970) Birds of Big Eagle Creek Valley: summer and fall, 1969. *Indiana Audubon Quarterly* 48:72–77.
———— (1976) *Birds of Eagle Creek Park.* Indianapolis Department of Parks and Recreation Pamphlet. 4 pp.

30.
SOUTH WESTWAY PARK, INDIANAPOLIS

DESCRIPTION AND BIRDING AREAS: Formerly known as Maywood Bottoms, South Westway Park consists of a series of old riverbed sloughs and heavily timbered secondary forests and is bordered by the west fork of the White River. Now, heavily grazed and semi-commercialized (e.g., pay lake) the area is not quite as attractive to birds as it was some thirty years ago. Nevertheless, it still produces good numbers of migratory hawks and warblers, which follow the ridges that line the west bank of the White River.

To reach the area take Highway 67 to Mann Road about 5 miles southwest of the Indianapolis city limits. Continue on Mann Road south approximately 6 miles to the southernmost corner of South Westway golf course and follow the unpaved road back to the river. Old Maywood Bottoms lies immediately south of this road. This is private land—permission to bird should be obtained before entering the property, either at the adjacent farm or the pay lake.

Some of the species recorded during the summer include Pileated Woodpecker, Prothonotary Warbler, White-eyed Vireo, and Summer Tanager. During migratory periods check the ridges for hawks, Common Flicker, and Blue Jay which follow them, during late April and once again in late September or early October.

Unusual species recorded include Great and Snowy Egrets, Yellow-crowned Night Heron, Connecticut and Mourning Warblers, and, in the nearby fields, Dickcissel. During the winter large numbers of American Tree Sparrows inhabit these same fields, and on occasion Lapland Longspur have been recorded.

ACCOMMODATIONS: Motels at nearby Indianapolis.

31.
RACCOON LAKE (MANSFIELD RESERVOIR)

DESCRIPTION AND BIRDING AREAS: Raccoon Lake State Recreation Area is located on Highway 36 near Hollandsburg. It was established in 1961 as part of a U.S. Army Corps of Engineers flood control program to reduce flood hazards in the Wabash, Ohio, and Mississippi River basins. Five trails, covering about six and one-half miles and ranging from moderate to rugged, cross the area, often leading into ravines formed by inlets of the lake. They pass through varied habitat, open meadows and a disturbed beech—maple woodland. Typical nesting species include Gray Catbird, Brown Thrasher, Cardinal, Wood Thrush, Indigo Bunting, American Robin, American Goldfinch, and Eastern Kingbird. Warblers include Cerulean, Kentucky, Common Yellowthroat, and Yellow-breasted Chat.

The lake itself is generally host to good numbers of waterfowl in season with Great Blue and Green Herons occurring frequently. Both Scarlet and Summer Tanagers nest in the area and the Pileated Woodpecker is often seen.

ACCOMMODATIONS: Campgrounds, some equipped with electricity and trailer hookups, are located within the area. Motels available at nearby Greencastle.

REFERENCES:
Campbell, M. F. (1965) Birding at Raccoon Lake. *Indiana Audubon Quarterly* 43:75–77.

32.
WAVELAND AREA

DESCRIPTION: The Waveland Area consists of Lake Waveland, a shallow, semi-private lake located on U.S. 47 13 miles west of Crawfordsville, and Shades State Park and Pine Hills Nature Preserve, located about 5 miles due north. It is mostly gently rolling farmland except in the region bounded by Sugar Creek, which has spectacular sandstone bluffs. Together, the 2,960-acre Shades State Park and the 600-acre Pine Hills Nature Preserve form a unique natural and scenic area rivaled by few others within the State.

One local resident, Alan Bruner, has recorded over 200 species of birds here since 1972, and another, Dorothy Luther, listed 20 species of warblers which nest, or may nest, in the area. Included in Luther's list were Black-throated Green, Chestnut-sided, Mourning, and Canada Warblers—indeed unusual nesting species in this area. Observers should be aware of the potential for new southernmost breeding records for these species.

BIRDING AREAS (see map):
Lake Waveland
1. West end of dam. Good place for observation of waterfowl and general overall view of the lake.
2. Beach area (admission fee). Nesting Rose-breasted Grosbeaks; migrating Savannah, Sharp-tailed, and LeConte's Sparrows in cattails and field adjoining lake during March, April, and October.
3. Housing area. Offers view of narrow inlet and mid-portion of lake.

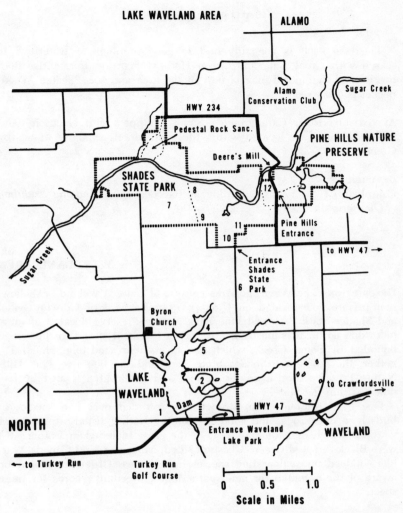

LAKE WAVELAND AREA

ALAMO

Alamo Conservation Club

Sugar Creek

HWY 234

Pedestal Rock Sanc.

Deere's Mill

PINE HILLS NATURE PRESERVE

SHADES STATE PARK

8

7

9

12

11

10

Pine Hills Entrance

to HWY 47 →

Entrance Shades State Park

6

Sugar Creek

Byron Church

4

3

5

LAKE WAVELAND

2

Dam

1

to Crawfordsville

HWY 47

NORTH

← to Turkey Run

Turkey Run Golf Course

Entrance Waveland Lake Park

WAVELAND

0   0.5   1.0

Scale in Miles

4. North end of lake. Herons, dabbling ducks, and shorebirds during migration. Sedge Wrens have nested.

5. Mixed hardwoods. Good area for resident Great Horned Owls and migratory warblers.

6. Pasture. Lesser Golden Plover seen during early spring.

Shades–Pine Hills

7. Nesting Prairie Warblers

8. Nesting Blue-winged Warblers
9. Nesting Bell's Vireos
10. Superintendent's Lot
11. Nesting Henslow's Sparrows
12. Warbler Woods (nine species of resident warblers including Northern Parula and Worm-eating).

During mild winters large numbers of Turkey Vultures can be found at the Shades and/or Turkey Run State Parks.

ACCOMMODATIONS: Camping is allowed in Shades State Park and nearby Turkey Run State Park. There are an excellent Inn and cabins at Turkey Run, and motels in Crawfordsville about 13 miles east of Waveland.

REFERENCES:
Bruner, A. (1974) Birds of Lake Waveland, fall 1972. *Indiana Audubon Quarterly* 52:116–120.
Lindsey, A. A. et al. (1969) *Natural areas in Indiana and their preservation* (Lafayette: Indiana Natural Areas Survey), pp. 334–346.
Luther, D. (1976) Annotated listing of warblers that have nested, or may nest, in the Shades State Park area. *Indiana Audubon Quarterly* 54:75–82.
Mason, J., and Mason, A. (1966) The Vultures of Turkey Run. *Indiana Audubon Quarterly* 44:14–15.

33.
TURKEY RUN STATE PARK

DESCRIPTION: Established in 1916, Turkey Run State Park consists of 2,182 acres of deep gorges that were formed by the action of glacial streams that cut deep fissures into sandstone. Stands of virgin timber cover an area of 285 acres and include fine specimens of tulip poplar, walnut, oak, cherry, hemlock, sycamore, and maple.

The name "Turkey Run" is derived from reports of early residents that thousands of wild turkeys once collected in great flocks under the natural protection of overhanging cliffs along Sugar Creek. The turkeys have long since vanished, and in their place are hundreds of Turkey Vultures which now roost along those same overhanging cliffs.

Much has been written concerning the birdlife of the area; ornithologically, it has been one of the more extensively studied regions in Indiana. Branham (1964, 1965) listed 11 species of warblers that nest in the park: Prothonotary, Worm-eating, Yellow, Cerulean, Yellow-throated, and Prairie Warblers; Ovenbird; Louisiana Waterthrush; Kentucky Warbler; Common Yellowthroat; and Yellow-breasted Chat. He also listed 4 probables: Black and White, Blue-winged, and Hooded Warblers plus American Redstart. Recently it has been suggested that the Northern Parula Warbler may nest there also (*fide* M. Forsyth).

BIRDING AREAS: A series of ten trails originate within the park, ranging from easy (Trail 6) to moderate (Trails 1, 4, 5, 7, 8, 10) to rugged (Trails 2, 3, 9). Trail 3, bordering Sugar Creek, is an excellent trail for viewing native nesting species, particularly in the early morning when males are more vociferous. Most of the nesting warblers can be heard and seen from the trail, and an early- to mid-May trip is very rewarding for migratory species. It is one of the few places within the State that Black-throated Blue Warblers can usually be seen. Check the steep slopes in the ravines for Worm-eating, while the floors of the gorges themselves are very good for Louisiana Waterthrush and Hooded Warbler. The treetops often reveal Prothonotary and Northern Parula Warblers. Trails 1 and 7 are excellent trails for viewing the immense virgin timber and are well worth the effort.

A word of caution concerning the rugged trails; some contain ladders and steep slopes, so be particularly careful when these are wet.

ACCOMMODATIONS: Turkey Run Inn is open year-round; there are cabin units available from April 15 through November 15. A new campground is available that can accommodate trailers. There are no individual water or sewer hookups, but there is electricity. In addition, there is a Rally campground. For further information write: Reservation Clerk, Turkey Run Inn, Marshall, Indiana 47859.

REFERENCES:
Branham, J. P. (1963) Some notes on the summer avifauna of Turkey Run State Park, Part 1. *Indiana Audubon Quarterly* 41:46–49.
——— (1964) Some notes on the summer avifauna of Turkey Run State Park, Part 2. *Indiana Audubon Quarterly* 42:10–15.
——— (1965) Some additional notes on the summer avifauna of Turkey Run State Park: Picidae and Parulidae. *Indiana Audubon Quarterly* 43:17–18.
——— (1965) Some notes on the summer avifauna of Turkey Run State Park, Part 3. *Indiana Audubon Quarterly* 43:79–82.

Luther, D. (1967) A 1942 Pileated Woodpecker recorded at Turkey Run State Park. *Indiana Audubon Quarterly* 45:24–25.

Mason, J., and Mason, A. (1966) The Vultures of Turkey Run. *Indiana Audubon Quarterly* 44:14–15.

Mumford, R. E. (1948) Summer resident warblers of Turkey Run State Park. *Indiana Audubon Yearbook* 26:50–52.

Overlease, W. R., and Overlease, E. (1974) Winter bird studies at Turkey Run State Park, Marshall, Indiana 1953–1973. *Indiana Audubon Quarterly* 52:63–65.

Test, F. H. (1928) Summer resident birds of Turkey Run State Park. *Proc. Ind. Acad. Sci.* 37:467–472.

———— (1929) Additional notes on summer birds of Turkey Run State Park. *Proc. Ind. Acad. Sci.* 38:329–331.

34.
BRAZIL SEWAGE LAGOONS

DESCRIPTION AND BIRDING AREAS: Located south of Brazil, Indiana, the Brazil Sewage Lagoons can be reached by traveling north of the Interstate 70–State Highway 59 interchange 1.8 miles to Paradise Lake Road; turn right (east) and proceed 0.9 mile to first crossroad (small general store on right); turn left (north) and travel 0.5 mile to entrance. Stop at caretaker's house and obtain permission to enter the sewage lagoon area.

Four large transfer basins, each about 30 to 40 acres in extent, are highly attractive to migratory waterfowl. Some of the species recorded include: Canada Goose, Mallard, American Black Duck, Common Pintail, Green-winged Teal, Blue-winged Teal, American Wigeon, Northern Shoveler, Wood Duck, Redhead, Canvasback, Greater and Lesser Scaup, Ring-necked Duck, Bufflehead, Common Goldeneye, Oldsquaw (once), Black Scoter (once), Common Merganser, Hooded Merganser, and Red-breasted Merganser. In addition, occasional shorebirds frequent the lagoon edges. Five Northern Phalaropes were recorded during the fall of 1976. Both Ring-billed and Herring Gulls have been recorded. In winter watch for Rough-legged Hawk, while during the spring the swallow migration can be quite spectacular.

ACCOMMODATIONS: Motels in nearby Brazil.

35.
SHAKAMAK STATE PARK

DESCRIPTION AND BIRDING AREAS: Established in 1929 as a gift from the people of Clay, Greene, and Sullivan Counties, Shakamak State Park is located on Indiana 48 near Jasonville, and contains 1,766 acres of reclaimed strip mines, abandoned fields, and secondary forests. The area has not been heavily birded and is ripe for intensive observation and exploration.

The authors spent a week there during the summer of 1967 but recorded no unusual resident species. Eastern Pewee, Acadian Flycatcher, Cerulean and Yellow Warblers, Summer Tanager, and Rufous-sided Towhee were common. With the creation of a large impoundment joining Lake Lenape to Shakamak Lake, the area probably is attractive to migrating waterfowl. Four trails wind through the park, affording views of a variety of habitats.

ACCOMMODATIONS: Camping accommodates trailers, with electricity available. A series of moderately priced family housekeeping cabins can be rented during April through October and are located in secondary woods adjacent to one of the arms of the lake. Luncheons, sandwiches, and dinners are served at Shakamak Pavilion.

36.
OWEN-PUTNAM STATE FOREST AREA

DESCRIPTION: The Owen–Putnam State Forest Area, which includes Cataract Lake and Falls, Lieber State Park, and Owen–Putnam State Forest, is west of Highway 43, south of Highways 343–243, and north of Highway 46. Because it offers a wide diversity of habitat, it can provide the birder with an optimum variety of southwest-central Indiana birdlife.

Cataract Lake, also called Cagle Mills Reservoir, is a 1,500-acre flood control impoundment on Mill Creek in Owen and Putnam Counties. If filled to capacity it would cover an area of 4,840 acres. South of the lake where Mill Creek enters the reservoir is Cataract Falls, the largest falls of its type in Indiana. Lieber State Park consists of 8,283 acres and lies on the north shore of Cataract Lake. The beach area during early spring, before public use, is one of the better vantagepoints of the lake.

Owen–Putnam State Forest consists of several thousand acres adjacent to Lieber State Park and south from the lake in loose, disjointed parcels

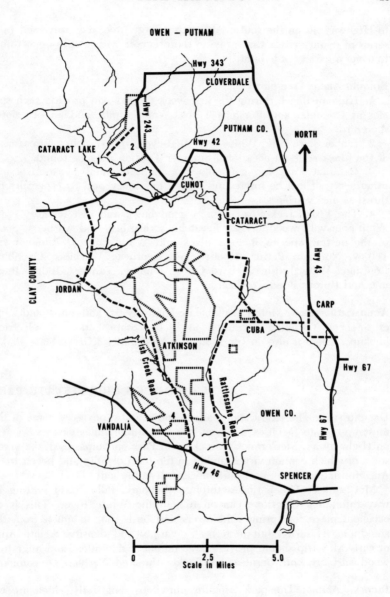

OWEN – PUTNAM

Hwy 343

CLOVERDALE

Hwy 243

PUTNAM CO.

CATARACT LAKE

Hwy 42

2

NORTH

CUNOT

3 CATARACT

Hwy 43

CLAY COUNTY

JORDAN

CARP

CUBA

ATKINSON

Fish Creek Road

Rattlesnake Road

Hwy 67

OWEN CO.

Hwy 67

VANDALIA

4

Hwy 46

SPENCER

0   2.5   5.0
Scale in Miles

to Highway 46 on the south. Although a large area, it is traversed by a series of county roads that provide the observer with ample opportunity to cover a variety of habitat.

BIRDING AREAS (see map):
1. Hulman Beach during the first week of May can provide such species as Common and Forster's Terns, Water Pipits, and an occasional shorebird.
2. Lieber State Park. White-eyed, Red-eyed, and Warbling Vireos nest; at the forest edge an occasional Summer Tanager may be found.
3. Cataract Falls are generally heavily frequented by tourists and fishermen, but can be interesting during migratory periods especially for thrushes and warblers.
4. The Fish Creek Road area is good hawk and owl territory, with Whip-poor-will, woodpeckers, flycatchers, thrushes, and warblers. Some of the nesting species include Black and White (once), Blue-winged, Yellow, Northern Parula, Hooded and Kentucky Warblers, Ovenbird, Louisiana Waterthrush, Orchard Oriole, Summer Tanager, Indigo Bunting, and Rufous-sided Towhee.

ACCOMMODATIONS: Motels available on Highway 67, both north and south of Spencer. Camping permitted in Lieber State Park with electrical hookups. There is also an Inn at nearby McCormick's Creek State Park.

37.

McCORMICK'S CREEK STATE PARK

DESCRIPTION: The oldest state park in Indiana also possesses some of the most up-to-date facilities. Located two and a half miles east of Spencer on Highway 46, McCormick's Creek State Park encompasses 1,752 acres, some of which contain virgin timber in the form of tulip and beech trees. An information center and park office is near the gate.

McCormick's Creek rushes through the park, falling and cutting its way through a limestone canyon to join the White River. This is an excellent place for spring wildflowers and birds, not so much from the standpoint of rarity, but in terms of variety and density. A late April or early May trip should provide large numbers of resident and migratory wood warblers. Both Cerulean and Yellow-throated Warblers are common.

BIRDING AREAS: The park contains numerous foot trails which are excellent for birding. Trail 7, which leads to the White River, is particularly good in the spring for warblers. Along Trail 3, which parallels McCormick's Creek, are areas where Louisiana Waterthrush and Hooded Warbler can be found. The forested slopes are good for Kentucky Warbler and Scarlet Tanager. During the winter, Evening Grosbeak are sometimes attracted to the feeding station near the Inn, often remaining until the first week in May. In early summer a trip along some of the country roads in the area could produce sightings of Blue Grosbeak and Lark Sparrow.

ACCOMMODATIONS: There is an all-electric campground with good facilities nestled among pine trees, as well as a primitive campground under spreading beech trees. Some campsites are available for reservation and a Rally campground is also available. A fifty-meter swimming pool is open to the public, and a saddle barn offers trail rides, surrey, buggy, and hack rides through a special area of the park reserved only for these vehicles. The Inn and family cabins have been refurbished and remodeled. For reservations write: Reservation Clerk, Canyon Inn, Spencer, Indiana 47460.

REFERENCES:
Michaud, H. H. (1938) Preliminary nesting studies in Indiana state parks. *Indiana Audubon Yearbook* 53–57.
────── (1942) More on the nesting birds of Indiana state parks. *Indiana Audubon Yearbook* 6–10.
Overlease, W. R. (1974) Winter bird studies at McCormick's Creek State Park, Spencer, Indiana, 1952, 1954, 1955, 1961, 1973. *Indiana Audubon Quarterly* 52:58–61.
Thompson, M. T. (1946) Echo from McCormick's Creek Canyon. *Indiana Audubon Yearbook* 24:59.
Wilson, D. (1942) A field trip to McCormick's Creek State Park. *Indiana Audubon Yearbook* 30–32.

38.
MORGAN-MONROE STATE FOREST
LAKE LEMON

DESCRIPTION: The largest state forest in Indiana, Morgan-Monroe encompasses 24,000 acres of unglaciated woodlands, hills and ravines. Three exceptionally long trails begin from the forest: Yellowwood, Tulip Tree Trace, and the Ten O'Clock Line. In addition, there are three small lakes and a medium-sized one, Lake Lemon, which adjoins the property.

Long noted for Ruffed Grouse and Pileated Woodpeckers, the forest still retains good numbers of both of these species, which can usually be seen from one of the trails.

Lake Lemon, at times, is an excellent area for spring waterfowl migration and, in dry autumns, exceptional for shorebirds. Rarities include Western Grebe, Baird's, Stilt, and Buff-breasted Sandpipers. During the winter Rough-legged Hawk, Yellow-bellied Sapsucker, and Hermit Thrush can usually be seen.

BIRDING AREAS: The sheltered Bean Blossom Lake often has Gadwall and Hooded Merganser during mild winters. A group of pine trees near the picnic area is usually good for Red-breasted Nuthatches (flight years) and Golden-crowned and Ruby-crowned Kinglets. As mentioned above, Ruffed Grouse can usually be seen from one of the three trails. A favorite habitat is the dense woods, where they will often startle the observer by flushing at one's feet, then flying off into dense cover. In early spring (April) drumming males can be heard and, with careful stalking, it may be possible to get quite close.

Lake Lemon is a developed lake approximately 4 miles south of the back entrance. While it contains a large number of private cottages, there are areas where one can observe the wider portions which are particularly good in early spring during waterfowl season. In the fall, during dry periods, large mudflats are left exposed when the water level recedes. Good numbers of shorebirds occur, including Baird's, Western, Stilt, and Buff-breasted Sandpiper. Access to these flats is best obtained on the northeast side, but permission from some of the resident property owners should be obtained before entering any private land. This area is also good for herons and an occasional Double-crested Cormorant.

ACCOMMODATIONS: Camping is allowed within specified areas of the forest. Motels are available in Martinsville and Bloomington.

39.
ATTERBURY

DESCRIPTION: Atterbury is one of the newest and most promising areas in Indiana for birdwatching. Originally the northern section of Camp Atterbury, it consists of flat, scrubby open woodlands and extensive overgrown and neglected fields, so is conducive to species whose habitat requirements favor the use of this type of biotope (e.g., Upland Sand-

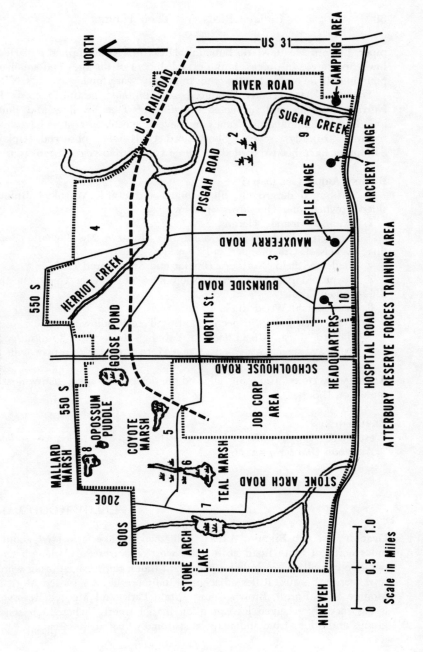

ATTERBURY

NORTH

US 31

CAMPING AREA

RIVER ROAD

SUGAR CREEK

9

US RAILROAD

2

PISGAH ROAD

1

MAUXFERRY ROAD

RIFLE RANGE

ARCHERY RANGE

4

3

HERRIOT CREEK

550 S

BURNSIDE ROAD

NORTH St.

10

HEADQUARTERS

HOSPITAL ROAD

ATTERBURY RESERVE FORCES TRAINING AREA

GOOSE POND

SCHOOLHOUSE ROAD

550 S

OPOSSUM PUDDLE

JOB CORP AREA

MALLARD MARSH

8

COYOTE MARSH

5

STONE ARCH ROAD

200E

6

TEAL MARSH

600S

7

STONE ARCH LAKE

NINEVEH

Scale in Miles

0   0.5   1.0

piper, Eastern Meadowlark, Bobolink, Dickcissel, Grasshopper, and Henslow's Sparrow). In process is the establishment of marshes and small impoundments favorable to attracting migratory waterfowl.

The area has recently produced southernmost nesting records for Northern Harrier and suspected breeding of Tree Swallow and Bobolink. In addition, Sandhill Cranes and several species of raptors have been recorded. In 1975 several Short-eared Owls were observed. Upland Sandpiper have been recorded for three consecutive years, 1976–1978.

BIRDING AREAS (see map):
1. Scrubby undergrowth. Blue-winged and Prairie Warblers, Rufous-sided Towhee, and Henslow's Sparrow.
2. Extensive marsh. Herons.
3. Neglected fields. Upland Sandpiper, Eastern Meadowlark, Bobolink, Dickcissel, Grasshopper and Henslow's Sparrows.
4. Neglected field. Northern Harrier and Short-eared Owl.
5. Coyote Marsh. Small established flock of Canada Geese, nesting Blue-winged Teal.
6. Teal Marsh. Wood duck.
7. Stone Arch Lake. Suspected nesting Tree Swallow.
8. Mallard Marsh. Mixed flocks of dabbling ducks during migration.
9. Extensive secondary woods. Great Horned Owl, Whip-poor-will.

ACCOMMODATIONS: Camping allowed in designated area; many nearby motels on U.S. 31.

REFERENCE:
West, H. C. (1974) Marsh Hawks nesting in Johnson County. *Indiana Audubon Quarterly* 52:71.

40.
YELLOWWOOD LAKE

DESCRIPTION AND BIRDING AREAS: Yellowwood Lake is located about 2 miles north of State Road 46 8 miles west of Nashville. Although comparatively small and secluded it can be, at times, impressive during waterfowl season. Because it lies adjacent to the more heavily birded Morgan–Monroe State Forest, Brown County State Park, and Monroe Reservoir, it has recently received less attention than formerly, when high school groups and others from Indianapolis seasonally visited the area.

Species recorded include Ruffed Grouse, Pileated Woodpecker, Eastern Bluebird, Hooded Warbler, and Summer Tanager. In open winters Common Goldeneye, Hooded Merganser, and White-winged Scoter (once) occur.

ACCOMMODATIONS: Nearby motels at Nashville and camping available at the Lake.

41.
BROWN COUNTY STATE PARK

DESCRIPTION: Among the attractions of Brown County, made famous by Kin Hubbard's character Abe Martin, are the picturesque town of Nashville, with its art galleries and its antique and gift shops, and the largest state park in Indiana, which contains 15,543 heavily-forested acres of typical southern-Indiana hill land. Throngs of visitors from all over the world come here to marvel at the spectacular autumn foliage; those who prefer tranquility to fall color will find it advisable to avoid the October-weekend crowds and visit the park at other times of the year.

The park is known for Ruffed Grouse, Pileated Woodpecker, and Hooded Warbler, all of which nest within its confines. It is particularly good for spring warblers; an early-morning walk along any of the trails during mid-May should produce many sightings of these sprightly species. It is also noted for the approximately twenty-five mature yellowwood trees that grow along Trail 5. Yellowwood (*Cladrastis lutea*), a tree native to the southeastern United States, is found no other place in Indiana. The trunk of the largest yellowwood (located on the down slope of Trail 5) measures 22.7 inches in diameter. Difficult to identify, particularly in winter, it has pinnately compound leaves resembling those of an ash tree.

BIRDING AREAS: The park offers a system of eight well-marked trails that provide good observation points and lead the birder through a variety of habitats.

Trails 1 and 2, in the vicinity of the lodge, lead through oak, hickory, sassafras, beech, and maple trees. Trail 3 passes the saddle barn and amphitheatre and returns to the lodge. Check the ravines for Hooded Warbler and Ovenbird. Trail 4 starts near the service area and leads through upland terrain (Prairie Warbler and Summer Tanager) to a deep ravine at the headwaters of Lake Ogle. Trail 5, north of the Service Area, connects to Trail 7 and passes down a wooded slope where the rare yellowwood tree can be found. These trails are good for Ruffed Grouse and Pileated Woodpecker. Trail 6 encircles Jimmie Strahl Lake where waterfowl (early spring, late fall) may often be seen. Trail 8 extends from the west gate house eastward to the west overlook and then south to Lake Ogle. A view from the overlook affords the observer an unparalleled view of the park. Here a patient observer can sit quietly and scan the treetops for migrating warblers.

ACCOMMODATIONS: On Highway 135 south of Nashville are the Brown County Inn and a Ramada Inn. Abe Martin Lodge, located within the park, is open from April through November. A campground is also located within the park. For further information write: Reservation Clerk, Abe Martin Lodge, Nashville, Indiana 47448.

REFERENCES:

Esten, S. R. (1930) Observations made in Brown County, May 20–28. *Indiana Audubon Bulletin* 36–39.

Lindsey, A. A. et al. (1969) *Natural areas in Indiana and their preservation* (Lafayette: Indiana Natural Areas Survey), pp. 210–211.

Michaud, H. H. (1938) Preliminary nesting studies in Indiana state parks. *Indiana Audubon Yearbook* 53–57.

———— (1942) More on the nesting birds of Indiana state parks. *Indiana Audubon Yearbook* 6–10.

Zimmerman, H. A. (1954) Hooded Warbler nest noted in Brown County. *Indiana Audubon Quarterly* 32:57–58.

———— (1964) Birding in Brown County. *Indiana Audubon. Quarterly* 42:71–72.

42.
MARY GRAY BIRD SANCTUARY

DESCRIPTION: In 1940, 240 acres of land were donated to the Indiana Audubon Society by Mrs. Finley Gray to be used as a bird sanctuary to be named in memory of her daughter Mary. Six years later, an additional 400-plus acres were added with the settlement of the Finley Gray estate, and this was augmented in 1976 by additional small acreage acquired through purchase. Today the Mary Gray Bird Sanctuary totals about 700 acres of rolling land crossed by small, wooded streams. It is located about 3.5 miles south of State Road 44, just west of Connersville (see map).

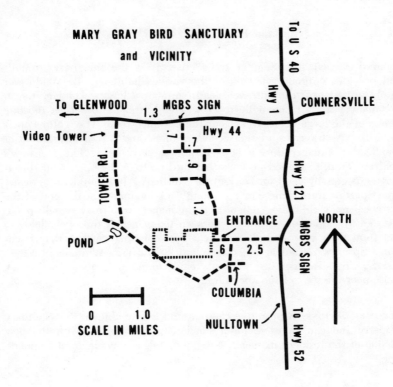

MARY GRAY BIRD SANCTUARY
and VICINITY

To U S 40

To GLENWOOD 1.3 MGBS SIGN

Hwy 1

CONNERSVILLE

Video Tower→ Hwy 44 .7

TOWER Rd. .9

Hwy 121

1.2

ENTRANCE NORTH

POND

MGBS SIGN

.6 2.5

COLUMBIA

NULLTOWN

To Hwy 52

0 1.0
SCALE IN MILES

Much of the Sanctuary was logged at one time, and this left few good-sized trees except those that were considered unmarketable. Despite that fact, or perhaps because of it, the sanctuary provides sufficient varied habitat for a variety of nesting species. Some of these include, or have included, Pileated Woodpecker, White-eyed Vireo, Cerulean Warbler, Prairie Warbler, Orchard Oriole, Summer Tanager, Henslow's Sparrow, and Bachman's Sparrow.

The Indiana Audubon Society conducts its annual spring meeting here on the first weekend in May; it features a varied and interesting program. At Brooks Hall (so named in honor of Earl Brooks, an indefatigable former sanctuary chairman), various exhibits and a large library are housed. Also on the sanctuary grounds is the residence of the present managers, Denzil and Deanna Barricklow. It is because of them and the sanctuary committee, headed by Clifford Gough, that the property has maintained its excellent system of picnic areas, campground, and trails. Visiting birders are welcome.

BIRDING AREAS: A system of trails crisscrosses the sanctuary grounds and provides optimum viewing of the various habitats. The Wildflower Trail, located near the entrance, leads through a large secondary forest. For many years a resident Barred Owl could often be observed roosting in one of the large beech trees near the entrance road. The Tulip Poplar Trail likewise traverses a large secondary forest and is a favorite haunt of the Scarlet Tanager during late April and early May. The Henslow's Sparrow Trail, so named because that bird nests in the open field that it crosses, is equally good for Dark-eyed (Northern) Junco and (American) Tree Sparrow during the winter. A long walk beginning at the end of the entrance road continues down a maintenance trail to a small pond. Pileated Woodpeckers can often be seen flying across the open fields to and from their nest sites. It was near the maintenance trail that Bachman's Sparrow nested at one time. Prairie Warbler, White-eyed Vireo, and Summer Tanager are residents close to an old, abandoned brick house near the start of the above trail.

ACCOMMODATIONS: A primitive campground is available on the sanctuary property and can be used, for a small maintenance fee, with the permission of the resident manager. Nearby motels are available at Connersville.

REFERENCES:

Gough, M. (1976) Breeding bird census, Mary Gray Bird Sanctuary. *Indiana Audubon Quarterly* 54:32.

Keller, C. E. (1962) Composite list of birds of Mary Gray Sanctuary. *Indiana Audubon Quarterly* 40:24–25.

Lindsey, A. A. et al. (1969) *Natural areas in Indiana and their preservation* (Lafayette: Indiana Natural Areas Survey), pp. 219–222.

Webster, J. D. (1961) Three years of breeding bird censuses at the Sanctuary. *Indiana Audubon Quarterly* 39:52–54.

Webster, J. D. et al. (1962) Beech-maple forest. *Audubon Field Notes* 16:370.

——— (1963) Beech-maple forest. *Audubon Field Notes* 17:366.

——— (1965) Tornado-disturbed beech-maple forest. *Audubon Field Notes* 19:423–424.

Wise, K. (1951) A breeding bird census at Mary Gray Bird Sanctuary. *Indiana Audubon Quarterly* 29:55–58.

Zimmerman, H. A. (1967) Sanctuary nests. *Indiana Audubon Quarterly* 45:54–55.

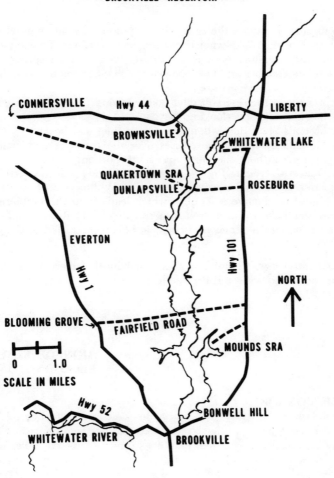

BROOKVILLE RESERVOIR

43.
BROOKVILLE RESERVOIR
WHITEWATER STATE PARK

DESCRIPTION AND BIRDING AREAS: The comparatively new, 5,260-acre Brookville Reservoir is located northeast of Brookville, on State Road 101. The 1,515-acre Whitewater State Park is located off that same state road about 3 miles southwest of Liberty. Both can be visited in one day.

In its short existence the reservoir has produced some unusual records: Western Grebe, White-winged Scoter, and Northern Phalarope. Large numbers of migratory waterfowl visit the area in both spring and fall, and the late October and early November flight of Snow Geese has been impressive.

Four areas of the reservoir offer good viewing (see map):

1. Bonwell Hill—overlooking the dam.
2. Mounds State Recreation Area—large inlet and beach.
3. Fairfield Road Bridge—crosses over the reservoir and enables the observer to scan both the north and south portions.
4. Quakertown State Recreation Area and Bridge—at the northern end.

A series of six trails is available within Whitewater State Park. One of the most productive is Trail 6, which leads from the southern end of Whitewater Lake to an overview of the Brookville Reservoir. For many years an annual Chirstmas bird count has been conducted in the park.

ACCOMMODATIONS: Camping available at both the reservoir and the park. Motels at Connersville and Brookville.

44.
MONROE RESERVOIR
BLOOMINGTON AREA

LAKE MONROE

DESCRIPTION: Bordering U.S. 37 on the west and State Road 46 on the north, Lake Monroe is the largest lake (10,750 acres) within Indiana. Many side roads provide ready access to most of its 125 miles of shoreline. There are spectacular views of the surrounding primitive countryside. Although heavily developed in some areas, it is nonetheless very attractive to migratory waterfowl and shorebirds. Maps of the lake are available at the Paynetown information center and at various other locations in the vicinity.

Birders anticipating a trip here should be prepared to spend considerable time exploring the lake's many inlets. These offer haven to herons and dabbling ducks, which can become abundant during spring and fall. During the winter, when the water begins to freeze over, Golden and Bald Eagles are often observed. Nearly 200 species of birds have been recorded.

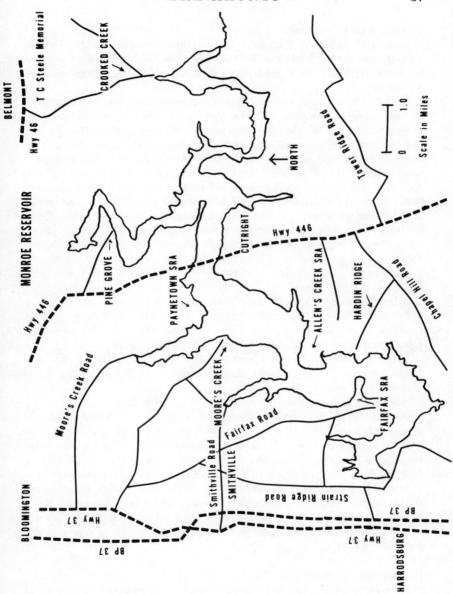

BIRDING AREAS (see map):
Dam and Spillway: Common Loon, Horned Grebe, White Pelican (once), and diving ducks can be observed. The limestone ledges created when the spillway was constructed host many nesting Rough-winged Swallows.

Fairfax: Steve Glass, who has birded the area extensively, has furnished the following information: "Fairfax Recreation Area is located near the southwestern end of Monroe Reservoir on the north side. Here a low narrow peninsula juts out 3,000 feet into the reservoir, extending over halfway to the opposite (eastern) shore. At the base of the peninsula is a large paved parking area, bathhouse, and pay beach. Up the hill, on Fairfax Road, there is a small, unpaved parking area where one can park free. The varied habitat and location of this peninsula make it one of the best birding spots for its size in Indiana. I have seen over 140 species of birds on or up the hill from the peninsula, including 17 species of ducks, 10 species of raptors, 22 species of shorebirds, 8 species of gulls and terns, and 10 species of warblers. The best time for birding the peninsula is late summer through the fall season when the water level is usually below normal pool level."

Moore's Creek: Overlooks the widest portion of the reservoir.

Paynetown: North and east of Moore's Creek. Has primitive camping facilities. State Road 446 crosses the reservoir just east of Paynetown. Here you can see both the upper and lower portions of the lake.

Crooked Creek: Located about 3 miles south of Belmont off State Highway 46 on T. C. Steele Road. Excellent area for wading birds (herons) and waterfowl.

Allen Creek: A rugged area just east of Hardin Ridge.

Hardin Ridge: A favorite of backpackers and hikers, the area abounds in scenic beauty.

Hickory Ridge Tower: A delightful scenic drive along Tower Ridge Road leads into a primitive area. At the tower, park your car and walk the trail north to the reservoir. (The Sassafras Audubon Society publishes a booklet called *A Hiker's Guide to Nebo Ridge* that is available at newsstands, bookstores, and bait shops in Monroe and Brown Counties. Many of the trails it describes begin at or near the Hickory Ridge Fire Tower.) Near the tower are extensive pine plantings where Pine Warblers are believed to nest.

BLOOMINGTON AREA

Besides Monroe Reservoir, there are many other excellent birding spots near Bloomington, some of which are treated separately (see

Morgan-Monroe State Forest, Brown County State Park, etc.). Two other places that offer good birding, one to the northeast of the city and one to the northwest, are:

1. Griffy Lake. A small storage reservoir nestled among rolling hills north of the Indiana University campus, about a mile east of the junction of old State Road 37 and the SR 46 Bypass. From the junction, drive east on the Bypass ⁸⁄₁₀ mile to the Indiana State Police Post, then turn north onto Matlock Road and continue in a northerly direction approximately one more mile to the lake. Cross the bridge, park the car, and proceed eastward, birding as you go, along the north shore of the lake, through the swamp, across the creek, and into the meadow on the south side. Along this route Amy Perry, Lynn Lightfoot, and Bobbi Diehl have recorded, among other sightings, Eastern Bluebirds, a Green Heron, several species of warblers, and, in 1976, a Yellow-headed Blackbird. Another local birder, Steve Glass, has found drumming Ruffed Grouse in the surrounding hills and, during the winter of 1976–77, a flock of 50–100 Evening Grosbeaks at a nearby feeding station.

2. Bloomington Sewage Plant. From the junction of old 37 and the SR 46 Bypass, drive west 1 mile. Turn north onto the 37 Bypass and drive 3 miles to the Bottom Road sign, just south of the overpass. Turn left onto Bottom Road and go north 1.1 mile to Maple Grove Road, where a large, heated storage pond, set in high banks, is a gathering place for waterfowl during the winter when other bodies of water are frozen over. Walk carefully up to the fence that surrounds the pond. Large numbers of Common Goldeneyes, Bufflehead, and other waterfowl can generally be seen during December, January, and February. In late March and continuing into May check the surrounding low-lying fields for shorebirds. Here Tom Potter found hundreds of Common Snipe, Lesser Yellowlegs, and Pectoral Sandpipers in early April.

ACCOMMODATIONS: Numerous camping facilities in the Lake Monroe area. Both lodging and food available at the comfortable and convenient Inn of the Fourwinds at the lake. Many less expensive motels and eating places in Bloomington.

REFERENCE:

Newhall, S. (1976) White Pelican at Monroe Reservoir in September 1975. *Indiana Audubon Quarterly* 54:11.

45.
VERSAILLES STATE PARK

DESCRIPTION AND BIRDING AREAS: Established in 1943, Versailles State Park was acquired through the U.S. Department of Interior's National Park Service. Unusual topographic features of this 5,897-acre park include Laughery Creek and Fallen Timber Creek, which are bordered by scenic hillsides of limestone outcroppings. A 230-acre lake has been created at the junction of these creeks; two moderate hiking trails provide opportunities to scan the surrounding countryside. Located north of U.S. Highway 50 near Versailles in the southeastern corner of the state, it has not been extensively birded.

ACCOMMODATIONS: Campgrounds are available within the park.

46.
MUSCATATUCK NATIONAL WILDLIFE REFUGE

DESCRIPTION: Muscatatuck, Indiana's only national wildlife refuge, is located 3 miles east of Seymour south of U.S. Highway 50. Interstate Highway 65 and U.S. Highway 31 parallel the west boundary. The refuge is easily reached from Indianapolis, Louisville, or Cincinnati.

A short drive from the entrance is a modern information center where visitors can obtain maps and a bird list of approximately 232 species known to occur in the area. Radiating from the center are foot trails designed to provide the birder with varied habitat, including a boardwalk into a large secondary forest marsh. American Woodcock, Great Horned Owl, and Pileated Woodpeckers are frequently seen from this area. Another foot trail, screened by multiflora rose bushes, provides an overview of a marsh immediately behind the visitor center.

The word "Muscatatuck" is derived from the language of the Piankeshaw Tribe of the Algonquin Indians and means "Land of the Winding Waters." Formerly an area of unspoiled marshes and woodlands, it became in later years spot farms and deforested woodlands. Poor farming practices stripped much of the land of its cover, resulting in erosion and loss of fertility. The consequent high acidic soil reduced farming, with resultant abandonment. In 1966 land was acquired by the U.S. Fish and Wildlife Service and restoration initiated. Today the refuge encompasses 7,702 acres of water, marsh, timber and croplands in Jackson and Jennings Counties of south-central Indiana.

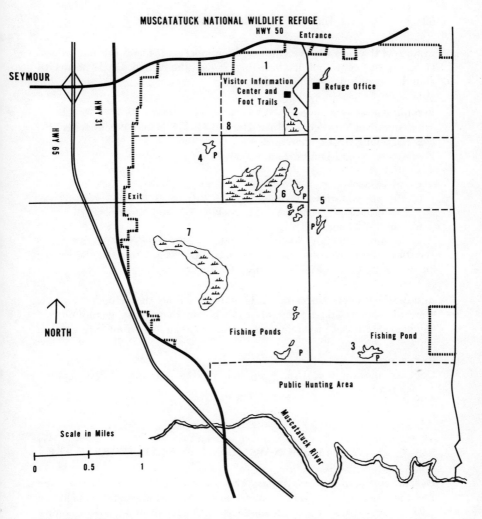

MUSCATATUCK NATIONAL WILDLIFE REFUGE

Habitat development plans include the construction of six impoundments totaling over 1,000 acres of permanent water and over 1,200 acres of temporary water areas. These temporary water areas will be in the form of green tree reservoirs and moist soil units which will be flooded in the fall and spring and drained in early summer to allow plant growth. Waterfowl populations are expected to peak at 50,000 ducks and 3,000 geese in response to this habitat development. Of prime importance is the provision of habitat for the many species of nesting and migrating waterfowl that use the area during the annual spring and fall migrations. Here, in the center of its breeding range, the Wood Duck occurs in abundance and may easily be observed.

BIRDING AREAS (see map):
1. American Woodcock, Great Horned Owl, Pileated Woodpecker
2. Dabbling ducks, shorebirds
3. Geese, Wood Ducks, American Kestrel
4. Waterfowl
5. Sparrows
6. Herons, waterfowl, shorebirds
7. Waterfowl (especially Wood Ducks), Pileated Woodpecker
8. Sandhill Cranes

In addition, feeding stations near the visitor center often attract a variety of the more common species plus, "in season," some of the winter finches (e.g., Purple Finch, Evening Grosbeak).

ACCOMMODATIONS: No camping is allowed within the refuge; however, there are motels and restaurants available in the nearby community of Seymour. State and private campgrounds are available within a few miles.

REFERENCE:
Dept. of the Interior, U.S. Fish and Wildlife Circular #RF–33540–1 March 1976.

47.
JACKSON-WASHINGTON STATE FOREST AREA

DESCRIPTION AND BIRDING AREAS: This area includes Starve Hollow Lake and the discontinuous Jackson-Washington State Forest. Starve Hollow Lake is located about 3 miles southeast of Vallonia on a marked county road which junctions at State Road 135. The State Forest area begins about 3 miles southeast of Brownstown, on State Road 250. Immediately southeast of the lake, below the dam, is the Vallonia Fish Hatchery. This area has produced some outstanding shorebird records, particularly when the pond is low. Some of these include: Semipalmated Plover, Lesser Golden Plover, Willet, both Yellowlegs, White-rumped Sandpiper, Baird's Sandpiper, Dunlin, Stilt Sandpiper, Western Sandpiper, and Northern Phalarope.

The lake itself, although comparatively small (145 acres), is at times quite productive. Eight species of herons have occurred, including: Little Blue, Yellow-crowned Night Heron, and the Least Bittern, which nested in 1954 (Mumford, 1965). Twenty-two species of waterfowl have occurred, including a Surf Scoter. In the surrounding fields Short-eared Owl, Dickcissel, Bachman's Sparrow (nesting), and Lapland Longspur have been observed.

The state forest area is excellent for migratory species with some thirty species of warblers being recorded; some of these include: Worm-eating, Golden-winged, Blue-winged, Orange-crowned, Cape May, Blackburnian, Bay-breasted, and Wilson's Warblers.

ACCOMMODATIONS: Starve Hollow Lake has 200 "Class C" campsites. Motels available near Seymour, about 12 miles from Vallonia.

REFERENCES:

Fleetwood, R. J. (1931) Notes from Jackson County. Indiana Audubon Yearbook 83.
———— (1933) Birds of Jackson County, Indiana. The American Midland Naturalist 14:(1)17–35.
Mumford, R. E. (1965) Additions to the birds of Jackson County, Indiana. Indiana Audubon Quarterly 43:40–48.

48.
CRANE NAVAL AMMUNITION DEPOT AND MARTIN STATE FOREST

DESCRIPTION AND BIRDING AREAS: On the grounds of the Crane Naval Ammunition Depot, located about 10 miles south of Bloomfield on State Highway 231, a variety of habitat coupled with the large Lake Greenwood attracts many species. Annual Christmas Counts are held there and from time to time groups may obtain access to the area—by permission from the Commandant only. The 1975–76 Christmas Count produced a Red-throated Loon.

Southeast of the Depot, Martin State Forest is a little-explored area that potentially would seem to offer ideal habitat for arboreal species; it is one of the most scenic spots in Indiana and well worth investigating.

Just southeast of Shoals are the Hindostan Falls. They are located on Highway 550, which parallels a meandering creek that provides the source for these falls. The senior author remembers a spectacular May migration in this area when birds were literally in every tree and bush.

ACCOMMODATIONS: Motels available at Shoals.

49.
GREENE-SULLIVAN STATE FOREST

DESCRIPTION AND BIRDING AREAS: This is a noted fishing area consisting of 5,488 acres of land and water in Sullivan and Greene Counties in west-central Indiana. All of the mined land on the property was reclaimed by coal companies and later donated to the Department of Natural Resources for a state forest. Over 112 lakes provide habitat for waterfowl during migratory periods. Access to the forest is via State Highway 159 south of Dugger.

ACCOMMODATIONS: Over 100 primitive camping sites border several of the lakes.

50.
CLIFTY FALLS STATE PARK

DESCRIPTION: Established in 1920, this very scenic 1,309-acre park overlooks the Ohio River and the historic town of Madison. Its star attraction is Clifty Falls itself, plummeting 70 feet into a narrow gorge; other natural wonders include canyons, fern-covered cliffs, wooded ravines, and additional waterfalls. It also possesses eleven miles of moderate to rugged hiking trails, an Olympic-size swimming pool, and a wading pool.

BIRDING AREAS: The nine trails that intersect the park offer a variety of habitat. Trail 1 is of moderate difficulty; it winds along the canyon rim past the observation tower overlooking the Ohio River, and returns to the park road. From the tower one can look down on nearby treetops, obtaining excellent views of arboreal species. Here too can be seen Turkey and the rarer Black Vultures, migrating hawks, and at times migrating passerines. Trail 2 joins with Trail 1 at the source, then winds down the creek bed at the mouth of the canyon to the foot of Clifty Falls. This trail gives the viewer unexcelled observation of Louisiana Waterthrush, Ovenbird, and Hooded Warbler. Trail 3 leads through similar habitat, but ends near a picnic area. Trail 4, beginning at Hoffman Falls, overlooks the rim, enabling observers to scan the treetops, especially productive during migration periods. Trail 8 offers essentially the same type of viewing as Trail 5. The road leading to Cragmont Shelter is bordered by large, neglected open fields. Sharp-tailed, Grasshopper, and Savannah Sparrows can be found by careful searching during the fall.

ACCOMMODATIONS: In the park, the relatively new Clifty Inn and Motor Lodge has air-conditioned rooms plus a modern dining room. Two campgrounds, one with modern facilities, will accommodate trailers. Further information can be obtained by writing: Reservation Clerk, Clifty Inn, P.O. Box 387, Madison, Indiana 47250. There are also hotels in nearby Madison.

REFERENCE:
Michaud, H. (1942) More on the nesting birds of Indiana state parks. *Indiana Audubon Yearbook*, 6–10.

51.
FALLS OF THE OHIO

DESCRIPTION AND BIRDING AREAS: Considered by many to be part of the state of Kentucky, the Falls of the Ohio can only be reached from the Indiana shore. Indeed, there is some question, due to changing river boundaries, about the exact ownership of this historically important area. It is also important ornithologically. Residents of nearby Louisville have birded the Falls for many years, and there is a host of published accounts of its unusual attraction for migratory waterfowl and shorebirds. Both Alexander Wilson and John James Audubon visited the Falls, and portions of their works mention many of the birds encountered. It is believed that the latter author completed many of his paintings nearby.

The Falls are located west of the Interstate 65 bridge along a street that parallels the river. They can be reached during periods of low water levels by carefully wading from the Indiana shore. When the water level is high, access is possible only by boat. Water levels are controlled by the operation of locks located above the Falls. They are usually closed during the fall when river level is low. It is then that your chances of seeing the rarer birds are best.

Some of the species seen at the Falls include White Pelican, Wood Stork, Whistling Swan, Bald Eagle, Osprey, Peregrine Falcon, Black-legged Kittiwake, and Glaucous Gull. It is the fall migration of shorebirds, however, that makes the area unique. On the algae-coated rocks and in the small pools of semi-stagnant water fair numbers of migrant shorebirds gather, providing the observer with unprecedented views as they doze and feed. Some of the 26 species recorded include Lesser Golden Plover, Black-bellied Plover, Willet, Ruddy Turnstone, Wilson's Phalarope, Northern Phalarope, Red Phalarope, Short-billed Dowitcher, Red Knot, Sanderling, Western, White-rumped, and Baird's Sandpipers, Dunlin, Stilt Sandpiper, and Buff-breasted Sandpiper.

The willows that line the north side of the river were former nesting sites for Black-crowned Night Heron, and during the summer they host occasional Little Blue Heron, Snowy and Great Egrets.

ACCOMMODATIONS: There are numerous hotels and motels along Interstate 65, but no campgrounds.

REFERENCES:

Able, K. P. (1965) Notes on the occurrence of some birds at the Falls of the Ohio during the fall of 1964. *Indiana Audubon Quarterly* 43: 49–51.

Audubon, J. J. (1840–1844) *The Birds of America* (Dover Reprints Edition, 1967). 7 vols.

Kemsies, E., and Randle, W. (1958) *Birds of Southeastern Ohio* (privately published).

Lovell, H. B. (1951) Water birds at the Falls of the Ohio. *Indiana Audubon Quarterly* 29:2–7.

Mengel, R. M. (1965) *Birds of Kentucky*. Ornithological Monograph #3 (American Ornithologists' Union), 581 pp.

Monroe, B. L. (1939) Bird life at the Falls of the Ohio. *Indiana Audubon Yearbook* 14–18.

Monroe, B. L., and Monroe, B. L., Jr. (1961) Birds of the Louisville region. *The Kentucky Warbler* 37:23–42.

Monroe, B. L., Jr. (1976) Birds of the Louisville region. *The Kentucky Warbler* 52:39–64.

Stamm, A. L., Brecher, L., and Croft, J. (1967) Recent studies at the Falls of the Ohio. *The Kentucky Warbler* 43:3–12.

Wilson, A. (1808–1814) *American Ornithology*. 9 vols.

52.

HARDY LAKE–CROSLEY STATE FISH AND WILDLIFE AREA

DESCRIPTION AND BIRDING AREAS: The newly-created 750-acre Hardy Lake State Recreation Area is located just south of State Road 250 and east of Interstate 65. Recent bird sightings by members of the Beckham Bird Club of Louisville have aroused considerable interest in the area, and visitors to the nearby Crosley State Fish and Wildlife Area or Muscatatuck National Wildlife Refuge can easily include a side trip to this region.

Hardy Lake has produced White-winged Scoter, Leconte's and Sharp-tailed Sparrows, and Snow Bunting. Good birding locations are the overlook area near the dam, Sunnyside Beach, and the Wooster Campground.

Crosley State Fish and Wildlife Area lies astraddle State Road 3 just south of Vernon. Its 4,042 acres contain six ponds and border the Muscatatuck River. Its main claim to fame was a recent nesting record for the Long-eared Owl.

ACCOMMODATIONS: Camping is available at both the above locations with motels at the Interstate 65 exchange near Crothersville.

REFERENCE:
Mumford, R. E. (1976) Nesting of the Long-eared Owl in Indiana. *Indiana Audubon Quarterly* 54:95–97.

53.
CLARK STATE FOREST

DESCRIPTION AND BIRDING AREAS: The discontinuous Clark State Forest is located on U.S. Highway 31, 10 miles south of Scottsburg or one mile north of Henryville just off I-65. It has not been extensively birded except for Deam Lake which lies just north of State Highway 60 about 6 miles southeast of New Providence. Here, members of the Beckham Bird Club of Louisville have periodically visited and recorded small numbers of waterfowl and an occasional Common Loon. Three other lakes are included in the forest: Schlamm, Franke, and Bowen Lakes. A fish hatchery located near Hardy Road just north of Schlamm Lake may be attractive, at times, to shorebirds.

ACCOMMODATIONS: Campgrounds are located near the main entrance, with motels at nearby Scottsburg.

54.
HARRISON-CRAWFORD STATE FOREST

DESCRIPTION AND BIRDING AREAS: Harrison-Crawford State Forest is located on State Road 462, 6½ miles west of Corydon. Affording a splendid panorama of the Ohio River countryside at its southern terminus, it will give both naturalist and sightseer respite from the hustle and bustle of everyday life. It is in this part of the State that Chuck-will's-widow can usually be found. Drive the scenic country roads at dusk and listen carefully for the typical call note of this species. The "chuck" part of the call is usually inaudible (unless close at hand), but the "will's widow" is diagnostic and may be heard from late April into July. Just recently, Black Vultures have nested in the area.

In the forest area are the Wyandotte Caves, located on U.S. 460 west of Wyandotte. Open from 8:45 A.M. to 3:45 P.M. during the spring, autumn, and winter, these consist of a large complex of underground passages with a variety of magnificent rock formations.

Neither area has been heavily birded, especially in recent years, so that any ornithological work would be of great benefit in furthering our understanding of bird distribution in this region.

ACCOMMODATIONS: Camping facilities are available and motels can be found in nearby Corydon.

REFERENCES:
Kahl, P. (1953) The status of the Chuck-will's-widow in southern Indiana. *Indiana Audubon Quarterly* 31:72–75.
Lovell, H. B. (1950) Chuck-will's-widow is invading southern Indiana. *Indiana Audubon Quarterly* 28:57–58.
Mumford, R. E. (1974) Black Vultures nesting in Crawford County, Indiana. *Indiana Audubon Quarterly* 52:67–69.

55.
SPRING MILL STATE PARK

DESCRIPTION: Located 3 miles southeast of Mitchell along the north side of Highway 60 in Lawrence County, Spring Mill State Park contains some 1,319 acres. Outstanding features include a large stone gristmill and pioneer village, Virgil Grissom memorial, Donaldson and Twin Caves, and the 80-acre Donaldson Woods. The latter consists of native virgin timber among which are a tulip tree with a fifty-two inch girth and several white oaks exceeding thirty-six inches in girth, all worth seeing in themselves. The gristmill produces stoneground cornmeal that is a favorite of many cornbread fanciers. The two large caves are famous Midwest attractions, which visitors may tour on conducted trips only. There is also a series of six trails, ranging from moderate to rugged, that are carefully laid out to ensure maximum viewing of the surrounding area.

Some of the birds recorded in the area as resident include: Tufted Titmouse, Carolina Chickadee, White-eyed, Red-eyed, and Warbling Vireos, Common Yellowthroat, Yellow-breasted Chat, and Summer Tanager.

BIRDING AREAS: Trail 1 begins from the Inn, runs along Donaldson Branch and Lake, and returns to the Inn. Check the lake for Green Heron and Wood Duck. Trail 2 connects the village parking area to the picnic area and boat docks and is especially good for migrating Wood Warblers. The more rugged trail 3 begins near the Inn cabins and passes through Donaldson Cave gorge and several sink holes to Donaldson Woods and Twin Caves, and returns via another beautiful stand of virgin woods. Check the various ravines for Hooded Warblers and the virgin woods for Wood Thrush and Scarlet Tanager.

Trail 4, also quite rugged, may be entered from Trail 6 at the picnic area; it goes by Donaldson Cave and Hamer Cemetery. This is an excellent trail during early spring for migrating species—particularly the area paralleling the small stream that emanates from the cave and eventually flows into the lake. All *Catharus* thrushes are common during early May and once again in mid-September. Trail 5 circles the lower section of the lake from the bridge to the boat docks. Trail 6 connects the village with the primitive campground. It borders the mill creek, where Louisiana Waterthrush may be found.

ACCOMMODATIONS: The recently remodeled Spring Mill Inn offers good accommodations and meals that are tasty and usually quite reasonable. The campground is amply equipped except for modern hookups. There is also a primitive campground. Naturalist service is available year-round. For more information call 812–849–4129.

REFERENCES:

Lindsey, A. A. et al. (1969) *Natural areas in Indiana and their preservation* (Lafayette: Indiana Natural Areas Survey), pp. 170–175.

Michaud, H. H. (1942) More on the nesting birds of Indiana state parks. *Indiana Audubon Yearbook* 6–10.

Overlease, W. R., and Overlease, E. (1974) Winter bird studies at Spring Mill State Park. *Indiana Audubon Quarterly*, 52:61–63.

56.
HOOSIER NATIONAL FOREST

DESCRIPTION: The huge Hoosier National Forest contains some 180,000 acres in south-central Indiana. Located in the Crawford and Norman uplands of that region, it stretches from Lake Monroe on the north to the Ohio River at the south and lies within a day's drive of the metropolitan centers of Cincinnati, Louisville, Evansville, and Indianapolis. Despite its nearness to these cities it still retains a variety of habitats—rolling hills with sharp ridge lines, lakes and streams, colorful stands of hardwoods, and a rich, green background of pine and cedar.

Major roads leading to the region are State Highway 37 (from Indianapolis), U.S. Highways 150 and 460 (from Louisville), U.S. Highway 50, and State Highway 64. An impressive list of nearly 250 species of birds has been recorded.

BIRDING AREAS: Proceeding from the north to the south, the following areas are interesting:

1. Nebo Ridge Wilderness Area. A favorite of backpackers and campers lying just south of Monroe Reservoir (see Monroe Reservoir: Hardin Ridge and Hickory Ridge Tower).

2. Avoca State Fish Hatchery. Located just west of State Highway 37 on State Highway 54. Ponds attract large numbers of migrating swallows during late April and early May and, when low or drained, occasional shorebirds.

3. Springs Valley State Fish and Game Area. Located about 6 miles west of State Highway 37 on the Youngs Creek Road. A small reservoir just south of French Lick is good during waterfowl migration.

4. Ferdinand State Forest. Located northeast of the State Highway 162–64 interchange on State Road 264 west of the Forest boundary. A nearby fish hatchery may provide good habitat for shorebirds. Neither has been heavily birded.

5. Ohio River Overlook. Located just west of the small town of Rome off Highway 66, it provides a panoramic view of the river and surrounding countryside.

ACCOMMODATIONS: Camping is available at the following sites:

1. Buzzard Roost Overlook: West of Alton.
2. German Ridge Recreation Area: On State Highway 66 about 6 miles east of Tell City.
3. Hardin Ridge Recreation Area: About 3 miles east of State Highway 446 and 3 miles south of the Monroe Reservoir overpass.
4. Lake Celina: Three miles west of State Highway 37 near Saint Croix.
5. Saddle Lake Recreation Area: Southwest of State Highway 37 junction with State Highway 70.

Motels in most large cities and towns nearby.

REFERENCE:

Schrodt, P., Riddle, M., and Lynch, M. P. (1975) *Nebo Ridge—Wilderness for Indiana*. Hoosier Group of the Sierra Club Publication. 105 pp.

57.
GLENDALE FISH AND WILDLIFE AREA

DESCRIPTION AND BIRDING AREAS: Located about 6 miles west of U.S. Highway 231, Glendale Fish and Wildlife Area is one of the better locations for waterfowl observation in southwestern Indiana. Dogwood Lake offers shelter for migrating Gadwall and Hooded Merganser, especially during late fall before the water freezes over, while during the summer both White-eyed Vireo and Summer Tanager are fairly easy to observe. The area is not heavily birded and may offer some potential for the enterprising explorer.

ACCOMMODATIONS: Camping is available.

58.
EASTERN GIBSON AND WESTERN PIKE COUNTIES

DESCRIPTION AND BIRDING AREAS (see map): Recent intense observation of several areas within eastern Gibson and western Pike Counties by local observers (e.g., Charles Mills, Marietta Smith, et al.) has resulted in several unusual and important bird records for Indiana. While it could be argued that each of these areas is deserving of individual treatment, it seems simpler, because of their proximity, to include them in this overall discussion. Avid birders could survey this entire region in a good day's birding.

1. Buckskin Bottoms. Lying astraddle State Road 57 immediately south of the small town of Buckskin in southwestern Indiana is this large area of swampy secondary forest land (some of which is literally impenetrable). Good area for Wood Duck and several species of heron.

2. Hemmer Woods. Take County Road 950E from Mackey, 2 miles south to 1050E and then north for ¼ mile to Hemmer's Lane. The area is particularly good during spring migration for warblers.

3. Cedar Valley. Take 1150S 4 miles east of Mackey to the junction of 150W. A heavily pined strip pit area of the Patoka Fish and Wildlife Area.

4. Blue Grosbeak Nesting Area. Just north of Summerville, and opposite the Blue Diamond Lounge. Take county road 450S three miles east to an area bordered by rolling, open, hilly land on the south and strip-mined, planted area on the north. Check both sides of the road for Blue Grosbeak. Males generally perch in treetops or on telephone wires where

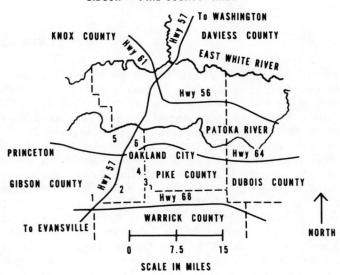

GIBSON – PIKE COUNTY AREA

To WASHINGTON

KNOX COUNTY
Hwy 57
Hwy 61

DAVIESS COUNTY

EAST WHITE RIVER

Hwy 56

PATOKA RIVER

PRINCETON
OAKLAND CITY
Hwy 64

5
6

GIBSON COUNTY
Hwy 57
4
PIKE COUNTY
DUBOIS COUNTY

3
2
Hwy 68

1

WARRICK COUNTY

To EVANSVILLE

NORTH

0   7.5   15

SCALE IN MILES

they sing their characteristic warbling song. In the area south of the road, walk back on one of the numerous side roads and watch for Lark Sparrow. Approximately four to six pairs have been sighted here during late spring and early summer. Young were observed by Tim Keller in 1977.

5. Patoka River Bottoms: Take State Road 57 3.2 miles north of State Road 64 junction, turn west on County Road 50N 1.7 miles to the bottomland area. From this point a county road leads north through the bottomlands, affording the observer excellent vantagepoints for viewing herons, waterfowl, and shorebirds. Where the river crosses the road check for Prothonotary Warblers. Some recent sightings include: Little Blue Heron, Great Egret, Snowy Egret, Yellow-crowned Night Heron (common), Cinnamon Teal (spring, 1977), Sandhill Cranes, Long-billed Dowitcher, and Pectoral Sandpiper. The area is especially attractive to shorebirds when it is flooded.

6. Oakland City Lake and Strip Pit Area: Southeast of Oakland City. The lake produces good numbers of waterfowl, while in the strip pit area just east of the lake, Bell's Vireo and Lark Sparrow occur.

ACCOMMODATIONS: Primitive camping in Patoka Fish and Wildlife Area, with motels at Petersburg.

59.
LAKE GIBSON

DESCRIPTION AND BIRDING AREAS: One of the major attractions for migratory waterfowl in southwestern Indiana is the newly-created 2,000-acre storage reservoir of the Gibson County Power Plant (Lake Gibson). The plant is located 9.5 miles west of Princeton on State Road 64 just east of the Wabash River. Before entering the area, you must register at the southern end of the lake located on a side road that leads to Skelton. That same side road passes a series of runoff ponds that are semi-marshy and provide adequate foraging for dabbling ducks, herons, and some shorebirds. During the late fall and in winter the surrounding fields often host Short-eared Owl, Water Pipit, Lapland Longspur, and Snow Bunting.

Some of the species recorded from the storage reservoir include: Common Loon, Double-crested Cormorant, Canada Goose, Snow Goose, large concentrations of Mallard and Black Ducks (especially during the late fall), Ring-necked Duck (July record), Lesser Scaup, Oldsquaw, and Common Goldeneye.

ACCOMMODATIONS: Motels at nearby Princeton.

60.
HOVEY LAKE

DESCRIPTION AND BIRDING AREAS: Hovey Lake State Fish and Wildlife Area consists of 4,400 acres located in the extreme southwestern portion of the State near Mt. Vernon. It borders State Road 69 south of that city. Long known for its extensive bald cypress stands and other rare flora and fauna, it lost some of its attractiveness after the recent construction of the Wabash Island Dam. That dam has raised the water level about seven feet, which is killing the cypress that acted as a haven for many species of unusual birds. At one time, Double-crested Cormorant, Osprey, and Prothonotary Warbler nested in this location, and Great Egrets were common visitors during the late summer and early fall.

Main attraction of the lake now is the thousands of Canada Geese and other waterfowl that pass through during fall and early spring, some of which have wintered when weather allowed them to do so. A persistent rumor that Swainson's Warbler nested here is derived from data of Ridgway, but nesting of this species has never been proved and the bird remains on the hypothetical list for the State.

ACCOMMODATIONS: Motels and restaurants are located at nearby Mt. Vernon.

REFERENCES:
Buskirk, W. (1966) Summer bird notes from Hovey Lake and vicinity. *Indiana Audubon Quarterly* 44:100–101.
Esten, S. R. (1933) Hovey's Lake, summer bird paradise. *Indiana Audubon Yearbook* 15.
Hicks, L. E. (1935) The Wood Ibis observed in southern Indiana. *Wilson Bulletin* 56(2):125.
Mumford, R. E. (1950) Osprey nesting at Hovey Lake. *Indiana Audubon Quarterly* 28:32–33.
Perkins, S. E. (1932) Hovey Lake in August. *Indiana Audubon Yearbook* 86–87.
Skarr, P. (1951) Posey County expedition. *Indiana Audubon Quarterly* 29:13–14.

61.
WESSELMAN PARK

DESCRIPTION AND BIRDING AREAS: The city of Evansville can be justifiably proud of this 400-acre parcel of land located within its city limits, west of Stockwell Road and north of Division Street. Concerning the 205-acre wooded section, Lindsey et al. (1969) writes "that the average acre contains 6.25 trees over 30 in. dbh. Also, the numerous trees of the same and other species between 20 and 30 in. make this a splendid forest; a stand of this size and quality within a city or town is not found elsewhere in Indiana, if anywhere."

As might be expected in a forest this size, species such as Great Horned Owl, Pileated Woodpecker, Acadian Flycatcher, Cerulean Warbler, and other arboreal species can usually be found. The main attraction, however, is the unique nature center located on the west side of the forest. Here an enclosed observation room enables the visitor to view, at close hand, many species that are enticed by a generous supply of suet, cracked corn, and other feed. Photographers will find an unexcelled opportunity to ply their skills with the many willing subjects that abound, particularly during the winter and early spring. Some of these include Common

Flicker, Red-bellied Woodpecker, Yellow-bellied Sapsucker, Hairy and Downy Woodpeckers, Carolina Chickadee, Tufted Titmouse, White-breasted Nuthatch, Carolina Wren, Yellow-rumped Warbler, Evening Grosbeak (occasional), Purple Finch, American Goldfinch, Rufous-sided Towhee, Northern Junco, White-throated Sparrow, Fox Sparrow, and Song Sparrow.

Programs geared to nature study and/or conservation are frequently held, and the Evansville Audubon Society has periodic meetings that are open to the public. Check with the personnel at the center for dates and times.

ACCOMMODATIONS: Numerous hotels and motels are located in Evansville.

REFERENCE:
Lindsey, A. A. et al. (1969) *Natural areas in Indiana and their preservation* (Lafayette: Indiana Natural Areas Survey), pp. 126–130.

62.
SCALES LAKE

DESCRIPTION AND BIRDING AREAS: Scales Lake lies just north of Highway 460 and ½ mile east of Boonville. A reconverted strip-mine area with a small lake and numerous pine plantings, it is, at times, attractive to waterfowl and to some migrating land birds. Immediately east and slightly south of the lake is a series of fish hatchery ponds that are excellent for shorebirds when the water level is low.

Some of the birds recorded were Bufflehead, Hooded Merganser, (Lesser) Golden Plover, both Yellowlegs, Pectoral and Least Sandpiper. During fall and winter check the pines that line the main park road for Red-breasted Nuthatch. An occasional Brown Thrasher and large numbers of White-throated and White-crowned Sparrows may be found wintering in the surrounding multiflora rose hedges. It was near this area that one of the authors found a Saw-whet Owl, and any small, dense pine planting should be thoroughly checked for that species.

ACCOMMODATIONS: Camping is allowed in specified areas; motels are available in Boonville.

63.
LINCOLN STATE PARK

DESCRIPTION AND BIRDING AREAS: Lincoln State Park commemorates the boyhood of Abraham Lincoln, who lived in the area from 1816–1830. The 1,731 acres consist of typical southern Indiana upland. Not too well known ornithologically, it offers a fertile field for investigation and study. The authors spent two days here in the summer of 1968 and found large numbers of resident White-eyed Vireos and Summer Tanagers.

An 85-acre artificial lake, stocked with game fish, is well known throughout southern Indiana for its fishing, and four hiking trails lead around the lake and to a fire tower. Within the park is Little Pigeon Primitive Baptist Church, built on the site of the early building in which the Lincoln family worshipped. Sarah Lincoln Grigsby, Lincoln's only sister, is buried in that church's cemetery.

Both Lincoln State Park and Lincoln Boyhood National Memorial are located on Indiana 162 near Lincoln City. About 10 miles southeast of the park is the town of Santa Claus, a focal point for Christmas mailings. A small amusement park and craft shops may provide visitors with diversion after a hard day's birding.

ACCOMMODATIONS: A campground is located within the park; some sites accommodate trailers. Motels and restaurants are located in nearby Santa Claus.

Part II

The Birds

Order Gaviiformes
Family Gaviidae: Loons

Common Loon
Gavia immer

FORMER STATUS: "The Loon is a regular migrant throughout the State in some numbers. They sometimes remain through the winter, but most of them do not" (Butler, 1898). He quotes an Hon. R. Wes McBride and others with breeding data for northern Indiana.

CURRENT STATUS: **North** Fairly common migrant; casual in winter and summer. 10 April–15 May; 15 October–20 November. One bird seen from 1 January–12 January 1973, St. Joseph Co. (N. Rea). One bird in winter plumage, 18 July 1976, Allen Co. (J. Haw). **Central** Fairly common migrant; casual in winter and summer. 1 April–5 May; 25 October–5 December. Four birds, 24 January 1976, Monroe Res. (S. Glass). Two seen 11 August 1975 in Delaware Co. (L. Carter). An estimated flock of 100, 19 November 1978, Eagle Creek Res. (A. Starling). **South** Fairly common migrant; very rare in winter and casual in summer. 25 March–30 April; 5 November–10 December. One, 11 January 1976, Gibson Co. (C. Mills). One, 9 July 1978, Gibson Co. (C. Mills–M. Brown).

REMARKS: Loons are extremely vulnerable to pesticide ingestion and avian diseases. As such they are good biologic indicators of environmental changes. An estimated 1,000–3,000 were found dead along southern Lake Michigan during the fall of 1976 (Kleen, 1977).

Arctic Loon
Gavia arctica

STATUS: **North** Accidental. Two records: 20–21 May 1961, Tippecanoe Co. (Burr, 1961); 15–16 May 1974, Huntington Co., documented by Neil Case and seen by many observers. **Central** Accidental. One record: 14 April 1949. Henry Co., specimen in Joseph Moore Museum at Earlham College (Cope, 1951).

Red-throated Loon
Gavia stellata

FORMER STATUS: "Rare winter resident and occasional migrant" (Butler, 1898). He presented data from four areas within the State.

81

CURRENT STATUS: **North** Generally a casual migrant; casual in winter. Some years (e.g., 1952–1957) could be considered a very rare migrant in counties bordering Lake Michigan. 10 October–15 December. Of the nine contemporary records only one, 18–22 April 1953, Michigan City (Segal, 1953) is for the spring. Ray Grow recorded one, 8 January 1955 at Michigan City (Burr, 1955). **Central** Casual migrant, 25 October–30 November. Of the five contemporary records only one, 20 April 1957, Geist Reservoir, by Satter and West, is for the spring (Keller, 1959). **South** Casual in winter. Only one contemporary record: 29 December 1975 at Lake Greenwood, Martin Co., by Mumford et al. (Masons, 1976). Probably a casual migrant.

REMARKS: Paucity of recent data suggests decline in population.

Order Podicipediformes
Family Podicipedidae: Grebes

Red-necked Grebe
Podiceps grisegena

FORMER STATUS: Butler (1898) termed it a rare migrant and a possible winter resident. West (1956) summarized the existing data accumulated since then and added about twelve records.

CURRENT STATUS: **North** Casual migrant and winter visitant. 20 March–10 April; 20 October–5 December. One seen 2 January 1956 at Michigan City by R. Grow (Smith, 1956). **Central** Casual migrant and winter visitant. 15 March–15 April; three late November dates since 1949. Latest is a bird seen near Nashville 27 November 1971. West found two 13 May 1967 at Geist Reservoir (Keller, 1967). One seen on White River in Marion Co. 24 December 1941 (West, 1956). **South** Casual migrant and winter visitant. Three seen at Lake Gibson 11 March 1979 (Kellers et al.).

REMARKS: This species recorded less frequently than the Western Grebe during recent years.

Horned Grebe
Podiceps auritus

FORMER STATUS: "Regular migrant in some numbers, but never abundant. Some are winter residents in suitable localities. In the northern part of the State among the lakes and marshes it breeds" (Butler, 1898). West (1956) refuted nesting data in his summary.

CURRENT STATUS: North Uncommon spring and fairly common fall migrant; very rare in winter. 15 March–1 May; 1 October–1 December. One observed on the St. Joseph River in South Bend, 13 February 1974, by Virgil Inman. Central Uncommon migrant; casual in winter. 10 March–20 April; 5 October–5 December. There are several winter dates. South Uncommon migrant; casual in winter. 5 March–15 April; 10 October–5 December. Charles Mills found two in Gibson Co., 2 February 1975.

REMARKS: Availability of open water is the determinative factor for winter birds.

Eared Grebe
Podiceps nigricollis

FORMER STATUS: Butler (1898) termed it an accidental visitor or rare migrant. West (1956) agreed essentially with that evaluation and added an additional ten records.

CURRENT STATUS: North Casual migrant and winter visitant. Some years (e.g., 1956–1959) could be considered a very rare migrant in counties bordering Lake Michigan. 20 March–15 April, 10 October–1 December. Several December dates. One late July date at Jasper-Pulaski (West, 1956). One remained near Hammond 19 August–25 November 1978. Central Casual migrant 25 March–15 April. Only two fall dates: 5 November 1886 (Butler, 1898) and 6 December 1952 (West, 1956). A bird found at Geist Reservoir by Al Starling 11 May 1968 (Oswalt & Wilson, 1969). South No data.

REMARKS: Fall birds very difficult to identify; bird must be seen in ideal conditions.

Western Grebe
Aechmophorus occidentalis

FORMER STATUS: Butler (1890) listed it as accidental on the basis of a supposed specimen. He refuted this data in his later work (Butler, 1898) and transferred it to hypothetical status. Apparently the first record for the State was one seen 27 October 1945 at Indiana Dunes State Park (DuMont and Smith, 1946). West (1956) listed five additional records.

CURRENT STATUS: North Casual fall migrant; casual in winter. 30 October–6 December. A bird seen by Ray Grow, 23 December 1956, at Michigan City (Ward, 1957). Central Casual migrant. Two widely separated spring dates: 2 April 1955, Lake Lemon (Keller), and 21 May 1967 (2 birds), Geist Reservoir (Keller–Starling). Two fall dates; 9 November 1976, Brookville Reservoir (Cope, Whitney, et al.) and 23 November 1975, Prairie Creek Reservoir (Carter–Wise). **South** No data.

REMARKS: Recent influx of records for eastern United States suggests change in migratory pattern.

§ **Pied-billed Grebe**
Podilymbus podiceps

FORMER STATUS: Butler (1898) reported: "throughout the greater part of the State it is seen regularly, but not very commonly, during the migrations, and is, perhaps, more commonly observed in spring. . . . It has never been reported as wintering in Indiana. . . ." West (1956) enlarged upon these statements by furnishing winter data and nesting data from 19 counties within the State.

CURRENT STATUS: North Common migrant; rare summer resident; very rare in winter. 10 April–10 May; 1 September–15 November. There are numerous winter dates. **Central** Common migrant; very rare summer resident; very rare in winter. 1 April–1 May; 10 September–30 November. Numerous winter data. **South** Fairly common migrant; recent breeding data lacking; very rare in winter. 20 March–25 April; 15 September–5 December. Numerous winter data.

REMARKS: Nesting records for central and southern regions are sparse.

Order Procellariiformes
Family Hydrobatidae: Storm Petrels

Band-rumped Storm Petrel
Oceanodroma castro

STATUS: Accidental, one record: 15 June 1902, specimen taken in Morgan Co. and deposited in the National Museum of Natural History (Butler, 1906).

Order Pelecaniformes
Family Pelecanidae: Pelicans

American White Pelican
Pelecanus erythrorhynchos

FORMER STATUS: "Almost every year one or more are noted from some place in the State, yet few are the persons who ever saw one alive" (Butler, 1898). West (1958) gave data for 23 counties and agreed with Butler's earlier evaluation.

CURRENT STATUS: **North** Casual migrant. Twelve records suggest mid-May and September are migratory periods. **Central** Casual migrant. Essentially the same migratory pattern as above. Most recent record, a bird seen near Martinsville, Morgan Co., 25 November 1976 (T. Alexander *fide* S. Glass), is also the latest record for the State. **South** Casual migrant. Migratory pattern for spring as above. Fall expanded into October.

Brown Pelican
Pelecanus occidentalis

STATUS: Accidental. A specimen taken in Marion Co. 28 March 1907 (Blatchley, 1907), present whereabouts of which is unknown. One seen at Fish Lake, Lagrange Co., during the spring of 1978 (*fide* R. Mumford).

Family Sulidae: Boobies and Gannets

Northern Gannet
Morus bassanus

STATUS: Accidental. One killed on Lake Michigan during November 1904, about two miles from Michigan City (Butler, 1906). Another specimen, found in Jay Co. 5 December 1947, is in the Purdue Wildlife Laboratory Collection (Kirkpatrick, 1948).

Familiy Phalacrocoracidae: Cormorants

§ **Double-crested Cormorant**
Phalacrocorax auritus

FORMER STATUS: "Regular migrant, more or less common along the larger streams. Doubtless occasionally winter resident in southern part of the

State . . ." (Butler, 1898). Sixty years later, West (1958) summarized the existing data and added breeding records for Posey Co. and a nesting attempt for Newton Co.

CURRENT STATUS: North Very rare migrant. Casual in winter. Attempted to breed in Newton Co. during 1953 but Mumford believed this attempt was unsuccessful (West, 1958). 10 April–1 June; 15 August–1 December. Central Very rare migrant. 1 April–25 May; 25 August–1 December. South Very rare migrant; casual in winter. Bred at Hovey Lake in 1934 and again from 1949–1954. 15 March–15 May; 15 August–5 December. Used to winter at Hovey Lake. A recent record of 27, Gibson Co., 23 April 1978 (C. Mills).

REMARKS: Status has changed considerably over the past 20 years probably due to this species' being at the top of a food chain affected by pesticides, etc. A slow increase is evident, particularly in southern Indiana, with many recent records by Charles Mills et al. in Gibson Co. area.

Family Anhingidae: Darters

American Anhinga
Anhinga anhinga

STATUS: Accidental. Two killed in 1858 and another (no date) near Indianapolis (Butler, 1898). One seen on the Ohio River about 5 miles above Jeffersonville 4 June 1964 by Floyd S. Carpenter and Morrison Hicks (Carpenter, 1964). On 14 August 1976, Mr. and Mrs. Charles E. Norton (*fide* B. Gill) observed two birds soaring around a small pond on their farm 3 miles north of Franklin. The birds descended into two small trees and were observed for about half an hour through binoculars.

Family Fregatidae: Frigatebirds

Magnificent Frigatebird
Fregata magnificens

STATUS: Accidental. One shot, Shelby Co., 14 July 1896 (Butler, 1898). One seen, Michigan City, 27–28 April 1957 by Landing et al. (West, 1958).

Order Ciconiiformes
Family Ardeidae: Herons and Bitterns

§ **Great Blue Heron**
Ardea herodias

FORMER STATUS: "Common migrant and summer resident. Rare winter resident southward. Breeding abundantly in suitable localities in the northern half of the State and in Knox and Gibson counties (Ridgway, Chansler)" (Butler, 1898). Keller (1966) agreed essentially with that report and summarized nesting data for 32 counties.

CURRENT STATUS: **North** Fairly common migrant; casual in winter. Active nest sites decreasing. 10 March–15 November. **Central** Fairly common migrant; very rare in winter. Active nest sites decreasing. 1 March–30 November. **South** Fairly common migrant; rare in winter. Recent nesting data lacking. 25 February–5 December.

REMARKS: Status has changed somewhat from the analysis of Keller in 1966. Difficult to assess summer population because of dispersion of birds into the State from outside areas.

§ **Green Heron**
Butorides striatus

FORMER STATUS: Butler (1898) simply termed it a summer resident in the State and Keller (1966) called it a fairly common summer resident. He summarized nesting data for 16 counties.

CURRENT STATUS: **North** Fairly common migrant; rare summer resident. 25 April–10 October. **Central** Fairly common migrant; rare summer resident. 20 April–5 October. **South** Fairly common migrant; very rare summer resident. 15 April–10 October.

REMARKS: Breeding data for southern Indiana sparse, probably due to lack of observation.

Little Blue Heron
Florida caerulea

FORMER STATUS: Butler (1898) listed it as a summer resident in southern Indiana. Later, Keller (1966) questioned this data in view of the fact that the nearest known breeding colony is Reelfoot Lake in Tennessee.

CURRENT STATUS: **North** Casual spring migrant; very rare summer visitant. 15 April–30 September. R. C. Tweit found two in Porter Co., 28 June 1975, and one was seen near South Bend by Philip Wagner, 8 June

1976. **Central** Casual spring migrant; very rare summer visitant. 15 April–30 September. Max Forsyth et al. found two in Marion Co., 30 April 1975. **South** Very rare spring migrant; rare summer resident. 15 April–10 October. Charles Mills has consistently observed this species in the Patoka River Bottoms, Gibson Co., during the spring. A blue-phased bird was seen here by the authors, 11 July 1977.

REMARKS: Post-breeding dispersal of birds during the summer to Indiana is not as prevalent as it was twenty years ago.

Cattle Egret
Bubulcus ibis

FORMER STATUS: Keller (1966) termed it very rare and gave but two records.

CURRENT STATUS: **North** Very rare migrant. At least ten records since 1965; 8 spring, 2 fall. Data suggests 30 April–30 May; 15 October–15 November. **Central** Very rare migrant. At least nine records. Barnes (1971) found a group of 16 in Green Co., 6 May 1971. Tom Potter and Steve Glass found 13 in Monroe Co., 16 May 1978. **South** Very rare migrant. Data lacking. A sight record of 12, 14 November 1974, in Gibson Co. (C. Mills).

REMARKS: Large flocks seen near East St. Louis, Illinois, suggest that it is only a question of time until the species becomes more frequent in our area. Breeding may possibly occur.

§ Great Egret
Casmerodius albus

FORMER STATUS: "Regular migrant and summer resident, formerly tolerably common, becoming rare. Breeds in some numbers locally in the northern part of the State and in the lower Wabash Valley . . ." (Butler, 1898). Keller (1966) terms it a fairly common to very common summer visitant and cites breeding data for Newton County in 1953.

CURRENT STATUS: **North** Casual spring to rare fall migrant. 30 April–5 June (some non-breeding records in July); 15 August–30 October. **Central** Casual spring to rare fall migrant. 30 April–25 May; 10 August–10 November. **South** Casual spring to rare fall migrant. 20 April–20 May; 1 August–15 November.

REMARKS: Twenty years ago, post-breeding flocks of as many as a hundred birds—sometimes more—were common. Residential construction near breeding areas along with suspected pesticide poisonings can probably be blamed for the decrease. No breeding records since 1953.

Snowy Egret
Egretta thula

FORMER STATUS: "Migrant and summer resident in southern part of the State; not common; breeding locally in the lower Wabash Valley" (Butler, 1898). Keller (1966) termed it an occasional, very rare to rare summer visitant; accidental in the spring and questioned possible breeding data presented by Butler.

CURRENT STATUS: **North** Casual migrant or summer visitant. Two spring records: (2) 14 May 1956, Wabash Co., by Snyder (Burr, 1956); 22 May 1974, Clinton Co., by R. Murrey. 10 August–15 October. **Central** Casual migrant or summer visitant. Three spring records: 30 April 1975 Geist Reservoir by M. Forsyth; 7 May 1976 Marion Co. by Keller; and one seen at Eagle Creek Reservoir 9 June 1978, Marion Co. (Kellers et al.). 1 August–20 October. **South** Casual migrant or summer visitant. Two spring records: 2 April 1948, Posey Co., by Barnes et al.; 26 April 1953, Vanderburgh Co. (Visher *fide* Mumford, 1953). 25 July–1 November.

REMARKS: No documented summer visitation records during last five years.

Louisiana Heron
Hydranassa tricolor

FORMER STATUS: Butler (1898) termed it a rare summer visitor and gave two records: June 1876, Starke Co., by F. T. Jencks and during the summer of 1894, Knox Co., by Chansler. Keller (1966) called it accidental and cited an additional record: 27 July 1964, Tippecanoe Co., by Burr et al. Later Mumford and Keller (1975) reduced its status to hypothetical because of the lack of acceptance criteria.

CURRENT STATUS: Casual. Two recent records did not meet the acceptance criteria: 8 May 1971, Vigo Co., by James and Amy Mason (Wilson, 1971); 24–27 May 1976, Tippecanoe Co., by Mr. and Mrs. John McCain (*fide* Hopkins). A bird was observed in western Gibson Co. on 9 July 1978 by Dennis Jones et al. (documented). That observation officially adds it to the State List.

§ **Black-crowned Night Heron**
Nycticorax nycticorax

FORMER STATUS: "Regular migrant and summer resident" (Butler, 1898). Keller (1966) termed it a locally abundant summer resident, uncommon to very common post-breeding visitant, and irregular to very rare winter resident. He gave breeding data for 18 counties.

CURRENT STATUS: **North** Rare migrant; casual in winter. Only known active breeding colony located near Gary where Ray Grow found 50 pairs 13 May 1978. 1 April–10 October. **Central** Rare migrant; casual in winter. No recent breeding data. 25 March–15 October. **South** Rare migrant; casual in winter. No recent breeding data. 20 March–1 November.

REMARKS: A blue-listed species that has not regained its former abundance. Like all blue-listed species, this bird should be carefully watched.

§ **Yellow-crowned Night Heron**
Nyctanassa violacea

FORMER STATUS: "Common summer resident in some localities in the lower Wabash Valley. Breeds in colonies" (Butler, 1898). Keller (1966) termed it: "A rare to uncommon spring and fall transient; in the northern portion of the State it is very rare." He cited breeding data for Delaware Co. (*fide* Zimmerman).

CURRENT STATUS: **North** Casual migrant; no breeding data. Five dates spanning late April to late September. A current record: 8 May 1976, Allen Co. (J. Williams *fide* J. Haw). **Central** Casual migrant; four breeding records: Delaware Co. 1958, 1963 (Zimmerman *fide* Keller, 1966). Martin Co. 1971, 1975 (Weeks, 1976). **South** Rare migrant; locally common in the Patoka River Bottoms, where it breeds. Breeding data cited for the above location by Weeks (1976) during 1973 and 1976 where it is believed to have nested for several years. 1 April–1 October.

REMARKS: Probably nests in suitable areas over most of the State but is usually unrecorded because of isolated nature of nesting sites.

§ **Least Bittern**
Ixobrychus exilis

FORMER STATUS: "Regular migrant; generally rare, but locally somewhat common. Summer resident in suitable localities; some places common" (Butler, 1898). Keller (1966) agreed essentially with Butler's evaluation.

CURRENT STATUS: North Rare migrant, locally uncommon summer resident. 10 May–5 September. Central Very rare migrant, casual summer resident. 5 May–1 September. South Casual migrant; no nesting data. Data sparse but migrating period probably similar to central district.

REMARKS: Keller (1966) gave nesting data for 15 Indiana counties, most of which were in the northern district. Southern area observers should explore the possibility of nesting near the larger lakes.

§ American Bittern
Botaurus lentiginosus

FORMER STATUS: "Regular migrant; tolerably common; summer resident in suitable localities, especially in the northern part of the State, where, in some places, it breeds commonly" (Butler, 1898). Keller (1966) used somewhat the same status except for breeding data.

CURRENT STATUS: North Rare migrant and very rare summer resident. Casual in winter. 25 March–25 October. Winter data for December, January and February. Central Rare migrant; casual summer resident. Casual in winter. 20 March–1 November. One January date. South Very rare migrant; no recent breeding data. Casual in winter. 15 March–15 November. Winter data for December and January.

REMARKS: Keller (1966) listed breeding data for 15 Indiana counties. Recent breeding data lacking.

Family Ciconiidae: Storks

Wood Stork
Mycteria americana

FORMER STATUS: "Summer visitor or summer resident, more or less irregular, in the lower Wabash Valley; throughout the remainder of the southern two thirds of the State, rare summer visitor" (Butler, 1898). Keller (1966) classified it as an occasional very rare summer visitant with last reported occurrence in 1944. He listed data for 13 counties (3 North, 6 Central, 4 South).

CURRENT STATUS: Accidental. A recent report of two seen in Morgan Co., July 1976 (*fide* A. Starling), is the only record since 1944.

REMARKS: Future sightings dependent upon breeding success in Florida.

Family Threskiornithidae: Ibises and Spoonbills

Glossy Ibis
Plegadis falcinellus

FORMER STATUS: Listed as hypothetical by Butler in 1898. This was based on its reported occurrence in Illinois, Ohio, and Michigan. Keller (1966) listed it as accidental on the basis of a sight record at the Indianapolis Sewage Disposal Plant, 20 May 1962, Marion Co., which was observed by many.

CURRENT STATUS: Casual. One recent record: Two observed in Pulaski Co. 17–18 April 1968, one of which was collected and deposited in the National Museum of Natural History (Mumford and Lehman, 1969).

REMARKS: Species is well known to wander during the spring; possibly exploring for suitable nesting sites.

White Ibis
Eudocimus albus

FORMER STATUS: Butler (1898) recorded it as a rare summer visitor. Keller (1966) listed it as accidental, citing four records: Clark Co., July 1925; Knox Co. in 1864 and 1878; and Posey Co., 18 August 1925.

CURRENT STATUS: No recent records.

Roseate Spoonbill
Ajaia ajaja

FORMER STATUS: "Accidental visitor" (Butler, 1898). Keller (1966) listed Butler's data for Jay, Knox, and Vigo counties with last reported occurrence in 1889.

CURRENT STATUS: Status remains the same as Butler's analysis.

Order Anseriformes
Family Anatidae: Swans, Geese, and Ducks

§ **Mute Swan**
Cygnus olor

FORMER STATUS: The domestic swan of aviaries, cemeteries, and zoos has established itself on the East Coast and in northern Michigan. While free-flying escapees occur, the proliferation of recent reports, especially in northern Indiana (where Michigan birds are most likely to occur), seems to indicate that this species deserves recognition for inclusion within this list.

CURRENT STATUS: **North** Casual migrant and winter visitant. A pair constructed a nest (no young) in Steuben Co. in 1975 and were believed to have hatched young in 1977 (*fide* Casebere). A flock of eleven, 8–31 December 1976, St. Joseph River at South Bend, was seen by many. **Central** Casual migrant and winter visitant. Several recent records. Two free-flying birds were seen at Atterbury Fish and Wildlife Area by the authors, 20 February 1977. **South** Casual during winter. A pair (free-flying) seen near Corydon, 24 January 1976 (H. Bruner).

Whistling Swan
Olor columbianus

FORMER STATUS: Butler (1898) termed it not common and a rare winter resident.

CURRENT STATUS: **North** Rare migrant. Casual in winter. 15 March–25 April; 25 October–5 December. A flock of 52 at Pigeon River, 12 November 1976 (Weldon). One, 2–8 May 1976, Noble Co. (Heller–Haw). **Central** Very rare migrant. Casual in winter. 10 March–15 April; 5 November–10 December. One, 2 January 1975, Monroe Reservoir (Glass). **South** Casual migrant. Recent data lacking. Older records from Hovey Lake suggest migratory periods occur roughly 5 days earlier in spring and 5 days later during the southward migration.

REMARKS: Species' main migratory routes lie slightly east of Indiana.

Trumpeter Swan
Olor buccinator

FORMER STATUS: "Rare migrant and probably winter resident. . . . Formerly summer resident and bred (Butler, 1898). Schorger (1964) mentions the Kankakee Marshes and Beaver Lake, Newton Co., as former nesting areas in 1860s and before.

CURRENT STATUS: Extirpated. Last reported during the late 1890s.

§ Canada Goose
Branta canadensis

FORMER STATUS: "Common migrant; sometimes winter resident in the northern part of the State; resident in some numbers. They often breed"

(Butler, 1898). Mumford (1954) stated that no wild breeding birds remain in the State except a nesting population at Jasper-Pulaski that were permanent residents.

CURRENT STATUS: North Common migrant; rare in winter. Breeding confined to Jasper-Pulaski Game Reserve and a few isolated areas (not well documented) 1 March–15 April; 15 September–5 December. A pair nested in a small marsh near South Bend in 1976 (Wagner). Eight recorded, 14 May 1973, Steuben Co. (Casebere). Central Uncommon migrant; rare in winter. Breeding populations at Eagle Creek Reservoir probably remnant of Lake Sullivan captive flocks. Restocking program initiated at Atterbury during 1977. 25 February–10 April, 20 September–10 December. South Uncommon migrant; rare in winter. 20 February–5 April; 1 October–15 December.

Brant
Branta bernicla

FORMER STATUS: Butler (1898) termed it an accidental visitor on the basis of a report by Dr. Rufus Haymond for the Whitewater Valley.

CURRENT STATUS: Accidental. All reports from the Lake Michigan area: Three, Michigan City, 19 October 1957. Two remained until 27 October 1957, one of which was collected. One seen 16 October 1969 by Brattain and Carmony at the Indiana Dunes (Oswalt and Wilson, 1970). Seventy-five to one hundred, 14 December 1975 at Beverly Shores by Brock and Underborn et al.

Greater White-fronted Goose
Anser albifrons

FORMER STATUS: Butler (1898) listed it as a rare migrant in the State and cited three records for northern Indiana.

CURRENT STATUS: North Casual spring and fall migrant. Several records (most during the first week of April) for Willow Slough and Jasper-Pulaski. A recent record of one 9 April 1975 at Pigeon River (*fide* Haw). Twelve, 11 October 1977, in the above location (5 adults, 7 immatures) were seen by P. Meyer, J. Hampshire (*fide* Casebere), and one, 5 November 1977 (Haw, Weldon, et al.), also at Pigeon River. Central Casual spring migrant. One record of a bird seen 4 April 1954 by C. E. Keller at Geist Reservoir. South No data.

Snow Goose
Chen caerulescens

FORMER STATUS: Butler (1898) listed the Lesser Snow Goose (*Chen hyperborea*), Greater Snow Goose (*Chen hyperborea nivalis*), and Blue Goose (*Chen caerulescens*) as rare migrants within the State. The lumping together of the Blue–Snow Goose complex has reduced the above three birds to one species.

CURRENT STATUS: **North** Very rare spring and uncommon fall migrant. 20 March–15 April; 5 October–15 November. Two birds, 3–8 May 1976, St. Joseph Co., by Jane Bebb. **Central** Very rare spring and uncommon fall migrant. Casual in winter. 25 March–10 April; 10 October–20 November. One bird, 30 December 1973, Whitewater State Park, by L. Carter. **South** Very rare spring and rare fall migrant. Casual in winter. 30 March–10 April; 15 October–1 December. Recent data lacking.

Ross' Goose
Chen rossii

STATUS: Accidental. One bird, 30 December 1965, at the Willow Slough Fish and Wildlife Area by Mumford et al. (Mumford, 1966).

Fulvous Whistling Duck
Dendrocygna bicolor

STATUS: Accidental. One seen by many at Lake Sullivan from 28 May to early September 1960. Two were seen by John Louis at Jasper-Pulaski, 16 May 1964 (Mumford and Keller, 1975).

§ **Mallard**
Anas platyrhynchos

FORMER STATUS: "Abundant migrant; winter resident in varying numbers, and locally, particularly in the northern part of the State, resident in some numbers" (Butler, 1898). Mumford (1954) listed 19 counties where the species had bred at one time but stated: "the numbers of birds which nest annually in the southern half of Indiana is quite small."

CURRENT STATUS: **North** Common migrant; fairly common in winter. Uncommon summer resident. Bulk of the migration occurs: 20 February–10 April; 10 October–30 November. **Central** Common migrant; fairly common in winter. Rare summer resident. 15 February–5 April; 10 October–

5 December. **South** Common migrant and winter visitant. Recent breeding data lacking. 10 February–1 April; 15 October–15 December. Large numbers winter in southwest Indiana.

§ **American Black Duck**
Anas rubripes

FORMER STATUS: Butler (1898) called it a not common migrant; occasional in winter and a rare summer resident. Mumford (1954) gave breeding data for seven Indiana counties.

CURRENT STATUS: **North** Fairly common migrant, rare in winter. Recent breeding data lacking. 15 February–10 April; 5 October–5 December. **Central** Fairly common migrant; rare in winter. Casual breeder. 20 February–5 April; 10 October–10 December. **South** Fairly common migrant and winter visitant. No breeding data. 25 February–1 April; 15 October–15 December.

REMARKS: Status undergoing some change due to interbreeding with Mallard, which appears to be diluting the specific strain.

Gadwall
Anas strepera

FORMER STATUS: Butler (1898) called it a rare migrant and gave but two records.

CURRENT STATUS: **North** Rare migrant and very rare winter visitant. 25 March–20 April; 20 October–30 November. **Central** Rare migrant and winter visitant. 20 March–15 April; 25 October–5 December. A flock of 133 wintered at Indian Lake during 1949–50. **South** Very rare migrant and winter visitant. 15 March–10 April; 1 November–15 December. Charles Mills found three in Gibson Co., 11 January 1976.

REMARKS: Species seems to prefer sheltered, small lakes. Indian Lake near Indianapolis, Bryants' Creek Lake and Bean Blossom Lake in Morgan-Monroe State Forest annually harbor some numbers during open winters.

§ **Common Pintail**
Anas acuta

FORMER STATUS: "Abundant migrant in spring; not common migrant in fall. Perhaps occasionally winters" (Butler, 1898).

CURRENT STATUS: **North** Fairly common spring migrant and uncommon fall migrant. Very rare winter visitant. A female with 6 young seen, Whitley Co. during mid-June 1958, by Mrs. Earl Bordner (Nolan, 1958). Woodruff (1907) cites Nelson for a nesting record for the Calumet River in northern Indiana. 25 February–5 April; 20 September–15 November. **Central** Uncommon migrant. Very rare winter visitant. 20 February–25 March; 25 September–25 November. **South** Uncommon migrant and winter visitant. 15 February–20 March; 1 October–5 December.

§ **Green-winged Teal**
Anas crecca

FORMER STATUS: "Common migrant; also, winter resident; may be locally a rare summer resident in northern part of the State" (Butler, 1898).

CURRENT STATUS: **North** Fairly common migrant; rare in winter. 5 March–15 April; 15 September–1 December. Tim Manolis found two in Tippecanoe Co. 24 August 1975. A female with four young found near Decatur 24 July 1978 by Larry Parker. **Central** Fairly common migrant; rare in winter. 25 February–10 April; 20 September–5 December. **South** Uncommon migrant and winter visitant. 20 February–5 April; 25 September–10 December. Charles Mills found 25 in Gibson Co. 11 January 1976.

REMARKS: The speedy little Green-wing, one of the hardiest of our ducks, will remain in an area as long as there is open water. Hovey Lake in the southwestern portion of Indiana annually harbors small numbers of this species during the winter.

§ **Blue-winged Teal**
Anas discors

FORMER STATUS: Butler (1898) listed it as a common migrant and a local summer resident. Mumford (1954) noted breeding in 16 Indiana counties, 14 of which were confined to the northern region.

CURRENT STATUS: **North** Common migrant and uncommon summer resident. 25 March–5 October. Breeds across the northern tier of counties. **Central** Common migrant and very rare summer resident. 20 March–10 October. Breeds as far south as Atterbury Fish and Wildlife Area and Muscatatuck National Wildlife Area. **South** Common migrant; recent breeding data lacking but may breed in suitable habitat. 15 March–15 October. Charles Mills found 500 in Gibson Co. 20 March 1976.

REMARKS: Winter data suspect; not known to winter this far north.

Cinnamon Teal
Anas cyanoptera

FORMER STATUS: Butler (1898) listed it as hypothetical on the basis of its nearby occurrence in Illinois.

CURRENT STATUS: **North** Accidental. Brodkorb (1926) reported this species near Hammond 10 August 1926. **Central** Accidental. One photographed by Ed Wagner at Muscatatuck National Wildlife Refuge in April 1972. **South** Accidental. A male taken in Lawrence Co. 4 May 1940, and another seen (documented) by Charles Mills, 7 April 1977, in the Patoka River Bottoms, Gibson Co.

REMARKS: All above data is for adult male birds; female birds cannot be safely identified in the field.

Eurasian Wigeon
Anas penelope

FORMER STATUS: Butler (1898) called it an accidental visitor on the basis of four records, all of which were from English Lake. Three of these were during spring migration while the fourth was simply listed for 1881 or 1882. Ford (1956) gave three more records: 17 April 1930, Wolf Lake (Lewy); 9 May 1943, Kankakee State Game Preserve (Clark); 20 April 1949, Wolf Lake (Campbell).

CURRENT STATUS: **North** Casual spring migrant; no fall data. Most recent record: 22 March 1964 in Starke Co. (Burr, 1964). **Central** Casual spring migrant. One seen by the senior author at Geist Reservoir, 29 March 1947. One in Wayne Co., 23 September 1949 (Wright, 1950). **South** No data.

REMARKS: There is a definite paucity of records for the Midwest region since 1949.

American Wigeon
Anas americana

FORMER STATUS: "Common migrant, and rare summer resident in the northern part of the State" (Butler, 1898).

CURRENT STATUS: **North** Fairly common spring migrant; uncommon in fall. Casual in winter. 5 March–25 April; 1 October–20 November. **Central** Fairly common spring migrant; uncommon in fall. Casual in winter. 1 March–20 April; 10 October–30 November. **South** Fairly common spring migrant; uncommon in fall. Very rare in winter. 25 February–15 April;

15 October–5 December. Small numbers winter during open winters in southwestern Indiana.

REMARKS: An almost constant consort of the American Coot, *Fulica americana*, which species it victimizes when feeding.

§ Northern Shoveler
Anas clypeata

FORMER STATUS: "Migrant, not uncommon; rare summer resident; possibly winter resident, some winters southward" (Butler, 1898). Reported by him to breed in Lake and Starke Cos. Ford (1956) gave a breeding record for Lake George in Lake Co., 26 June 1936. Smith (1936) records a nest with 9 eggs in that same location, 14 July 1935.

CURRENT STATUS: North Fairly common spring migrant; uncommon in fall. Casual in winter. Bred in northwestern Indiana in 1965 (Mumford, 1966). 15 March–15 November. Central Fairly common spring migrant; uncommon in fall. Casual in winter. Larry Carter found two in Delaware Co. 27 January 1974. 10 March–1 May; 25 September–20 November. South Fairly common spring migrant; uncommon in fall. Very rare in winter. 5 March–25 April; 1 October–25 November. Charles Mills found 500 in Gibson Co. 20 March 1976.

§ Wood Duck
Aix sponsa

FORMER STATUS: Butler (1898) related: "Migrant and summer resident in some numbers. Breeds in suitable localities throughout the State." Mumford (1954) listed 66 counties where they were known to breed and stated further that he believed they nest in every Indiana county.

CURRENT STATUS: North Common migrant; casual in winter. Breeds. 20 March–10 October. Central Common migrant; rare in winter. Breeds. 15 March–15 October. Found frequently at Muscatatuck National Wildlife Refuge during the winter. South Common migrant; rare in winter. Breeds. 10 March–20 October.

REMARKS: A remarkable success story, the "Woodie" has regained its common status within the last 30 years probably as a result of wise conservation practices and the establishment of numerous state fish and game areas.

Redhead
Aythya americana

FORMER STATUS: "Common migrant in suitable localities. It may occasionally remain during the summer and breed" (Butler, 1898). He based the breeding assumption on data that a male bird was taken during June in nearby Ohio.

CURRENT STATUS: **North** Fairly common spring and rare fall migrant. Casual in winter. 1 March–10 April; 15 October–25 November. Charles Clark found two adults and 8 young at Lake Calumet in nearby Illinois, 6 July 1975. **Central** Fairly common spring and rare fall migrant. Very rare in winter. 25 February–5 April; 20 October–1 December. Steve Glass found as many as five at Monroe Reservoir from 17 December 1975 until 11 February 1976. **South** Fairly common spring and rare fall migrant. Very rare in winter. 20 February–1 April; 25 October–5 December. Two were seen in Gibson Co. 2 February 1975 (C. Mills).

§ Ring-necked Duck
Aythya collaris

FORMER STATUS: "Tolerably common migrant; in the northern part of the State it is common in the spring and fall" (Butler, 1898). Nested in Lake County according to J. D. McCall and a suspected nest with 6 eggs was found in Tippecanoe Co. 2 July 1949 (Mumford & Keller, 1975).

CURRENT STATUS: **North** Common spring and rare fall migrant. Very rare in winter. No recent breeding data but numerous records of summer birds. 10 March–15 April; 5 October–20 November. **Central** Common spring and rare fall migrant. Very rare in winter. 5 March–10 April; 10 October–25 November. **South** Fairly common spring migrant and rare fall migrant. Rare in winter. 1 March–5 April; 15 October–5 December. Michael Brown found a male in Gibson Co. during July of 1977.

Canvasback
Aythya valisineria

FORMER STATUS: Butler (1898) called it a regular migrant but rare.

CURRENT STATUS: **North** Rare migrant; casual in winter. 1 March–15 April; 5 October–25 November. **Central** Rare migrant; uncommon in winter. 20 February–10 April; 15 October–1 December. Steve Glass found 200 plus at Monroe Reservoir 20 February 1975. **South** Rare migrant; rare in winter. 20 February–5 April; 25 October–5 December.

THE BIRDS　　　　　　　　　101

REMARKS: Species winters in fair numbers in the Monroe Reservoir area. Main requisite appears to be open water.

Greater Scaup
Aythya marila

FORMER STATUS: Butler (1898) termed it a rare migrant, particularly in the fall.
CURRENT STATUS: **North** Uncommon migrant; winter status uncertain. Data difficult to assess but believed to occur with some degree of fre‐ quency on Lake Michigan. Jim Haw found one, 9 May 1974 in Allen Co. **Central** Very rare spring migrant; fall and winter status uncertain. Migration seems to parallel that of Lesser. **South** Lack of data to as‐ certain status.
REMARKS: Difficulty in identification and/or misidentification leaves status questionable. Generally seen in small groups; possibly 2–3 indi‐ viduals.

§ Lesser Scaup
Aythya affinis

FORMER STATUS: "Very abundant migrant and rare summer resident" (Butler, 1898). Later, Mumford (1954) gave breeding data for Lake Co. in 1952.
CURRENT STATUS: **North** Common spring migrant; uncommon in the fall; very rare in winter. 15 March–5 May; 10 October–20 November. **Central** Common spring migrant; rare in the fall; very rare in winter. 10 March–1 May; 15 October–25 November. **South** Common spring mi‐ grant; rare in the fall; rare in winter. 5 March–25 April; 20 October–1 December. Charles Mills notes it with some degree of regularity in Gibson Co. during the winter. He found 50 there on 2 February 1975 and 100 on 24 January 1976.

Tufted Duck
Aythya fuligula

STATUS: Accidental. One seen 29 November 1978 at the Port of Indi‐ ana harbor in Porter Co. by Ken Brock, Russell Mumford, and Ted Cable (documented). This record has been accepted by the Indiana Audubon Verification Committee and is considered a valid addition to the avifauna of the State.

REMARKS: There has been an increase in sightings in the United States during the last 10 years, coupled with species' increase in Europe and critical observation by competent field workers.

Common Goldeneye
Bucephala clangula

FORMER STATUS: Butler's 1898 analysis, "On northern Lake Michigan this is the common winter duck, staying all winter," is essentially true for the northern two-thirds of the State.

CURRENT STATUS: **North** Fairly common spring migrant; uncommon in the fall; fairly common in winter. 5 November–10 April. **Central** Uncommon spring migrant; uncommon in the fall and winter. 15 November–10 April. **South** Uncommon spring migrant; rare in the fall and winter. 20 November–20 March. Some years, when the more northern lakes are frozen over, large numbers will move into the southern region.

Barrow's Goldeneye
Bucephala islandica

FORMER STATUS: Butler (1898) listed it as a rare visitor from the north in winter and spring on the basis of two records: one taken on the lower Wabash River in Gibson Co. in 1874 and a female taken in Carroll Co., 19 March 1885.

CURRENT STATUS: **North** Casual. Several records for St. Joseph Co. One photographed on 3 March 1962. Latest record; one seen from 3 December 1972–20 February 1973 (Van Huffel et al.). **Central** Two records; a bird seen during March 1933 in Marion Co. (Esten, 1933); one, 21 March–4 April Wayne Co. by J. Cope (Marks, Wright 1951). **South** No recent data.

Bufflehead
Bucephala albeola

FORMER STATUS: "Common migrant and winter resident" (Butler, 1898).

CURRENT STATUS: **North** Fairly common migrant; rare in winter except in the vicinity of Lake Michigan where it is common; particularly on Trail Creek when the lake is frozen over. 15 October–15 April. **Central** Fairly common migrant; rare in winter. 10 March–10 April; 20 October–25 November. **South** Fairly common migrant; rare in winter. 5 March–

5 April; 25 October–5 December. Charles Mills found 100, 2 February 1972, in Gibson Co.

Oldsquaw
Clangula hyemalis

FORMER STATUS: Butler (1898) called it a very common winter resident on Lake Michigan. Away from this area he termed it an exceedingly rare winter visitor. Ford (1956) agreed with this status, adding that it was "the most numerous of our wintering waterfowl on Lake Michigan."

CURRENT STATUS: **North** Rare migrant and winter visitant; formerly abundant, especially during the period of 1950–1960 in the vicinity of Lake Michigan. Species has apparently altered its winter distribution for some as yet unexplained reason. 1 November–10 April. **Central** Very rare migrant and winter visitant; formerly rare. 15 November–1 April. Larry Carter found 2, Prairie Creek Reservoir, 17 November 1973, and Alan Bruner observed a female at Lake Waveland, 24 January 1976. **South** Very rare migrant and winter visitant. 30 November–15 March. In Gibson Co., Charles Mills observed one, 14 March 1971 and 8–9 December 1972.

Harlequin Duck
Histrionicus histrionicus

FORMER STATUS: Butler (1898) listed it as hypothetical on the basis of occurrences in nearby states.

CURRENT STATUS: **North** Casual winter visitant. At least 8 records, all but one occurring on Lake Michigan. Date span is from 24 November–20 March. A specimen taken 3 January 1961 at Michigan City (Mumford, 1961). One was seen by many on the St. Joseph River in South Bend, 7 January–3 February 1973. Two remained at Michigan City from early December 1977 to the end of that month. First seen by Peter Grube, they appeared to be females but by the end of the period began showing plumage characteristics of males. They were last seen 29 December 1977 by Brock, Grube, and the Kellers. **Central** Accidental. One record: a male bird seen by Robert and William Buskirk and Henry West at Morse Reservoir, 24–25 December 1961 (Keller, 1962). **South** No data. It has been reported for the Louisville area.

Common Eider
Somateria mollissima

STATUS: Accidental. An immature bird reported to have been seen by many at Michigan City, 30 November–26 January 1958, no details (Burr, 1958). One reported to have been seen at Michigan City in February 1977, no details (Dierker *fide* Weber).

King Eider
Somateria spectabilis

FORMER STATUS: Butler (1898) placed this species on his hypothetical list and Ford (1956) quotes Smith about a specimen taken 6 November 1936 at Lake George.

CURRENT STATUS: **North** Casual late fall and winter visitant. One seen, 26 December 1956–12 January 1957 at Michigan City (Burr, 1957). An immature female taken on Lake Michigan, 16 December 1957, is in the Purdue Collection. One, 22 October 1959 at Michigan City, was seen by many (Burr, 1960). Four skins were given to Purdue during late November 1959 that had been shot at the south end of Lake Michigan (Mumford, 1960).

White-winged Scoter
Melanitta deglandi

FORMER STATUS: "Rare winter visitor. More numerous on Lake Michigan" (Butler, 1898). In speaking of the Chicago region, Ford (1956) called it a fairly common winter visitor.

CURRENT STATUS: **North** Uncommon fall migrant; rare winter visitant; very rare in spring. 15 October–1 April. **Central** Casual migrant and winter visitant. 20 October–20 March. One seen by many at Eagle Creek Reservoir, 7 November 1976. **South** Casual fall migrant and winter visitant. Date span uncertain; species was taken by hunters at Hovey Lake during the fall of 1946 and 1950 (Mumford, 1954).

Surf Scoter
Melanitta perspicillata

FORMER STATUS: Butler (1898) called it a rare winter resident on Lake Michigan and occasional elsewhere.

CURRENT STATUS: **North** Rare fall migrant; very rare spring migrant and winter visitor. 15 October–15 March. Ken Brock and Tim Keller

saw several 16 October 1977 at Michigan City. One, 19 April 1975, at
Fox Island, Allen Co. (Jim Haw et al.). **Central** Casual migrant and
winter visitor. Date span uncertain. A bird seen by James Cope, Bret
Whiting, et al. at Whitewater State Park from 9 November–28 November
1976. **South** Casual migrant and winter visitor. Date span uncertain.
Taken at Hovey Lake during the falls of 1951 and 1952 (Mumford,
1954).

REMARKS: Of the three scoters, data suggests that this is the rarest on
Lake Michigan.

Black Scoter
Melanitta nigra

FORMER STATUS: Listed as hypothetical by Butler (1898) on the basis
of its occurrence in nearby states.

CURRENT STATUS: **North** Rare fall migrant and winter visitor. Spring
data lacking. 15 October–15 December. A bird found dead 10 December
1959 at Gary is in the Purdue Collection (Mumford, 1960). **Central**
Casual fall migrant. Alan Bruner found one, 25 November 1975 at Lake
Waveland, Montgomery Co. **South** Casual fall migrant. One seen 6 November 1976 at Deam's Lake, Clark Co., by Jackie B. Elmore et al.

REMARKS: The rarest of the three scoters away from Lake Michigan.

§ Ruddy Duck
Oxyura jamaicensis

FORMER STATUS: Butler (1898) termed it a migrant, usually not common.

CURRENT STATUS: **North** Uncommon migrant; very rare in winter. 15
March–1 May; 10 October–25 November. Bred in Lake and Porter coun-
ties during the summer of 1953 (Mumford, 1954). Seen during June in
St. Joseph Co. during 1974 by Dorthy Buck. **Central** Uncommon migrant;
very rare in winter. 10 March–20 April; 15 October–1 December. **South**
Uncommon migrant; very rare in winter. 5 March–15 April; 20 October–
5 December. Nine were seen 11 January 1976 in Gibson Co. by Charles
Mills.

§ Hooded Merganser
Lophodytes cucullatus

FORMER STATUS: "Very abundant migrant, less common winter resident,
and locally resident in some numbers" (Butler, 1898). Mumford (1954)

gave breeding data for 17 counties and Keller suspected breeding in Marion Co. at Eagle Creek Reservoir during 1969.

CURRENT STATUS: North Fairly common migrant; very rare in winter and summer. 15 March–25 November. Ed Hopkins found a bird in Tippecanoe Co. 28–29 December 1973. Central Fairly common migrant; rare in winter and very rare summer resident. 10 March–5 December. Has a tendency to winter, when there is open water, in small secluded lakes that are well protected from the wind. Such habitat is found in south-central Indiana in the vicinity of Brown Co. South Fairly common migrant; rare in winter and very rare summer resident. 5 March–10 December.

Common Merganser
Mergus merganser

FORMER STATUS: In 1898 Butler considered it a common migrant and winter resident.

CURRENT STATUS: North Uncommon migrant and winter visitor. 1 November–20 March. Central Uncommon migrant and winter visitor. 15 November–15 March. South Uncommon migrant and winter visitor. 25 November–5 March. A flock of 150 were found by Charles Mills in Gibson Co. 2 February 1975.

REMARKS: Availability of open water is a prerequisite for wintering.

Red-breasted Merganser
Mergus serrator

FORMER STATUS: "Migrant and winter resident throughout the State. Generally rare, but occasionally, on the larger bodies of water, rather common" (Butler, 1898).

CURRENT STATUS: North Fairly common migrant, very rare in winter. 20 March–10 May; 25 October–1 December. At times, large flocks occur on Lake Michigan. Central Fairly common migrant; very rare in winter. 15 March–1 May; 1 November–5 December. Al Starling found 125 at Eagle Creek Reservoir, 25 March 1973. South Fairly common migrant; very rare in winter. 10 March–25 April; 5 November–10 December.

Order Falconiformes
Family *Cathartidae: American Vultures*

§ **Turkey Vulture**
Cathartes aura

FORMER STATUS: "Resident in southern Indiana, at least as far north as Vincennes and the lower Whitewater Valley. Some years they remain through the winter as far north as Brookville" (Butler, 1898).

CURRENT STATUS: **North** Rare migrant and very rare summer resident. Listed as breeding at Kankakee and Jasper-Pulaski Game Preserves by Charles Clark (Ford, 1956). 15 March–10 November. Species does not normally winter in this region but a record of two birds seen in DeKalb Co. 21 February 1976 by Ted Heemstra and Jim Williams may represent very early migrants. Probably nests in other areas in this region but data lacking. **Central** Common migrant and fairly common summer resident; normally very rare in winter except locally (i.e., Turkey Run–Shades) may be common. 1 March–1 December. **South** Common migrant and fairly common summer resident; rare in winter. 25 February–10 December.

§ **Black Vulture**
Coragyps atratus

FORMER STATUS: Butler (1898) relates: "Resident in the southern part of the State; generally not numerous, but, in the lower Wabash Valley, at least from Knox Co. southward, it is common. In the lower Whitewater Valley it is seen most commonly in winter, but also breeds."

CURRENT STATUS: **North** Casual summer visitant; a specimen was collected from a flock of 30 on 29 September 1912 and two were seen 3 May 1914 in Allen Co. (Butler, 1936). **Central** Casual summer visitant; formerly nested in Owen Co. (Butler, 1936). No recent records. The above author cited many occurrences for this region. **South** Very rare summer resident; casual in winter. Butler (1936) listed many records. Mumford and Whitaker (1974) gave breeding data for Crawford Co. in 1973. Harold Bruner found two 12–19 February 1976 in Harrison Co. and one 29 February 1976 Crawford Co.

REMARKS: Species has decreased in abundance in southern Indiana within the last forty years.

Family Accipitridae: Kites, Hawks, and Harriers

Swallow-tailed Kite
Elanoides forficatus

FORMER STATUS: Butler (1898) regarded it a rare summer resident in the southwestern portion of the state and rare to irregular northward. The same author cited several records. Ford (1956) gave two records: Tremont, Porter Co., 5 April 1921 (Belle Wilson), and in the same locality, 6 June 1948 (Bartel).
CURRENT STATUS: Accidental. No recent records.

Mississippi Kite
Ictinia mississippiensis

FORMER STATUS: Listed by Butler (1898) as a rare summer resident in the lower Wabash Valley and accidental elsewhere.
CURRENT STATUS: **North** Casual summer visitant. One seen 3 June 1973 in the Indiana Dunes by Jeffrey Sanders (Kleen, 1973). **Central** Casual summer visitant. At least three recent sight records, the latest being two birds, 4–5 July 1975, Marion Co. by J. J. Schuetz and Robert Rice (documented). **South** Casual summer visitant. Most recent record: one, 24 April 1976, by Marietta Smith (documented) at Woodruff Woods, southeast of Francisco, Gibson Co.
REMARKS: Species becoming common in southwestern Kentucky and may be moving northeast.

Northern Goshawk
Accipiter gentilis

FORMER STATUS: Butler (1898) termed it as a rare winter visitor.
CURRENT STATUS: **North** Very rare irregular winter visitant arriving in flight years from 15 October–1 April. **Central** Very rare irregular winter visitant arriving in flight years from 30 October–15 March. **South** Data lacking but probably a casual winter visitant.
REMARKS: Shortage of food supply farther north determines species' appearance within the State.

§ Sharp-shinned Hawk
Accipiter striatus

FORMER STATUS: "Resident. Most of them leave the northern part of the State in fall and return in spring" (Butler, 1898).

CURRENT STATUS: **North** Uncommon migrant; very rare in winter. Recent breeding data lacking. Main migratory periods coincide with the movement of small passerines (mainly warblers) upon which it preys. **Central** Uncommon migrant; very rare in winter. Recent breeding data lacking. Migration periods as above. **South** Uncommon migrant; very rare in winter. Recent breeding data lacking. Migration periods coincide with the movement of small passerines (mainly warblers) upon which it preys.

REMARKS: A female which hit a picture window in Tippecanoe Co. during September 1974 had been banded in Racine, Wisconsin, in September 1972 (D. Arvin).

§ Cooper's Hawk
Accipiter cooperii

FORMER STATUS: Butler (1898) wrote: "Resident in northern part of the State, rare in winter. Most numerous during migrations, and in summer."

CURRENT STATUS: **North** Uncommon migrant; very rare summer resident and very rare in winter. Migratory periods coincide with last named species. Nests located in Lagrange (J. Haw) and Allen (M. Weldon–Pat Bolman) counties during 1975–1976. **Central** Uncommon migrant; very rare summer resident and very rare in winter. Migratory periods as above. Nested in Marion Co. during late 1940s near Lake Sullivan. **South** Uncommon migrant; recent breeding data lacking; very rare in winter. Migratory periods as above.

§ Red-tailed Hawk
Buteo jamaicensis

FORMER STATUS: "Common resident; more numerous in southern two-thirds of the State, in most places, where it is the most abundant Buteo. In the region adjacent to Chicago all but a few have been destroyed. They are slightly migratory, perhaps more some years than others, as they are more numerous during the migratory periods, August, September, and March and April" (Butler, 1898).

CURRENT STATUS: **North** Fairly common migrant; rare summer resident; uncommon in winter. Difficult to assess true migratory periods but essentially the same as Butler's analysis. Mark Weldon noted nesting in Allen Co. in 1975. **Central** Fairly common migrant; rare summer resident; uncommon in winter. Migratory periods as above. **South** Fairly common migrant; rare summer resident; fairly common in winter. Migratory periods as above.

§ Red-shouldered Hawk
Buteo lineatus

FORMER STATUS: "Resident, varying in numbers, locally, and with the seasons. In some localities in northern Indiana they are abundant in summer, and breed commonly" (Butler, 1898).

CURRENT STATUS: **North** Uncommon migrant; very rare summer resident and very rare in winter. Migrants probably reach this area in early March and once again in September. Weldon found an abandoned nest in Allen Co. during the summer of 1974. **Central** Uncommon migrant; very rare summer resident, rare in winter. Migratory periods (see North). Young banded by Tim Keller at Eagle Creek Park during 1976–1977. **South** Uncommon migrant; very rare summer resident; rare in winter. Migratory periods (see North). Charles Mills and Willard Gray found a nest with 4 young in Buckskin Bottoms in 1976.

REMARKS: Status has changed since Butler's account. Species has been blue-listed in several areas.

§ Broad-winged Hawk
Buteo platypterus

FORMER STATUS: Butler (1898) called it not common; seen more in spring and fall. He listed several winter records which evidently were erroneous.

CURRENT STATUS: **North** Fairly common migrant and very rare summer resident. 25 April–5 October. A nest with one young found in Steuben Co. 1 July 1976 (Casebere–Weldon). **Central** Fairly common migrant and very rare summer resident. Nesting data lacking but noted often in south-central Indiana during the summer. 20 April–10 October. **South** Fairly common migrant. Summer status unknown. 15 April–15 October.

REMARKS: Winter records suspect; not known to winter this far north.

Swainson's Hawk
Buteo swainsoni

FORMER STATUS: Listed by Butler (1898) as hypothetical.

CURRENT STATUS: **North** No data. **Central** A bird seen (documented) 24 July 1977 at Monroe Reservoir by Jackie B. Elmore, Diane Elmore,

and Lene Rauth. Another seen 22 October 1977 approximately 7.5 miles ssw of Liberty (Union Co.) by William H. Buskirk and Bret Whiting. **South** No data.
REMARKS: Bird recorded several times in Illinois.

Rough-legged Hawk
Buteo lagopus

FORMER STATUS: "Winter visitor of irregular occurrence; usually rare, except along the western side of the State, where it is more or less common" (Butler, 1898).
CURRENT STATUS: North Irregularly fairly common to rare winter visitant. 5 October–10 April. **Central** Irregularly uncommon to very rare winter visitant. 15 October–25 March. **South** Irregularly uncommon to very rare winter visitant. 1 November–10 March.

Ferruginous Hawk
Buteo regalis

FORMER STATUS: Placed on the hypothetical list by Butler (1898) on the basis of its occurrence in Illinois.
CURRENT STATUS: North Accidental. An injured bird taken in Porter Co. 25 September 1934 by Lewis Robin (Ford, 1956). The bird was taken to the Chicago Natural History Museum, identified, banded, and released. One seen 31 December 1952–8 January 1953 by V. Reuterskiold in Porter Co. (Grow, 1954). **Central** No data. **South** No data.

Golden Eagle
Aquila chrysaetos

FORMER STATUS: Butler (1898) called it a winter resident; occurs regularly, but not common.
CURRENT STATUS: North Very rare winter visitant. 20 October–10 April. **Central** Very rare winter visitant except at Monroe Reservoir where it is rare to uncommon. 25 October–1 April. Has been reported every year since 1974 by Steve Glass, Tom Alexander, et al., at Monroe Reservoir. **South** Casual winter visitant. Few records. Charles Mills found one 23 November 1975 in Gibson Co.

Bald Eagle
Haliaeetus leucocephalus

FORMER STATUS: "Resident locally; formerly common resident throughout the State, and still generally distributed in fall, winter and spring" (Butler, 1898).
CURRENT STATUS: **North** Very rare winter visitant. 15 October–10 April. **Central** Very rare winter visitant except in the Monroe Reservoir Area where it is uncommon. 25 October–1 April. **South** Very rare winter visitant. Recent data lacking. Charles Mills and Marietta Smith found two 20–23 March 1976 in the Patoka River Bottoms of Gibson Co.
REMARKS: Has not bred in Indiana for at least 30 years.

§ **Northern Harrier**
Circus cyaneus

FORMER STATUS: Butler (1898) related: "Resident in northern Indiana; winter resident farther south. Breeds. Of rare or irregular occurrence in fall, winter and spring in the southeastern part of the State."
CURRENT STATUS: **North** Uncommon migrant and very rare summer resident. Uncommon in winter. Ford (1956) termed it a common resident. This certainly is not true today. An unsuccessful nest at Pigeon River during 1977 (L. Casebere and M. Weldon). **Central** Uncommon migrant and casual summer resident. Rare in winter. A nest found, photographed in Johnson Co. by Rolland Kontak during May 1974. **South** Uncommon migrant and rare winter visitor. 15 September–15 April.
REMARKS: Status has changed within the last 20 years when the bird was more common.

Family Pandionidae: Osprey

§ **Osprey**
Pandion haliaetus

FORMER STATUS: Butler (1898) stated: "Locally summer resident; regular migrant, and some winters rare. Winter resident in the southern part of the State."
CURRENT STATUS: **North** Rare migrant and uncommon summer visitant. Recent breeding data lacking. 25 April–1 October. **Central** Rare migrant and uncommon summer visitant. Very rare summer resident. 15 April–

15 October. Nest found in Parke Co. during the fall of 1972 (Luther, 1973). **South** Rare migrant and uncommon summer visitant. Very rare summer resident. 1 April–1 November. Formerly bred at Hovey Lake.

REMARKS: A blue-listed species which appears to be on the increase. No recent winter data.

Family Falconidae: Caracaras and Falcons

Peregrine Falcon
Falco peregrinus

FORMER STATUS: "Resident, not rare, in Lower Wabash Valley. Throughout the remainder of the State, rare. Migrant. Breeds" (Butler, 1898).

CURRENT STATUS: **North** Casual migrant. One seen, 13 May 1977, Willow Slough (M. Brown–T. Keller). **Central** Casual migrant; casual in winter. Tom Alexander found one 29 April 1976 at Indianapolis. **South** Casual migrant; casual in winter. One observed 28 November 1976 13 miles south of Elnora (T. Keller).

REMARKS: An endangered species whose status was drastically altered by pesticides. No date spans listed for the three regions because of paucity of recent records; however, generally coincides with waterfowl–shorebird migration.

Merlin
Falco columbarius

FORMER STATUS: Butler (1898) relates: "Regular migrant, and irregular winter resident, not common."

CURRENT STATUS: **North** Very rare migrant; casual in winter. 1 September–15 May. One observed by John and Dorthy Buck in LaPorte Co., 13 January–4 March 1975. **Central** Very rare migrant; casual in winter. 1 September–15 May. Recorded by Al Starling et al. at Eagle Creek Reservoir 30 August 1974 and 28 September 1975. **South** Very rare migrant; casual in winter. No recent data. Older data suggests date spans similar to above.

§ **American Kestrel**
Falco sparverius

FORMER STATUS: "Regular resident north to Wabash, Tippecanoe and Carroll counties. In winter, rare north from there, more numerous southward. Everywhere common in summer" (Butler, 1898).
CURRENT STATUS: **North** Common migrant and uncommon summer resident; uncommon in winter. **Central** Common migrant and uncommon summer resident; fairly common in winter. **South** Common migrant and uncommon summer resident; common in winter.

Order Galliformes
Family Tetraonidae: Grouse and Ptarmigan

§ **Ruffed Grouse**
Bonasa umbellus

FORMER STATUS: Butler (1898) listed it as resident; more abundant in the southern one-third of the State.
CURRENT STATUS: **North** Locally very rare permanent resident. Found in Steuben Co. by Casebere and in St. Joseph Co. by Virgil Inman et al. **Central** Locally uncommon permanent resident from Morgan, Brown, and Owen counties south. **South** Locally uncommon permanent resident. Hoosier National Forest and surrounding area.
REMARKS: Subject to restocking efforts by local and state conservation agencies. Center of abundance in south-central Indiana.

§ **Greater Prairie Chicken**
Tympanuchus cupido

FORMER STATUS: "Resident; formerly very abundant over the original prairie district, and now approximately confined to that district. In most places becoming scarce, in some very rare" (Butler, 1898). McKeever (1943) reported 100,000 in 1912, 1,000 in 1942, and 800 in 1943. Numbers reduced to 650 in 1951 (Barnes, 1952). Last seen in 1972–73.
CURRENT STATUS: Extirpated.

Family Phasianidae: Quails and Pheasants

§ **Common Bobwhite**
Colinus virginianus

FORMER STATUS: Butler (1898) called it a common resident.

CURRENT STATUS: Normally fairly common permanent resident, but subject to cyclic population changes, restocking, and severe winter depletions.

§ **Ring-necked Pheasant**
Phasianus colchicus

CURRENT STATUS: **North–Central** Status variable due to restocking, population declines, etc. More numerous in northwestern portion of State. Permanent resident. **South** May have been introduced locally but no recent data.

§ **Gray Partridge**
Perdix perdix

CURRENT STATUS: **North–Central** Locally very rare permanent resident. Reported from Tippecanoe Co. in the north and Johnson Co. in the central region. **South** No data.

Family Meleagrididae: Turkeys

§ **Wild Turkey**
Meleagris gallopavo

FORMER STATUS: Butler (1898) related: "Resident. Breeds. Formerly occurred in numbers throughout the State; now in most places extinct."

CURRENT STATUS: Locally restocked permanent resident. A small population at Pokagon State Park in the north. More numerous from south-central Indiana south to Ohio River.

Order Gruiformes
Family Gruidae: Cranes

Whooping Crane
Grus americana

FORMER STATUS: "Rare migrant; formerly more common" (Butler, 1898). They occurred in Porter Co. as late as the early 1900s (Baczkowski, 1955).
CURRENT STATUS: Extirpated.

§ **Sandhill Crane**
Grus canadensis

FORMER STATUS: "Regular migrant; sometimes common. Occasional summer visitor. Occasional summer resident in northwestern Indiana" (Butler, 1898).
CURRENT STATUS: **North** Locally abundant migrant (Jasper-Pulaski), elsewhere rare. Downy young observed during the summer of 1976 in northeastern Indiana (*fide* L. Casebere) just south of the Michigan state line. 1 March–20 April; 1 October–5 December. An estimated 13,000 at Jasper-Pulaski during the fall of 1976 (*fide* R. E. Mumford). **Central** Rare migrant. 1 March–5 April; insufficient fall data to ascertain date spread but probably similar to above. **South** Rare migrant. 1 March–1 April; fall data probably coincides with their J.-P. departure by one day. Charles Mills observed 325 in Gibson Co. 6 December 1975 while Harold Bruner found 100 on that same date in Harrison Co.

Family Rallidae: Rails, Gallinules, and Coots

§ **King Rail**
Rallus elegans

FORMER STATUS: Butler (1898) referred to it as a summer resident in the Wabash Valley and northward but rare in the southern half of Indiana.
CURRENT STATUS: **North** Very rare migrant and summer resident. 5 April–15 October. No recent nesting data but doubtless does so in several suitable areas. **Central** Very rare migrant; formerly bred and may still do so in suitable areas but data lacking. A bird was banded by Tim Keller at Muscatatuck during June of 1977. **South** Casual migrant. Adult and young seen in Gibson Co. 9 July 1978 (C. Mills et al.).

§ **Virginia Rail**
Rallus limicola

FORMER STATUS: "Rather common migrant, most numerous in spring; summer resident in some numbers locally, principally northward" (Butler, (1898).

CURRENT STATUS: **North** Rare migrant and summer resident. Casual in winter. 20 April–1 November. One bird seen in northwestern Indiana 20 December 1975 by Calvin Snyder. **Central** Rare migrant; possible summer resident (no recent data). Casual in winter. 15 April–5 November. **South** No recent data but probably a rare migrant.

§ **Sora**
Porzana carolina

FORMER STATUS: "Common migrant throughout the State; summer resident in the northern part, where it breeds commonly" (Butler, 1898).

CURRENT STATUS: **North** Fairly common migrant and rare summer resident. 20 April–15 October. **Central** Uncommon migrant; possibly rare summer resident (recent breeding data lacking). 15 April–1 November. Alan Bruner recorded 52 at Lake Waveland 5 September 1976. **South** Rare migrant. 10 April–10 November. Near Clarksville, Donald Parker observed as many as 3 birds from 24 October–19 November 1976.

Yellow Rail
Coturnicops noveboracensis

FORMER STATUS: "Rare migrant; summer resident, very local; probably breeds" (Butler, 1898).

CURRENT STATUS: **North** Very rare migrant. 1 April–5 May; 20 September–1 November. Fourteen were found dead on the beach of Lake Michigan during April 1960 (Segal, 1960). **Central** Casual migrant. One recent record in Morgan Co. (R. Gregory). **South** No data.

Black Rail
Laterallus jamaicensis

FORMER STATUS: Butler (1898) listed it as a local rare summer resident on the basis of two records, one of which involved a young bird taken near Greencastle.

CURRENT STATUS: **North** Casual migrant; possible summer resident. Two flushed by Mumford and Weeks at Willow Slough 6 July 1976

(Mumford and Weeks, 1977). **Central** Casual migrant. Last reported in Marion Co. (Keller, 1946). **South** No data.

REMARKS: Seldom seen, the Black Rail is unquestionably one of the rarest North American birds. Potential areas should be explored by several observers using a rope-drag.

Purple Gallinule
Porphyrula martinica

FORMER STATUS: Butler (1898) called it a rare spring visitor and perhaps a summer resident. He gave three records of its occurrence prior to 1883.

CURRENT STATUS: **North** Three records: 7–10 May 1964 in Tippecanoe Co. by the Trimbles (Burr, 1965); 16 June 1973 at Purdue Baker Wildlife Area by Hopkins and Mumford; and 23 June 1973 at Willow Slough by Hopkins. **Central** One found dead in Wayne Co., 29 April 1963 (*Audu. Field Notes* 1963:408). **South** No data.

REMARKS: Species nested recently in Illinois.

§ Common Gallinule
Gallinula chloropus

FORMER STATUS: "Regular migrant. Summer resident among the more extensive swamps and marshes. Locally common; some places abundant. Breeds" (Butler, 1898).

CURRENT STATUS: **North** Locally uncommon summer resident. 25 April–20 October. Dorthy Buck observed adults with young at North Liberty, St. Joseph Co., 18–24 July 1973–74, and Jim Haw found 6 adults with 4 immatures in Steuben Co., 22 August 1973. **Central** Very rare migrant; no recent breeding data. 20 April–20 October. Bred formerly at the now-defunct Bacon's Swamp. **South** Very rare migrant; no recent breeding data. 15 April–25 October. Found in Gibson Co. 26 April 1975 by Charles Mills.

§ American Coot
Fulica americana

FORMER STATUS: "Common migrant. Northward summer resident. Locally very common. It may sometimes, [in] favorable winters, winter southward" (Butler, 1898).

CURRENT STATUS: North Abundant migrant and common summer resident; casual in winter. 15 March–20 November. Central Abundant migrant; recent breeding data lacking, uncommon in winter. 10 March–1 December. South Abundant migrant; fairly common in winter. 5 March–10 December.

Order Charadriiformes
Family Recurvirostridae: Stilts and Avocets
American Avocet
Recurvirostra americana

FORMER STATUS: Bred at one time near Vincennes (Audubon, 1967). Butler (1898) gave a queried record for Calumet Lake, Indiana. Keller (1957) called it an accidental fall visitant and gave four records.

CURRENT STATUS: North Casual fall migrant. At least five recent records spanning 29 August–5 November. Central Casual migrant. Four records: 12 May 1971 at Geist Reservoir by M. Forsyth (Wilson, 1971); 1 November 1953 in that same area (Keller, 1957); 25 September 1975 Monroe Reservoir by M. Brown and S. Glass; 27 August 1972 Eagle Creek Reservoir by Al Starling. South Casual migrant. One record 27 October 1949 at Evansville (Keller, 1957).

REMARKS: Bird is becoming common on the East Coast, especially in the North Carolina Outer Banks where over 100 birds occur during the fall.

Family Charadriidae: Plovers
Semipalmated Plover
Charadrius semipalmatus

FORMER STATUS: "Migrant, generally rare, not uncommon at times in the vicinity of Lake Michigan" (Butler, 1898). Keller (1957) listed it as a rare to frequent migrant in spring and fall.

CURRENT STATUS: North Fairly common spring and uncommon fall migrant. 5 May–1 June; 20 July–1 October. Central Fairly common spring and uncommon fall migrant. 1 May–1 June; 25 July–5 October. South Fairly common spring and rare fall migrant. 25 April–1 June;

1 August–10 October. Charles Mills found 100 on 26 May 1973 in Gibson Co.

§ **Killdeer**
Charadrius vociferus

FORMER STATUS: "Common summer resident. Resident in greater or less numbers, some winters, in the southern part of the State" (Butler, 1898). Keller (1957) called it a common resident and abundant transient.
CURRENT STATUS: **North** Abundant summer resident; rare in winter. 25 February–10 December. **Central** Abundant summer resident; rare in winter. 20 February–10 December. **South** Abundant summer resident; uncommon in winter. 20 February–10 December.

§ **Piping Plover**
Charadrius melodus

FORMER STATUS: Butler (1898) called it a rare migrant, nesting along Lake Michigan, and Keller (1957) presented the last nesting record: 6 June 1955, two adults with one downy chick at Wolf Lake (Marvin Davis).
CURRENT STATUS: **North** Casual migrant. Russell (1973) mentions Wolf Lake–Dunes area as former breeding area into the 1960s but gave no data. Ed Hopkins found one 24 April 1977 at Willow Slough. **Central** Casual fall migrant. Three fall records. **South** No recent data.
REMARKS: It is very doubtful that this species is still breeding in Indiana. Recent sightings probably Michigan birds.

Lesser Golden Plover
Pluvialis dominica

FORMER STATUS: "Migrant. Formerly very abundant over the original prairie region, but are now seen in greatly reduced numbers, though still common, and to the east and south quite rare" (Butler, 1898). Keller (1957) termed it a common spring migrant and rare fall migrant.
CURRENT STATUS: **North** Common spring migrant (northwestern Indiana). Elsewhere uncommon; rare during the fall. 25 March–15 May; 25 August–15 October. D. Buck recorded 1,578 in LaPorte Co., 8 May 1976, and S. Rea et al. found 72 in St. Joseph Co., 30 September 1972. **Central** Rare migrant. 20 March–10 May; 1 September–20 October. **South**

Very rare migrant. 20 March–?; 5 September–20 October. Five seen 20 March 1976 in Gibson Co. (C. Mills).

REMARKS: Southbound migration route of most adult birds is along the east coast, but some individuals pass through the interior of the U.S. instead. Fall birds at the Indianapolis Sewage Disposal Plant were predominantly adults.

Black-bellied Plover
Pluvialis squatarola

FORMER STATUS: "Rare migrant, more numerous in the northwestern part of the State" (Butler, 1898).

CURRENT STATUS: **North** Rare spring and uncommon fall migrant. 5 May–1 June; 15 August–1 November. **Central** Rare spring and uncommon fall migrant. 1 May–1 June; 20 August–5 November. **South** Very rare migrant. Date spans uncertain but probably very similar to above. Charles Mills found 8 in Gibson Co. 18 May 1976.

Hudsonian Godwit
Limosa haemastica

FORMER STATUS: Butler (1898) called it a rare migrant but gave no records. He cited Nelson's and Brayton's analysis that it occurred. Keller (1958) called it accidental on the basis of one record in 1898.

CURRENT STATUS: **North** Casual migrant; at least five spring records: 19 May 1961, Tippecanoe Co. (Burr, 1961); 10 May 1959, LaPorte Co. (Burr, 1959); 23 April 1977, Tippecanoe Co. by E. Hopkins; 6–9 May 1978, Lake Co. by K. Brock et al.; 11 May 1978, Lake Co., an incredible 8 birds found by Ted Cable et al. A recent fall record: 26 August 1978 near Hammond by K. Brock et al. **Central–South** No data.

REMARKS: Normal spring migratory route is west of State; in the fall, off the east coast.

Marbled Godwit
Limosa fedoa

FORMER STATUS: "Rare migrant. In former years it was common, and possibly bred" (Butler, 1898). Keller (1958) cited seven additional records and called it a rare migrant.

CURRENT STATUS: **North** Casual migrant. Three spring records: 24 April 1947, Lake Co. (Ford, 1956); 6–7 May 1977, Willow Slough (M.

Brown–E. Hopkins); 10–11 May 1978, Lake Co. (K. Brock et al.). Four fall records spanning late July to early September. **Central** Casual fall migrant. Two records: 1–2 September 1952, Geist Reservoir (Mumford, West, et al.), and 16 September 1975, Monroe Reservoir (M. Brown–S. Glass). **South** No data.

Eskimo Curlew
Numenius borealis

FORMER STATUS: Butler (1898) termed it a rare migrant. Bird was taken near Vincennes and Chalmers. Keller (1958) incorrectly called it extinct. There are recent sight records in Texas.
CURRENT STATUS: Extirpated.

Whimbrel
Numenius phaeopus

FORMER STATUS: Butler (1898) called it a rare migrant, much rarer than the Long-billed Curlew. Keller (1958) listed it as a very rare migrant and gave three records.
CURRENT STATUS: **North** Casual fall migrant. A bird remained at the sewage ponds at Woodburn from 17–21 September 1978. (Steve Albrecht, J. Haw–documented). **Central–South** No published data.

Long-billed Curlew
Numenius americanus

FORMER STATUS: "Rare migrant. Formerly more numerous and perhaps occasionally breeding in the northern part of the State" (Butler, 1898). Keller (1957) called it accidental with no records since 1896.
CURRENT STATUS: **North** Accidental fall migrant. One recent record: 31 August 1963 at Michigan City by James Landing (Burr, 1964). **Central–South** No data.

§ Upland Sandpiper
Bartramia longicauda

FORMER STATUS: Butler (1898) termed it a migrant and summer resident. Keller (1958) agreed essentially with Butler's analysis and indicated breeding for 17 counties.

CURRENT STATUS: North Rare migrant; very rare summer resident. 20 April–20 August. Weldon found it in Allen Co. 19 June 1975. **Central** Rare migrant; very rare summer resident. 15 April–25 August. James B. Cope recorded 190 in Wayne Co. 30 April 1948. Breeds at Atterbury Fish and Wildlife Area in Johnson Co. **South** Very rare migrant and summer resident. 15 April–25 August. Bred in Gibson, Knox, and Vanderburgh counties (Keller, 1958).

Greater Yellowlegs
Tringa melanoleuca

FORMER STATUS: "Migrant, tolerably common in suitable places, northward, but rare in the southern half of the State" (Butler, 1898). Keller (1958) referred to it as a fairly common migrant.

CURRENT STATUS: North Uncommon migrant. 10 April–10 May; 15 August–15 November. Dorthy Buck reported a group of 50 birds 8 May 1976 in LaPorte Co. **Central** Uncommon migrant. 1 April–5 May; 20 August–20 November. There were 8 birds at Monroe Reservoir 24 October 1976 (S. Glass). **South** Uncommon migrant. 20 March–1 May; 1 September–1 December. Charles Mills found 3 in Gibson Co. 20 March 1976.

REMARKS: Bulk of migration occurs earlier in spring and later in fall than the Lesser Yellowlegs.

Lesser Yellowlegs
Tringa flavipes

FORMER STATUS: "Common migrant; much more numerous in the northern part of the State, where some are summer residents and breed" (Butler, 1898). Keller (1958) called it a common spring and fall migrant and cited Ford's (1956) belief that the species never bred in Indiana.

CURRENT STATUS: North Common migrant. 5 April–20 May; 20 July–10 November. **Central** Common migrant. 1 April–15 May; 25 July–15 November. **South** Fairly common migrant. 20 March–10 May; 1 August–20 November. Charles Mills observed 25 in Gibson Co., 20 March 1976.

Solitary Sandpiper
Tringa solitaria

FORMER STATUS: "Common migrant; summer resident in some numbers northward. Breeds" (Butler, 1898). Keller (1958) refuted Butler's breeding data and called it simply a common migrant.

CURRENT STATUS: **North** Common migrant. 25 April–20 May; 20 July–10 October. **Central** Common migrant. 20 April–15 May; 25 July–15 October. **South** Common migrant. 15 April–10 May; 31 July–20 October.

REMARKS: This species along with several other shorebirds returns early in the fall and was responsible for some misconceptions about breeding on the part of early authors. Some years they appear as early as 4 July in suitable areas, but this is not the migrational peak.

Willet
Catoptrophorus semipalmatus

FORMER STATUS: Butler (1898) termed it a rare migrant, possibly a rare summer resident. Keller (1958) called it a rare migrant.

CURRENT STATUS: **North** Very rare migrant. 25 April–15 May; 15 July–5 September. **Central** Very rare migrant. 25 April–10 May; insufficient fall data for date span but probably similar to above. A recent sighting in Morgan Co., 9 July 1978, by Charles & Shirley Keller. **South** Three recent records: 12 May 1954 in Orange Co. (Mumford–Crail); 2 July 1978 in Gibson Co. (D. Jones); and 16 July 1977 in that same county (M. Brown).

§ Spotted Sandpiper
Actitis macularia

FORMER STATUS: "Common summer resident; a well-known frequenter of the banks of streams, ponds and lakes, and of sandbars everywhere throughout the State" (Butler, 1898). Keller (1958) agreed with this analysis.

CURRENT STATUS: **North** Common summer resident. 1 May–15 October. **Central** Common summer resident. 25 April–20 October. **South** Common summer resident. 20 April–25 October.

Ruddy Turnstone
Arenaria interpres

FORMER STATUS: "Rare migrant. Except along Lake Michigan it is almost unknown" (Butler, 1898). Keller (1957) called it a rare migrant through the interior but fairly common in the vicinity of Lake Michigan.

CURRENT STATUS: **North** Uncommon migrant. 10 May–5 June; 20 August–10 November. Neil Cutright found 35 on 25 May 1976 and 125 on 15 October 1976 in Porter Co. **Central** Very rare migrant. 15 May–1

June; 25 August–15 October. **South** Very rare migrant. Date spans probably similar to above but data insufficient for analysis. Willard Gray
noted two in Warrick Co. 16 May 1973.

REMARKS: Late-lingering birds at Lake Michigan apparently pass un-
detected over the State.

Wilson's Phalarope
Steganopus tricolor

FORMER STATUS: "Rare migrant. Summer resident northward. Common in extreme northwestern part of the State. Breeds" (Butler, 1898).
Keller (1957) called it a rare migrant in the interior and a very rare
summer resident in Lake Co.

CURRENT STATUS: **North** Rare migrant; no breeding data since 1941.
25 April–25 May; 1 August-25 September. Fifteen were seen 8 May
1978 near Woodburn (J. Haw). **Central** Very rare migrant. 25 April–25
May; 5 August–5 October. **South** Casual migrant; only a handful of
records. Mumford found two in Orange Co. 12 May 1954, and Mills observed 24 in the Potoka River Bottoms 6 May 1978.

Northern Phalarope
Lobipes lobatus

FORMER STATUS: Butler (1898) called it a rare migrant while Keller
(1957) amplified this status to a rare migrant during the fall and a very
rare migrant during the spring.

CURRENT STATUS: **North** Very rare migrant. 25 May–5 June; 25 August–
25 September. There are at least two April records which lie outside of
the normal peak range for this species. **Central** Very rare migrant. 25
May–5 June; 25 August–20 September. Five birds were observed at the
Brazil Sewage Lagoons 15–18 September 1976 by L. Smith et al. **South**
Very rare fall migrant; spring data lacking. Donald Parker found one at
Hardy Lake 19–20 September 1976, and Mumford recorded two at
Hovey Lake 7 October 1949.

Red Phalarope
Phalaropus fulicarius

FORMER STATUS: "Rare straggler during migrations" (Butler, 1898).
Keller (1957) referred to it as a very rare late-fall or early-winter straggler
which occurred most often in the Lake Michigan region.

CURRENT STATUS: North One spring record: 10 April 1885, a bird was shot in Jasper Co. (Butler, 1898). Very rare fall migrant. Numerous records for Lake Michigan area spanning 18 September–27 December. Most often seen after 1 November until 5 December. Central Casual fall migrant. One record: 12 September 1975 at Monroe Reservoir by Steve Glass et al. (documented). South No data.

§ American Woodcock
Philohela minor

FORMER STATUS: "Summer resident. Common in suitable localities. Some years, at least, resident in the southwestern part of the State, especially the Wabash Valley, and perhaps about moist places that do not freeze throughout the State" (Butler, 1898). Keller (1958) listed it as a rare summer resident, rare migrant, and occasional during the winter.

CURRENT STATUS: North Fairly common migrant; uncommon summer resident; casual in winter. 25 February–15 November. Central Fairly common migrant; uncommon summer resident; casual in winter. 20 February–20 November. South Fairly common migrant; lack of breeding data to ascertain summer status; very rare in winter. 15 February– 1 December.

Common Snipe
Capella gallinago

FORMER STATUS: "Abundant migrant. Summer resident northward; some winters a few remain in suitable localities" (Butler, 1898). Keller (1958) agreed with most of Butler's evaluation but could not present recent breeding data.

CURRENT STATUS: North Common migrant; casual in winter. No recent breeding data; however, Lee Casebere noted "winnowing" over a large wet meadow 6 April 1974 in Steuben Co., and R. Krol noted birds in aerial display flights in Lake Co. during the spring of 1974. 20 March– 15 May; 25 August–20 November. Central Common migrant; very rare in winter. 15 March–10 May; 1 September–25 November. Steve Glass recorded 30 14 April 1976 at Monroe Reservoir. South Common migrant; rare in winter. 10 March–5 May; 10 September–5 December.

Short-billed Dowitcher
Limnodromus griseus

FORMER STATUS: Butler (1898) called it a rare migrant, most often seen during the fall. Keller (1958) was uncertain of its status and listed most of the records for the State under the Long-billed species. Subsequently (Keller 1964) he corrected that evaluation by defining migration at the Indianapolis Sewage Disposal Plant. This species (*griseus*) he proved to be the more frequent bird.

CURRENT STATUS: North Rare migrant. 1 May–25 May; 25 July–10 October. Irving Burr recorded 74 on 13 May 1972 in Tippecanoe Co. (Wilson, 1972). Central Rare migrant. 25 April–20 May; 1 August–15 October. Keller (1964) recorded it on 34 different occasions between 1959–1963 in Marion Co. South Insufficient data to ascertain exact status but probably similar to above. Charles Mills found 5 in Gibson Co. on 30 August 1976.

REMARKS: Field identification of this species: bare or spotted undertail coverts, longer primaries, and diagnostic "tu-tu-tu" call notes are definitive. Species migrates later in the spring and earlier in the fall than the Long-billed.

Long-billed Dowitcher
Limnodromus scolopaceus

FORMER STATUS: Butler (1898) related: "Rare migrant. Of all the references to Dowitcher only one refers to the short-billed form." Keller (1958), believing Butler's data, listed most of the accumulated data under this species. In Keller (1964) he corrected this assumption and listed the Short-billed as the more frequent species seen in the State.

CURRENT STATUS: North Very rare migrant. Insufficient data for evaluation. Two seen by Ed Hopkins 21 April 1974 in Warren Co.; Ken Brock, Tim Keller, et al. found 20 on 30 October 1977 in Lake Co. Central Casual migrant. 1 April–1 May; 25 September–1 November. Keller (1964) recorded this species on four different occasions between 1959–1963. Larry Peavler found one, 6–9 October 1975, in Marion Co. South Casual migrant. Insufficient data for evaluation. Charles Mills found 25 in Gibson Co., 27 March 1976.

REMARKS: Species is a much earlier migrant in the spring and generally a later migrant during the fall. Field identification marks of barred undertail coverts, shorter primaries, and peeping-type call are diagnostic.

Red Knot
Calidris canutus

FORMER STATUS: "Rare migrant. It seems, in the interior, to be almost exclusively found along the great lakes" (Butler, 1898). Keller (1958) called it a very rare migrant in the fall and gave but one spring record.

CURRENT STATUS: **North** Very rare fall migrant; only two records for the spring: 2 June 1917, Lake Co., and 23 May 1976 (3 birds), Michigan City (W. Buskirk). 25 August–30 September. **Central** Casual fall migrant; one spring record: 24 May 1968, Marion Co. (Keller). 25 August–20 September. Steve Glass recorded it at Monroe Reservoir 19 September 1972, 16 September 1973, and 29 August 1975. **South** No data.

Sanderling
Calidris alba

FORMER STATUS: "Migrant; most places rare, but very common in late summer and fall on the shore of Lake Michigan and perhaps along the Ohio River" (Butler, 1898). Keller (1958) listed it as an abundant migrant about Lake Michigan and of rare occurrence inland during the spring and fall.

CURRENT STATUS: **North** Very rare spring and rare fall migrant except in the vicinity of Lake Michigan where it is fairly common during the southbound migration. 15 May–5 June; 25 August–15 October. Ray Grow et al. found one 16 January 1954 near Gary (West, 1954). **Central** Casual spring and very rare fall migrant. Keller (1972) recorded it at the Indianapolis Sewage Disposal Plant 12–25 May. During the fall the date spans are generally 25 August–30 September. **South** No recent data.

Semipalmated Sandpiper
Calidris pusilla

FORMER STATUS: "Migrant; generally uncommon, but often common and perhaps summer resident in vicinity of Lake Michigan, and more numerous in spring than the Least Sandpiper, with which it is often found" (Butler, 1898). "Common migrant spring and fall" (Keller, 1958).

CURRENT STATUS: **North** Common migrant. 5 May–5 June; 15 August–15 October. **Central** Common migrant. 5 May–1 June; 15 August–20

October. **South** Exact status unknown because of lack of data. Charles
Mills found 45 on 19 May and 40 on 26 May 1973 in Gibson Co.

Western Sandpiper
Calidris mauri

FORMER STATUS: Butler (1898) listed it as hypothetical. Keller (1958)
called it a very rare spring and fall migrant. The first apparent state
record: 24–31 August 1941 at the Indianapolis Sewage Disposal Plant.
Mumford collected a specimen 8 September 1952 at Geist Reservoir.
CURRENT STATUS: **North** Difficult to assess; probably very rare or
casual. Keller (1958) gave two records, both of which were during the
fall. One seen 25 May 1976 in the Pigeon River area (J. Haw et al.).
Central Keller (1972) gave two spring records for Marion Co.: 19 May
1957 and 29 May 1954. He recorded this species on 49 different occasions in the fall with the bulk of the dates falling between 15 August–
30 September. **South** One record: 4–8 August 197? in Gibson Co. (C.
Mills).
REMARKS: Call note diagnostic (Keller, 1972). Rusty scapulars and
auricular patch helpful on some individuals during the fall.

Least Sandpiper
Calidris minutilla

FORMER STATUS: Butler (1898) listed it as a migrant, uncommon in
the spring while Keller (1958) called it a fairly common migrant.
CURRENT STATUS: **North** Common migrant. 25 April–20 May; 20
July–25 October. **Central** Common migrant. 20 April–20 May; 25 July–
25 October. **South** Fairly common migrant. 20 April–20 May; 25 July–
25 October.

White-rumped Sandpiper
Calidris fuscicollis

FORMER STATUS: Listed by Butler (1898) as hypothetical on the basis
of its occurrence in nearby states. Mumford (1953) summarized existing
data and collected the first specimen: 20 July 1950 at Wolf Lake in
Lake Co. Keller (1958) called it a rare spring and fall migrant.
CURRENT STATUS: **North** Rare migrant. 15 May–5 June; 1 September–
15 October. **Central** Rare migrant. 15 May–1 June; 25 August–20 October. There were 15 at Eagle Creek Reservoir 4 September 1972 (A.

Starling). **South** Very rare spring migrant. 15 May–1 June; fall data lacking. Charles Mills found one in Gibson Co., 26 May 1973.

Baird's Sandpiper
Calidris bairdii

FORMER STATUS: "Rare migrant. Up to this time it has been taken in Indiana but twice, both times in August" (Butler, 1898). Keller (1958) called it a very rare spring and rare fall migrant.

CURRENT STATUS: **North** Casual spring and very rare fall migrant. Insufficient spring data for date spans. One recent record: 8 May 1976, Starke Co. (D. Buck et al.). 25 August–25 September. **Central** Casual spring and rare fall migrant. Insufficient spring data for date spans. One recent record: 16 May 1976 at Eagle Creek Reservoir (Al Starling et al.). 30 August–1 October. **South** No data, but probably occurs.

REMARKS: Species normally rather solitary—prefers to feed away from other shorebirds. Spring birds are very difficult to identify unless seen well and compared with other birds of the same genus.

Pectoral Sandpiper
Calidris melanotos

FORMER STATUS: "Common, sometimes abundant, migrant, generally in flocks" (Butler, 1898). Keller (1958) referred to it as an abundant spring and fall migrant.

CURRENT STATUS: **North** Abundant migrant. 25 March–10 May; 25 July–25 October. **Central** Abundant migrant. 25 March–10 May; 20 July–1 November. Keller (1972) called it Indiana's most abundant shorebird based upon data collected by him at the Indianapolis Sewage Plant. He also demonstrated a bi-modal migration during the fall; presumably adults preceding the young. **South** Common migrant. 20 March–5 May; 25 July–10 November.

Purple Sandpiper
Calidris maritima

FORMER STATUS: Butler (1898) listed it as hypothetical. Keller (1958) called it a very rare irregular winter visitant to the breakwater at Michigan City.

CURRENT STATUS: **North** Very rare late fall and winter visitant. Casual in spring. 15 November–24 April. Brock (1977) published an excellent photograph taken 19 April 1977. All records confined to the Michigan City area except one seen by Tim Keller et al. during November 1977 at Beverly Shores. **Central–South** No data.

Dunlin
Calidris alpina

FORMER STATUS: "Migrant the latter part of May, rarely in June and October. Sometimes abundant about the lower end of Lake Michigan and the small lakes near there, in full breeding plumage, in May; elsewhere rare" (Butler, 1898). Keller called it a rare spring and fall migrant.
CURRENT STATUS: **North** Rare spring and uncommon fall migrant. 15 May–5 June; 25 September–20 November. Jim Haw found 40, 26 October 1974 in Steuben Co. **Central** Rare spring and uncommon fall migrant. 10 May–1 June; 25 September–25 November. There were 47 at Monroe Reservoir, 24 October 1975 (Steve Glass et al.). **South** Insufficient data for evaluation but probably similar to above.

Stilt Sandpiper
Micropalama himantopus

FORMER STATUS: Butler (1898) termed it a rare migrant and gave but one record. Keller (1958) called it a very rare spring and rare fall migrant.
CURRENT STATUS: **North** Casual spring and very rare fall migrant. One, Tippecanoe Co., 14–17 May 1950 by Burr et al. (Keller, 1958). 25 July–1 October. **Central** Very rare spring and rare fall migrant. 5 May–25 May; 25 July–5 October. **South** One record: 26 September 1954, Orange County, by R. E. Mumford (Keller, 1958).

Buff-breasted Sandpiper
Tryngites subruficollis

FORMER STATUS: "Rare migrant. Thus far has only been reported from this region in August and September" (Butler, 1898). Keller (1958) related: "Rare migrant in the fall; except for one record it is unknown in the spring."
CURRENT STATUS: **North** Casual spring and very rare fall migrant. One at Willow Slough, 1 June 1977 (E. Hopkins). 25 August–25 September. Nine were found on 26 September 1973 by Nancy Rea near Carlisle. This date is outside of the normal migration time span. **Central**

Casual spring and very rare fall migrant. An old spring record of one, 22 May 1926, in Marion Co. (Baumgartner, 1931). 25 August–20 September. The senior author found 18, 5 September 1960, in Marion Co. (Keller, 1972). **South** No data.

Ruff
Philomachus pugnax

FORMER STATUS: Listed by Butler (1898) as hypothetical. A specimen was taken, 12 April 1905, in Starke Co. by Deane (Ford, 1956).

CURRENT STATUS: **North** Accidental. Aside from the above specimen a bird was seen and photographed 18 April 1976 near Manchester by Mrs. Howard Book and Paul Steffen, and one was observed by Peter Grube et al. on 29 April 1978 in Porter Co.

Family Stercorariidae: Jaegers and Skuas

Pomarine Jaeger
Stercorarius pomarinus

FORMER STATUS: Butler (1898) gave one record. Landing (1966) summarized data for northwestern Indiana and called it "a periodic migrant through northern Indiana, especially near the southern edge of Lake Michigan, but never in great numbers."

CURRENT STATUS: **North** Casual fall migrant. 25 September–20 November. **Central** One record: One, 1 June 1946, at Geist Reservoir (C. E. Keller et al.). **South** No data.

REMARKS: The Pomarine is the second most encountered jaeger in Indiana. Probably more numerous than generally believed, but immature and dark-phased birds difficult to identify unless seen under ideal conditions.

Parasitic Jaeger
Stercorarius parasiticus

FORMER STATUS: Listed by Butler (1898) as hypothetical. Ford (1956) called it a casual visitor while Landing (1966) referred to it as a periodic migrant.

CURRENT STATUS: **North** Thus far all records obtained on Lake Michigan. Very rare fall migrant. 15 September–20 November. One light-phased bird seen by R. Grow at West Beach, 16 November 1977. **Central–South** No data.

REMARKS: Landing (1966) believes most jaeger migration may take off overland near West Beach in a southwesterly direction—possibly to the Mississippi River.

Long-tailed Jaeger
Stercorarius longicaudus

FORMER STATUS: Listed by Butler (1898) as hypothetical. Ford (1956) cites four records (see below).

CURRENT STATUS: North One collected by Herbert L. Stoddard at Dunes State Park, 21 September 1915. One seen at Miller, 20 August 1917. One found dead at Miller, 11 September 1917. An immature taken at Miller, 30 November 1918. There are no recent records. Probably a casual fall migrant. Most immature jaegers seen on Lake Michigan are unidentifiable, unless seen under ideal conditions. **Central–South** No data.

Family Laridae: Gulls and Terns

Glaucous Gull
Larus hyperboreus

FORMER STATUS: "Occasional visitor along Lake Michigan" (Butler, 1898). One collected at Miller, Lake Co., on 8 August 1897 (Woodruff, 1907).

CURRENT STATUS: All data from Lake Michigan area. Periodic rare to very rare winter visitor. Most dates fall between 15 December–15 March. Major winter invasion during the winter of 1976–1977, otherwise only a few recent records.

Iceland Gull
Larus glaucoides

FORMER STATUS: Butler (1898) called it an occasional winter visitor to the northern part of the State.

CURRENT STATUS: North Casual winter visitant and spring migrant. 1 January–10 May. One, 5 April–10 May 1958, at Michigan City (Burr, 1959). The junior author found one in the above location, 16 April 1977.

Central Accidental. One record: 2 April 1927 in Johnson Co. (Baumgartner, 1931). South No data.

Greater Black-backed Gull
Larus marinus

FORMER STATUS: Listed by Butler (1898) as hypothetical. Observed in Porter Co., 26 September 1895 (Eifrig, 1927).

CURRENT STATUS: North Casual winter visitor and migrant. Charles Clark found one at Wolf Lake on the unusual date of 15 June 1946 (Ford, 1956). Other dates span the period between 1 October–13 February. Two recent records: one 11 February 1977 at the Burr Street Dump, Hammond (D. Buck, M. Brown, A. Bruner); one 29 April 1978 at Michigan City (C.–T. Keller et al.). Central Accidental. One record; one seen, 2 April 1927 in Johnson Co. (Baumgartner, 1931).

Lesser Black-backed Gull
Larus fuscus

STATUS: Accidental. One collected at the Willow Slough Fish and Wildlife Area, 7 April 1962 (Mumford and Rowe, 1963). One seen by Mrs. Albert Campbell et al., 2 October 1948, Michigan City (K. Brock, *in press*).

Herring Gull
Larus argentatus

FORMER STATUS: "Common migrant throughout the State; locally, a winter visitor or winter resident" (Butler, 1898).

CURRENT STATUS: North Abundant migrant and winter visitant. Some are reported during the summer on Lake Michigan. Central Uncommon migrant; rare winter visitant (open winters). 15 November–15 April. South Uncommon migrant; rare winter visitant (open winters) except along the Ohio River where it is generally uncommon. 20 November–10 April.

Thayer's Gull
Larus thayeri

CURRENT STATUS: Uncertain, five recent records: 26 February 1978, Clark Co. (T. Keller & Alan Bruner); 18 March 1978, Burr Street Dump,

Lake Co. (T. Keller et al.); 4 May 1978 (T. Keller); 20 June 1978 (P. Grube–K. Brock); and 14 October 1978 (T. and C. Keller). The last three records are for Michigan City.

Ring-billed Gull
Larus delawarensis

FORMER STATUS: "Regular migrant and local winter resident in the same localities as the last mentioned species [Herring Gull]" (Butler, 1898).

CURRENT STATUS: **North** Abundant migrant and winter visitant. Fairly common in summer on Lake Michigan. Breeds at Lake Calumet, Illinois, just over the Indiana line. **Central** Common migrant and winter visitant (open winters). 1 November–25 April. **South** Common migrant and winter visitant (open winters). 10 November–15 April.

Black-headed Gull
Larus ridibundus

STATUS: Two records: one seen 20 August 1977 (documented) by Ken Brock, Ed Hopkins, et al., and two seen later that same day (documented) by T. Keller at Michigan City. There are several Chicago records.

Laughing Gull
Larus atricilla

FORMER STATUS: Listed by Butler (1898) as hypothetical.

CURRENT STATUS: **North** Casual. At least six records: one, 2 September 1957 by R. Grow and 15 October 1957 by Reuterskiold (Burr, 1958); one, 24 August 1959 by Landing (Burr, 1960); one, 31 August–1 September 1964 by Burr (Burr, 1965a). Three recent records include: 17 September 1977 (all above Michigan City area); 13 May 1978, Port of Indiana (K. Brock); and near Gary, 24 May 1978 (R. Grow). **Central** Accidental. One record: 8 May 1976, Lake Waveland, Montgomery Co. (Alan Bruner, Gene Meunch, M. Forsyth, et al.). **South** No data.

REMARKS: One was collected in Louisville Harbor 18 May 1967 by Able (Petersen, 1967).

Franklin's Gull
Larus pipixcan

FORMER STATUS: Butler (1898) called it an occasional migrant.
CURRENT STATUS: **North** Casual migrant, most often seen in fall. Insufficient spring data. A bird collected by J. G. Parker, 3 May 1898 (Butler, 1927). There are several dates between 25 August–15 November. **Central** Casual migrant, most often seen in fall. One seen 9–10 June 1951 at Geist Reservoir by Kahl and West (Kahl, 1951). Two observed by Al Starling at Eagle Creek Reservoir, 25 March 1973. 15 September–20 November. **South** No recent data but probably similar to above.

Bonaparte's Gull
Larus philadelphia

FORMER STATUS: "Common migrant and rare winter visitor" (Butler, 1898).
CURRENT STATUS: **North** Locally abundant migrant and rare winter visitant (Lake Michigan) elsewhere; a fairly common migrant. 1 October–15 May. **Central** Uncommon migrant. 1 April–10 May; 15 October–5 December. **South** Data sparse but probably similar to above.
REMARKS: Formerly (1950–1956) wintered in great numbers in Michigan City area.

Little Gull
Larus minutus

STATUS: Casual late fall and winter visitant. Nine recent records spanning 5 August–12 February. Most recent record is a documented sighting by Ken Brock, 28 October 1978. All data from Michigan City area.

Black-legged Kittiwake
Rissa tridactyla

FORMER STATUS: Listed by Butler (1898) as hypothetical.
CURRENT STATUS: **North** Casual fall migrant and winter visitor. Date spans fall between 20 November–20 March. All at Michigan City except one by T. Keller et al. near Hamlet, 20 March 1977. **Central** Casual late fall migrant. Two records: 26 November 1954, Marion Co., by H. C. West; 4 December 1976 by Forsyth, Keller, et al. at Geist Reservoir. **South**

Casual migrant. One record: one seen at Deam's Lake, Clark Co., by Jackie B. Elmore et al. (documented) on 7 November 1976.

Sabine's Gull
Xema sabini

FORMER STATUS: Listed by Butler (1898) as hypothetical.

CURRENT STATUS: All records from Lake Michigan area. Casual fall migrant. 5 December 1954, Lake Co., by Grow (Burr, 1955). 26 September 1958, Lake Co., by Louis (Burr, 1959). 25 October 1959, LaPorte Co., by Landing (Burr, 1960). Latest record is of one, possibly two, seen (documented), 14 October 1978 at Miller Beach (near Gary) and Michigan City by the Kellers, R. Grow, K. Brock, et al.

§ Forster's Tern
Sterna forsteri

FORMER STATUS: "Most places this tern is a rare migrant, but during the fall it is exceedingly abundant on Lake Michigan" (Butler, 1898).

CURRENT STATUS: North Abundant migrant in the vicinity of Lake Michigan; otherwise, uncommon. Very rare summer resident. Recorded as breeding in Lake Co. during 1957, 1958, and 1962. 25 April–15 October. Central Uncommon migrant. 20 April–20 May; 15 August–15 October. South Status not known but believed to be similar to above.

Common Tern
Sterna hirundo

FORMER STATUS: "Migrant; in some localities abundant" (Butler, 1898). Formerly bred in Lake Co. during 1934, 1935, and 1936 (Butler, 1937).

CURRENT STATUS: North Common migrant in vicinity of Lake Michigan; elsewhere, rare. 15 April–25 May; 15 August–1 November. Central Rare migrant. 15 April–20 May; 20 August–15 October. South Insufficient data but probably similar to above.

Arctic Tern
Sterna paradisaea

STATUS: Accidental. A bird (documented) seen 30 April 1978 at Michigan City by Tim Keller, Michael Brown, and Alan Bruner.

REMARKS: Several recently seen in Minnesota on Lake Superior.

Roseate Tern
Sterna dougallii

FORMER STATUS: Butler (1898) called it accidental on data given by Dr. Haymond. Herbert L. Stoddard collected an adult male in Lake Co., 14 August 1916 (Stoddard, 1917).
CURRENT STATUS: Accidental (see above). No recent reliable data.

Little Tern
Sterna albifrons

FORMER STATUS: "Rare migrant over most of the State. A few are summer residents in the northern part" (Butler, 1898).
CURRENT STATUS: North Casual migrant. Hopkins found one 19 June 1974 in Tippecanoe Co. and Bruce Fall recorded one 20 July 1963 in that same county (Burr, 1964). There are a few older records. Central Casual migrant. Recorded at Monroe Reservoir by Steve Glass 27 August 1973 and 25 September 1976. There are a few older records. South Casual migrant. There are some older records for Hovey Lake. The most recent were two observed by Denny Jones at the Gibson Co. Power Plant, 2 July 1978.

Caspian Tern
Hydroprogne caspia

FORMER STATUS: Listed by Butler (1898) as hypothetical. Ford (1956) called it an uncommon migrant. He listed a record by Smith and DuMont of 80 birds at Wolf Lake, 3 September 1944.
CURRENT STATUS: North Uncommon migrant in the vicinity of Lake Michigan; elsewhere, rare. 1 May–5 June; 15 August–1 October. Central Very rare fall migrant (no recent spring data). 25 August–25 October. South Casual fall migrant (no recent data).

§ **Black Tern**
Chlidonias niger

FORMER STATUS: "Regular migrant in the southern part of the State and a summer resident about marshy lakes, at least from the Kankakee River northward. In some localities it breeds commonly" (Butler, 1898).
CURRENT STATUS: North Abundant migrant and rare summer resident across the northern portion of the State; elsewhere, a fairly common mi-

grant. Breeds as far south as Kosciusko Co. 20 April–15 September.
Central Uncommon migrant. 20 April–25 May; 25 July–15 September.
Alan Bruner found 3, 19 June 1976, at Lake Waveland in Montgomery
Co. **South** Uncommon migrant. Date spans probably similar to above but
recent data lacking. N. Stocks found 30, 10 August 1973, in Warrick Co.

Family Alcidae: Alcids

Thick-billed Murre
Uria lomvia

FORMER STATUS: Accidental (Butler, 1898). A major "crash" occurred
during the winter of 1896–1897 with at least 10 records of this bird from
the Midwest. There have been no recent records.

Ancient Murrelet
Synthliboramphus antiquus

FORMER STATUS: Listed by Butler (1898) as hypothetical.
CURRENT STATUS: Accidental. One record: a dead bird found by Dave
Sobal ¾ mile west of the Lake Co.–Porter Co. line in Gary on 8 November
1976. The specimen (No. 1901) was prepared by James B. Cope and is in
the Joseph Moore Museum at Earlham College.

Order Columbiformes
Family Columbidae: Pigeons and Doves

§ **Rock Dove**
Columbia livia

STATUS: Normally omitted from most state lists because of its domestic
nature, this species has been noted nesting in the rock formations of
Montgomery Co. by Dorothy Luther. That would seem to indicate that
it has managed to utilize nesting habitats devoid of human association.
Whether it does so in other areas of the State has not been recorded. As
an exotic it is an abundant bird in all three regions.

§ **Mourning Dove**
Zenaida macroura

FORMER STATUS: "Common summer resident northward; southward, common resident. In the lower Wabash and lower Whitewater valleys they often spend the winter in small flocks, frequenting chosen places" (Butler, 1898).

CURRENT STATUS: Abundant resident except, perhaps, in the north during the winter.

Passenger Pigeon
Ectopistes migratorius

FORMER STATUS: "Migrant, formerly very abundant, but now rare; also rare resident" (Butler, 1898).

CURRENT STATUS: Extinct.

Common Ground Dove
Columbina passerina

STATUS: **North** No data. **Central** Accidental. One found dead in Hendricks Co., 23 November 1961, by R. S. Gregory, is now a specimen in the Joseph Moore Museum at Earlham College. **South** Accidental. One seen near Rockport, 27 October 1976 by Randall Cooley and Randall Madding, was documented (Kleen, 1977).

Order Psittaciformes
Family Psittacidae: Parrots

Carolina Parakeet
Conuropsis carolinensis

FORMER STATUS: "This beautiful little Parrot is now almost extinct. It will soon be entirely exterminated. At present it is probably to be found in small numbers in Florida and in a few favorable localities from there to northeastern Texas and Indian Territory" (Butler, 1898).

CURRENT STATUS: Extinct.

Order Cuculiformes

Family Cuculidae: Cuckoos, Roadrunners, and Anis

§ Yellow-billed Cuckoo

Coccyzus americanus

FORMER STATUS: "Common summer resident; less numerous northward" (Butler, 1898).
CURRENT STATUS: **North** Uncommon summer resident. 10 May–1 October. **Central** Fairly common summer resident. 5 May–15 October. **South** Fairly common summer resident. 1 May–20 October.

§ Black-billed Cuckoo

Coccyzus erythropthalmus

FORMER STATUS: "Summer resident; common northward; much less numerous southward, except during migrations, when it is common" (Butler, 1898).
CURRENT STATUS: **North** Fairly common summer resident. 10 May–1 October. **Central** Rare summer resident; fairly common migrant. 5 May–15 October. **South** Breeding status unknown; fairly common migrant. 1 May–20 October.

Order Strigiformes

Family Tytonidae: Barn Owls

§ Barn Owl

Tyto alba

FORMER STATUS: "Found throughout the State; locally resident; rare northward; more numerous in the Wabash Valley and southward. Breeds" (Butler, 1898).
CURRENT STATUS: **North** Casual resident. No recent breeding data. Found at Fox Island 16 November 1975 and during September 1976 by Pat Bolman. **Central** Casual resident. Young observed by authors in Marion Co. during 1975. **South** Casual resident. No recent breeding data. One observed, 16 February 1975, in Vanderburgh Co. (Anne Weaver *fide* N. Stocks).
REMARKS: A blue-listed species whose status has changed considerably since the 1930s. All records should be reported.

Family Strigidae: Typical Owls

§ **Common Screech Owl**
Otus asio

FORMER STATUS: Butler (1898) termed it an abundant breeding resident.
CURRENT STATUS: **North** Fairly common resident. Dorthy Buck has them roosting in an American Kestrel box from time to time in the winter at Hamlet. **Central** Fairly common resident. **South** Fairly common resident.

§ **Great Horned Owl**
Bubo virginianus

FORMER STATUS: Butler (1898) called it a common breeding resident.
CURRENT STATUS: **North** Fairly common resident. Delano Arvin found a nest with two young 18 March 1975 in Tippecanoe Co. **Central** Fairly common resident. Active nests at Eagle Creek Park and Geist Reservoir areas. **South** Fairly common resident.

Snowy Owl
Nyctea scandiaca

FORMER STATUS: "Winter visitor, of irregular occurrence" (Butler, 1898).
CURRENT STATUS: **North** Periodic winter visitant, usually very rare; but some years it can be fairly common. 15 November–15 March. **Central** Periodic winter visitant; usually very rare. 15 November–15 March. **South** Periodic winter visitant; usually casual. Dates probably similar to above.

Burrowing Owl
Athene cunicularia

FORMER STATUS: Two collected; one in Porter Co., 16 April 1924 (Hine, 1924), and another in Newton Co., 12 April 1942 (Kirkpatrick, 1942).
CURRENT STATUS: Accidental (see above).

§ Barred Owl
Strix varia

FORMER STATUS: "Common resident. Breeds. Not so common as it was formerly, and apparently not so numerous in the Whitewater Valley as elsewhere" (Butler, 1898).
CURRENT STATUS: North Fairly common resident. Noted with some degree of frequency in Tippecanoe Co. (D. Arvin). Central Fairly common resident. South Fairly common resident.

Great Gray Owl
Strix nebulosa

FORMER STATUS: Butler (1898) termed it accidental on the basis of reported observations by Dr. A. W. Brayton in northern Indiana and Mr. E. R. Quick in Franklin Co. One was supposedly taken near Fowler during the winter of 1897–98 (Perkins, *Auk*, 50:436) and another reportedly collected near Hovey Lake, Posey Co., prior to 1913. A specimen mounted and said to be on display in the Mt. Vernon Library in 1935 (Perkins, *Auk*, 52:465–466).
CURRENT STATUS: Accidental on the basis of the last named record. It would be most interesting to know the whereabouts of the above-mentioned specimen.

§ Long-eared Owl
Asio otus

FORMER STATUS: "Resident, not common in summer; more numerous in winter. Breeds" (Butler, 1898).
CURRENT STATUS: North Very rare summer resident; rare winter visitant. Nesting data summarized by Mumford (1976). He gave data for Porter, Newton, LaPorte, and Tippecanoe counties. Central Very rare winter visitant; casual summer resident. One breeding record: Jennings Co. at the Crosley Fish and Wildlife Area in 1973 (Mumford, 1976). South Casual winter visitant. One seen in Spencer Co., 22 November 1973 (N. Stocks).

Short-eared Owl
Asio flammeus

FORMER STATUS: "Resident in some numbers northward; elsewhere irregular winter resident in varying numbers. Some winters not seen. Oc-

casionally very abundant" (Butler, 1898). Nested in Allen Co. in 1938
(Price, 1938) and in Starke Co. (year ?) (*Ind. Aud. Soc. Yearbook*,
1940:87).
    CURRENT STATUS: **North** Rare winter visitant. Breeding status un-
known. 1 November–15 April. **Central** Very rare winter visitant. 15 November–10 April. Alan Bruner observed 4 in Montgomery Co., 25 November 1975. **South** Very rare winter visitant. Date spans uncertain.
Locally, Gibson Co., fairly common winter visitant (C. Mills).

§ **Saw-whet Owl**
Aegolius acadicus

    FORMER STATUS: "Not uncommon resident northward; irregular winter
resident south. Some winters common locally" (Butler, 1898). Edna
Banta (1953) summarized data for Mary Gray Bird Sanctuary and for
Indiana. Bred in St. Joseph Co. during 1959.
    CURRENT STATUS: **North** Casual winter visitant; casual summer resi-
dent. One seen 27 May 1974 near Willow Slough by E. Hopkins. 15
November–10 April. **Central** Casual winter visitant. 25 November–5
April. During the period of 1953–1965 they were observed at Mary
Gray Bird Sanctuary during the late fall to early spring. **South** Casual
winter visitant. A bird seen near Scales Lake in Warrick Co. 19 April
1959 by the senior author.

Order Caprimulgiformes
Family Caprimulgidae: Goatsuckers

§ **Chuck-will's-widow**
Caprimulgus carolinensis

    FORMER STATUS: "Summer resident in lower Wabash Valley, at least
as far north as Knox County. Breeds" (Butler, 1898).
    CURRENT STATUS: **North** Casual (resident ?). A recent record of a
bird heard and seen 20 May–28 May 1977 in Newton Co. by Ken
Brock, Ted Cable, Ed Hopkins, et al. (documented). Also recorded for
Newton Co. during spring, 1978. **Central** Very rare (resident ?). One
heard by Otto K. Behrens during the summer of 1975 in Marion Co.
Southernmost counties of this region generally believed to be the northern
fringe of their distribution. **South** Rare resident. 15 April–1 September.

In Gibson Co. in 1975 Charles Mills believed this species to be more common than Whip-poor-will.

§ Whip-poor-will
Caprimulgus vociferus

FORMER STATUS: "Common summer resident; breeds. Prefers more open woods overgrown with underbrush, or brushy pastures" (Butler, 1898).

CURRENT STATUS: **North** Uncommon summer resident. 25 April–1 September. Eight were heard on a breeding-bird census in Porter Co. 28 June 1975. **Central** Fairly common summer resident, particularly in south-central Indiana. 20 April–5 September. **South** Fairly common summer resident. 15 April–10 September. Delano Arvin heard one in Daviess Co. 31 August 1975.

§ Common Nighthawk
Chordeiles minor

FORMER STATUS: "Abundant migrant, most numerous in fall; in north-western Indiana a common summer resident; locally elsewhere in some numbers. Breeds in suitable localities" (Butler, 1898).

CURRENT STATUS: **North** Common spring migrant and summer resident; abundant fall migrant. 5 May–20 September. **Central** Common spring migrant and summer resident; abundant fall migrant. 1 May–25 September. **South** Common spring migrant and summer resident; abundant fall migrant. 25 April–1 October.

Order Apodiformes
Family Apodidae: Swifts

§ Chimney Swift
Chaetura pelegica

FORMER STATUS: Butler (1898) termed it an abundant summer resident.

CURRENT STATUS: Abundant summer resident. 20 April–15 October. Date spans may vary from 5 days later in the north to 5 days earlier for the south during the spring migration and conversely in the fall.

Family Trochilidae: Hummingbirds
§ **Ruby-throated Hummingbird**
Archilochus colubris

FORMER STATUS: "Common summer resident. Breeds" (Butler, 1898).
CURRENT STATUS: **North** Common summer resident. 1 May–20 September. Eighteen were observed on a breeding bird census in Porter Co. 28 June 1975. **Central** Common summer resident. 25 April–25 September. **South** Common summer resident. 25 April–25 September.

Order Coraciiformes
Family Alcedinidae: Kingfishers
§ **Belted Kingfisher**
Megaceryle alcyon

FORMER STATUS: "Resident southward, the extent and number depending upon the severity of the winter, and the number of open streams; common summer resident northward" (Butler, 1898).
CURRENT STATUS: **North** Common summer resident; rare during the winter (open water). 15 March–15 November. **Central** Common summer resident; rare during the winter (open water). 10 March–20 November. **South** Common summer resident; uncommon during the winter (open water). 5 March–1 December.

Order Piciformes
Family Picidae: Woodpeckers
§ **Common Flicker**
Colaptes auratus

FORMER STATUS: "Resident, very common southward. Rare in the north part of the State; common everywhere throughout the warmer parts of the year. Breeds" (Butler, 1898).
CURRENT STATUS: **North** Abundant summer resident; very rare in winter. 25 March–15 October. On a St. Joseph Co. bird count 79 were recorded 8 May 1975. **Central** Abundant summer resident; rare in

winter. 20 March–20 October. **South** Abundant summer resident; uncommon in winter. 15 March–1 November.

§ **Pileated Woodpecker**
Dryocopus pileatus

FORMER STATUS: "Resident, confined to the more heavily-timbered and more inaccessible portions of the State. Rarely breeds. It was formerly very common, but disappears before civilization" (Butler, 1898).

CURRENT STATUS: **North** Very rare resident. Arvin notes it with some degree of regularity in Tippecanoe Co. Farther north about Lake Michigan it is casual. In the northeast we have had no reports in the last 5 years. **Central** Uncommon resident except in south-central Indiana where it is fairly common. **South** Fairly common resident.

REMARKS: One of the truly remarkable success stories of our age, Pileateds are frequent visitors to feeding stations in central and southern Indiana. They nest in suburban Indianapolis, i.e., Eagle Creek Park and South Westway Park.

§ **Red-bellied Woodpecker**
Melanerpes carolinus

FORMER STATUS: "Resident, rare northward, more numerous southward, common in southern third of State" (Butler, 1898).

CURRENT STATUS: **North** Fairly common summer resident; rare during winter. Thirteen were observed 8 May 1976 on the St. Joseph Co. bird count and 9 were located in Porter Co. during a breeding bird census 28 June 1975. **Central** Fairly common summer resident. Uncommon during winter. James and Amy Mason found 40 on 29 April 1973 in Vigo Co. **South** Common summer resident; common in winter.

§ **Red-headed Woodpecker**
Melanerpes erythrocephalus

FORMER STATUS: Butler (1898) related: "It is liable to be found resident in any part of the State, but not always frequenting the same localities winter and summer. However, it usually migrates from the northern part when cold weather comes, and occasionally seems to leave the State almost entirely. The severity of the weather does not govern this removal. Food supply is the great factor . . . the abundance of mast keeps them."

CURRENT STATUS: **North** Locally abundant summer resident; generally less so in the winter depending on the available food supply. Arvin called them common during the winter of 1974–75 in Tippecanoe Co. and N. Rea called them common in St. Joseph Co. that same winter. **Central** Locally abundant summer resident; generally less so in the winter depending on the available food supply. H. C. West called them common during the summer of 1976 and almost absent during the winter of 1976–77. **South** Locally common summer resident; generally less so in the winter depending on the available food supply.

REMARKS: Blue-listed in some areas, the Red-head does not seem to warrant that status in Indiana.

§ Yellow-bellied Sapsucker
Sphyrapicus varius

FORMER STATUS: "Winter resident southward, and occasionally, over most of the State, varying in numbers; rare summer resident northward; common everywhere during migration" (Butler, 1898).

CURRENT STATUS: **North** Common migrant and casual summer resident; casual in winter. 5 April–1 November. Neil Cutright noted it 26 June 1974 and 27 July 1975 at the Indiana Dunes. A pair nested in Elkhart Co. in the summer of 1973 (M. Jacobs). **Central** Common migrant; very rare in winter. 1 April–5 May; 25 September–5 November. A bird found the last of June 1948 in Marion Co. (Mumford and Keller, 1975). **South** Common migrant; uncommon in winter. 1 October–1 May.

§ Hairy Woodpecker
Picoides villosus

FORMER STATUS: "Common resident; more numerous southward in fall, winter and spring. Breeds" (Butler, 1898).

CURRENT STATUS: Uncommon resident and appears to be decreasing in numbers.

§ Downy Woodpecker
Picoides pubescens

FORMER STATUS: Butler (1898) called it a common resident.
CURRENT STATUS: Abundant resident.

Black-backed Three-toed Woodpecker
Picoides arcticus

FORMER STATUS: Listed by Butler (1898) as hypothetical.
CURRENT STATUS: **North** Casual winter visitant. Stoddard (1917) reported one in 1917. In the period of 1917–1927 there were 10 records followed by two reports in September of 1949. All records thus far are from Lake and Porter counties. **Central–South** No data.

Ivory-billed Woodpecker
Campephilus principalis

FORMER STATUS: "Formerly resident, locally, in the southern part of Indiana; now extinct within our limits" (Butler, 1898).
CURRENT STATUS: Extirpated, if not extinct. Unverified or confidential sightings reported in Florida and Texas.

Order Passeriformes
Family Tyrannidae: Tyrant Flycatchers

§ **Eastern Kingbird**
Tyrannus tyrannus

FORMER STATUS: "A well known summer resident. Abundant. Breeds" (Butler, 1898).
CURRENT STATUS: **North** Abundant summer resident. 1 May–1 September. **Central** Abundant summer resident. 25 April–5 September. **South** Abundant summer resident. 20 April–10 September.

Western Kingbird
Tyrannus verticalis

FORMER STATUS: Listed by Butler (1898) as hypothetical.
CURRENT STATUS: **North** Casual. Burr listed it as very rare in Tippecanoe Co. in his checklist (Burr, 1962 mimeo). One was seen in LaPorte Co. 3 June 1951 by James Cope and Russell Mumford. There are a few unpublished records but none within the last 10 years. **Central** Casual. The senior author observed one, 2 November 1947, near Riverside Park. William Buskirk et al. found one on 6 September 1958 at Geist Reservoir and Palmer Skarr and Charles Marks found one on 7 September 1941

near Indianapolis. The latter is apparently the first state record. The most recent record is a bird seen (documented), 28 August 1977, at Eagle Creek Reservoir by the junior author. All above data is for Marion Co. **South** Casual. One collected in Jackson Co., 1 September 1953, by Mumford (*Ind. Audu. Quarterly* 32:16–18).

§ Scissor-tailed Flycatcher
Muscivora forficata

FORMER STATUS: Listed by Butler (1898) as hypothetical. Apparently the first reported sighting was in Lake Co. on 3–4 May 1947 (Bartel, 1948).

CURRENT STATUS: **North** Accidental. Two records: (see above) and 13 April 1963 in LaPorte Co. (Burr, 1964). **Central** Accidental. One record: Tom Alexander (*fide* S. Glass) found one bird in Clay Co. 11 May 1976 and 2 birds 28 July 1976 (documented). **South** Accidental. One record: a pair successfully built a nest and raised three young during 1974 in Daviess Co. (Howell and Thiroff, 1976).

REMARKS: Species appears to be utilizing strip-mine areas.

§ Great Crested Flycatcher
Myiarchus crinitus

FORMER STATUS: Butler (1898) called it a common summer resident.

CURRENT STATUS: **North** Common summer resident. 1 May–20 September. **Central** Common summer resident. 25 April–25 September. James and Amy Mason found 19, 11 May 1973 in Parke Co. **South** Common summer resident. 20 April–25 September.

§ Eastern Phoebe
Sayornis phoebe

FORMER STATUS: Butler (1898) said it was one of the earliest summer residents to arrive; rarely common before mid-April.

CURRENT STATUS: **North** Common summer resident; casual in winter. 1 April–1 November. One found 18 December 1976 in Tippecanoe Co. (R. W. Witerfield *fide* E. Hopkins). **Central** Common summer resident, casual in winter. 25 March–5 November. **South** Common summer resident, very rare in winter. 20 March–15 November. Charles Mills found them in Gibson Co., 23 December 1972 and 24 January 1976.

Yellow-bellied Flycatcher
Empidonax flaviventris

FORMER STATUS: "Rare migrant, and occasional summer resident. Breeds" (Butler, 1898). It is doubtful that it breeds in Indiana.

CURRENT STATUS: **North** Uncommon migrant. 10 May–1 June; 25 August–25 September. One heard at Kingsbury Fish and Wildlife Area, 17 July 1976, by Philip Wagner. **Central** Uncommon spring migrant; fairly common fall migrant. 5 May–1 June; 25 August–1 October. Steve Glass found one in Monroe Co., 17 September 1974. **South** Rare migrant. Insufficient data for time span but probably similar to above.

REMARKS: In 9 years of banding this has been the most common *Empidonax* during the fall in Marion Co.

§ Acadian Flycatcher
Empidonax virescens

FORMER STATUS: Butler (1898) related: ". . . in many localities it is very common, and is always more numerous during migrations."

CURRENT STATUS: **North** Common summer resident. 5 May–25 September. **Central** Common summer resident. 5 May–25 September. **South** Common summer resident. 1 May–30 September.

§ Willow Flycatcher
Empidonax traillii

FORMER STATUS: "Summer resident, generally distributed, and locally common. Breeds" (Butler, 1898).

CURRENT STATUS: **North** Common summer resident. 5 May–15 September. **Central** Common summer resident. 5 May–20 September. **South** Fairly common summer resident. 1 May–25 September.

REMARKS: See next species for overall discussion of the Willow–Alder complex.

Alder Flycatcher
Empidonax alnorum

FORMER STATUS: Butler (1898) included it as sub-specific to the Willow (Traill's) Flycatcher on the basis of its supposed occurrence in this area.

CURRENT STATUS: **North** Uncommon migrant; possibly summer resident. 10 May–?. Lee Casebere, Jim Haw, and Mark Weldon have located singing Alders and Willows in close proximity to each other in the Pigeon River area. On a canoe trip at that same location a total of 8 Willows and 4 Alders were observed. The Alder habitat is similar to the Willow in that area. Although no nest has been found, singing males occurred during June and July of 1975–1976. Other records include: Lake Co., 8 June 1975 (R. Krol); Porter Co., 12–31 May 1975 (N. Cutright) and 8 May 1976 in St. Joseph Co. **Central** Casual migrant. Al Starling noted one at Eagle Creek Reservoir during May 1976. **South** Casual migrant. Two recorded, 21 May 1978 in the Buckskin Bottoms of Gibson Co. (C. Mills).

§ **Least Flycatcher**
Empidonax minimus

FORMER STATUS: "Rather common migrant southward. Summer resident in some numbers northward" (Butler, 1898).

CURRENT STATUS: **North** Common migrant; uncommon summer resident. 1 May–1 October. **Central** Common migrant. One heard, 5 June 1977, in Montgomery Co. (Kellers–A. Bruner). 25 April–10 October. **South** Common migrant. 20 April–15 October.

§ **Eastern Pewee**
Contopus virens

FORMER STATUS: "A common summer resident in woods, pastures, orchards, and even about farms and other large lawns" (Butler, 1898).

CURRENT STATUS: **North** Common summer resident. 10 May–25 September. **Central** Common summer resident. 5 May–30 September. **South** Common summer resident. 1 May–5 October.

Olive-sided Flycatcher
Nuttallornis borealis

FORMER STATUS: "Migrant; generally rare, but found in some numbers about the lower end of Lake Michigan" (Butler, 1898).

CURRENT STATUS: **North** Rare migrant. 15 May–5 June; 1 September–25 September. **Central** Very rare migrant. 15 May–5 June; 1 September–30 September. **South** Very rare migrant; insufficient data for date spans but probably similar to above.

Family Alaudidae: Larks

§ **Horned Lark**
Eremophila alpestris

FORMER STATUS: "Resident, common northward, except in the extreme northern part; most numerous in winter, when it is found in flocks" (Butler, 1898).

CURRENT STATUS: **North** Common resident; abundant during the winter (when numerous sub-specific forms occur). **Central** Common resident; abundant during the winter. **South** Fairly common resident; abundant during the winter.

Family Hirundinidae: Swallows

§ **Tree Swallow**
Iridoprocne bicolor

FORMER STATUS: "The tree swallow is generally a migrant southward, but in the lower Wabash Valley and in northern Indiana it is a summer resident locally in suitable places. In some localities it is rare and in others very abundant" (Butler, 1898).

CURRENT STATUS: **North** Common migrant and fairly common summer resident. 20 March–1 November. **Central** Common migrant and rare summer resident. 15 March–1 November. A flock of 4,000, Geist Reservoir, 7 October 1978 (H. C. West–Kellers). **South** Common migrant and very rare summer resident. 10 March–5 November. Charles Mills observed one, 25 January 1975, in the Potoka River Bottoms.

§ **Bank Swallow**
Riparia riparia

FORMER STATUS: "Abundant summer resident, breeding in colonies wherever there are steep banks along streams or about ponds in which they can excavate holes for their nests" (Butler, 1898).

CURRENT STATUS: **North** Common migrant and locally abundant summer resident. 15 April–1 September. **Central** Common migrant and locally abundant summer resident. 10 April–5 September. **South** Common migrant and locally abundant summer resident. 10 April–5 September. Marietta Smith observed one, 13 March 1976, in Gibson Co.

§ **Rough-winged Swallow**
Stelgidopteryx ruficollis

FORMER STATUS: Butler (1898) called it a summer resident but not as common as the Bank Swallow.
CURRENT STATUS: **North** Common migrant and summer resident. 15 April–1 September. **Central** Common migrant and summer resident. 10 April–5 September. **South** Common migrant and summer resident. 10 April–5 September.

§ **Barn Swallow**
Hirundo rustica

FORMER STATUS: Butler (1898) called it an abundant summer resident.
CURRENT STATUS: **North** Abundant summer resident. 25 April–15 September. **Central** Abundant summer resident. 20 April–20 September. **South** Abundant summer resident. 15 April–25 September.

§ **Cliff Swallow**
Petrochelidon pyrrhonota

FORMER STATUS: Butler (1898) called it uncommon due to interference on nest sites by the House Sparrow.
CURRENT STATUS: **North** Uncommon migrant and summer resident. 1 May–1 September. **Central** Uncommon migrant and rare summer resident. 25 April–10 September. Nests locally in Montgomery Co. (A. Bruner–D. Luther). **South** Rare migrant; recent breeding data lacking. 25 April–15 September.
REMARKS: Competition for nest sites by House Sparrow is still a serious problem.

§ **Purple Martin**
Progne subis

FORMER STATUS: Butler (1898) called it a locally common summer resident.
CURRENT STATUS: **North** Common migrant and locally abundant summer resident. 5 April–1 September. **Central** Common migrant and locally abundant summer resident. 1 April–5 September. **South** Common migrant and locally abundant summer resident. 25 March–10 September.
REMARKS: Species subject to population fluctuations due to severity of weather.

Family Corvidae: Jays, Magpies, and Crows

§ **Blue Jay**
Cyanocitta cristata

FORMER STATUS: Butler (1898) called it a common and well-known resident.
CURRENT STATUS: Common resident and abundant migrant. Main period of migration occurs: 20 April–5 May; 15 September–10 October.

Black-billed Magpie
Pica pica

FORMER STATUS: Listed by Butler (1898) as hypothetical. A bird seen near Bicknell, Knox Co., from December 1907–February 1908 (Chansler, 1910).
CURRENT STATUS: **North** Accidental. One seen near Rochester, Fulton Co., in April 1951. **Central** Accidental. One photographed by R. H. Cooper in Delaware Co. in December 1959. A recent sight record in Marion Co. is believed to be a zoo escape. **South** Accidental. Three seen near Evansville in April 1956.
REMARKS: Birds commonly kept as pets and/or local zoo captives.

Northern Raven
Corvus corax

FORMER STATUS: Butler (1898) called it a rare resident, breeding in Martin Co. in 1894.
CURRENT STATUS: Accidental. One seen near Gary, 13 October 1953, by Mrs. Amy Baldwin (*Audu. Field Notes* 1954:22).

§ **American Crow**
Corvus brachyrhynchos

FORMER STATUS: "Very common throughout the State; resident, but not so common in winter northward" (Butler, 1898).
CURRENT STATUS: Common summer resident; locally abundant during the winter.

Family Paridae: Titmice

§ **Black-capped Chickadee**
Parus atricapillus

FORMER STATUS: Much of what Butler (1898) related is still true to-day: "Abundant resident in the northern part of the State; common winter resident for a little distance south of the area where it is resident. Not often seen in the southern part of the State, and then only as a winter visitor."

CURRENT STATUS: **North** Common resident. Exact limits of this species' range not clearly defined but believed to angle on a line from near Lafayette east to the vicinity of Fort Wayne. **Central** Rare winter visitant. 1 December–1 March. **South** Very rare winter visitant. Dates probably similar to above.

REMARKS: Some observers suspect occurrence of this species further south in the summer. Indeed, some chickadees banded by the authors and Tom and Sallie Potter south of Indianapolis have wing chord and tail measurements that fall within this species' range (i.e. > 60mm). Plumage characteristics, however, were more like those considered to be Carolina. Much work needs to be done before any real definitive explanation can be attempted.

§ **Carolina Chickadee**
Parus carolinensis

FORMER STATUS: Butler (1898) listed it as an abundant resident in southern Indiana.

CURRENT STATUS: **North** Occurs as far north as Lafayette and Fort Wayne. South of that area it is a common resident. **Central** Abundant resident. **South** Abundant resident.

Boreal Chickadee
Parus hudsonicus

FORMER STATUS: Butler (1898) placed this species on his hypothetical list due to its occurrence in nearby states.

CURRENT STATUS: **North** Accidental. Several seen from 25 November–17 April 1952 in the Dunes area. One was photographed and banded by Mrs. Floyd Maffitt. One, 8 May–8 June 1976 at Fox Island Nature Preserve near Fort Wayne (J. Haw et al.; photographed and documented). **Central** Accidental. A report of a bird near Bloomington, 31 October 1976, seen in comparison with Carolina Chickadees at a feeder (Tom Alexander *fide* S. Glass). **South** No data.

§ **Tufted Titmouse**
Parus bicolor

FORMER STATUS: "An abundant resident in southern Indiana and north, at least in the Wabash Valley, to Parke, Warren, Carroll, Tippecanoe and Wabash counties. Northward, in many localities, it is rare, and about the southern end of Lake Michigan it is apparently wanting" (Butler, 1898). CURRENT STATUS: **North** Common resident. Sixty-one were observed in Porter Co., 28 June 1975, on a breeding bird census. **Central** Abundant resident. **South** Abundant resident.

Family Sittidae: Nuthatches

§ **White-breasted Nuthatch**
Sitta carolinensis

FORMER STATUS: Butler (1898) called it a common resident.
CURRENT STATUS: Common resident.

Red-breasted Nuthatch
Sitta canadensis

FORMER STATUS: Butler (1898) noted it as irregular and gave nesting data for northern Indiana. There have been other nebulous reports of its nesting in that same area but definite data is lacking.
CURRENT STATUS: **North** Irregular migrant and winter visitant (sometimes common). 1 September–15 May. **Central** Irregular migrant and winter visitant (sometimes common). 10 September–10 May. **South** Irregular migrant and winter visitant (sometimes common). 15 September–5 May.

Family Certhiidae: Creepers

Brown Creeper
Certhia familiaris

FORMER STATUS: Butler (1898) called it a very common migrant and irregular winter visitant. He presented data for nesting in Steuben Co.

in 1882 and 1883. There are numerous recent summer records but no nests have been documented.
CURRENT STATUS: **North** Common migrant and very rare winter visitant. 30 September–20 April. **Central** Common migrant and rare winter visitant. 5 October–15 April. **South** Common migrant and uncommon winter visitant. 10 October–10 April.

Family Troglodytidae: Wrens

§ House Wren
Troglodytes aedon

FORMER STATUS: Butler (1898) called it a common summer resident except in extreme northwestern and southern Indiana.
CURRENT STATUS: **North** Common summer resident. 25 April–10 October. **Central** Common summer resident. 20 April–15 October. **South** Common summer resident. 15 April–20 October.

Winter Wren
Troglodytes troglodytes

FORMER STATUS: Butler (1898) called it a common migrant and a winter resident in the southern half of Indiana.
CURRENT STATUS: **North** Uncommon migrant and very rare winter visitant. 25 September–1 May. A bird responded to a tape at the Indiana Dunes State Park on the remarkable date of 12 June 1976 (*fide* R. Tweit). **Central** Uncommon migrant and rare winter visitant. 1 October–25 April. **South** Uncommon migrant and winter visitant. 5 October–20 April.

§ Bewick's Wren
Thryomanes bewickii

FORMER STATUS: Butler (1898) related: ". . . a common summer resident throughout the greater part of southern Indiana and in the lower Wabash Valley, at least, north to Knox County, is a resident, though much rarer in winter."
CURRENT STATUS: **North** Very rare summer resident. 25 April–25 September. Nested at the Indiana Dunes in 1948–1949 (Ford, 1956). **Central** Very rare summer resident; casual in winter. 20 April–5 October. A pair

nested in Morgan Co. at Bradford Woods during 1976 (V. Esten *fide* C. Tabbert). **South** Very rare summer resident; casual in winter. Recent breeding data lacking.

REMARKS: Species has decreased in abundance since Butler's analysis. Generally believed to be dominated by the House Wren.

§ Carolina Wren
Thryothorus ludovicianus

FORMER STATUS: "It is an abundant resident in southern Indiana, decreasing in numbers from there northward in some localities, notably the northwestern and the east central portion of the State, almost or entirely wanting" (Butler, 1898).

CURRENT STATUS: North Very rare resident. Formerly nested at the Indiana Dunes in 1948. **Central** Rare resident. **South** Rare resident.

REMARKS: The severe winter of 1976–77 greatly decimated resident populations in Indiana. In central Indiana during 1977 the species was virtually absent. It remains to be seen whether this species can rebound from that disastrous winter.

§ Marsh Wren
Cistothorus palustris

FORMER STATUS: Butler (1898) called it an abundant resident in marshes, otherwise rarely seen.

CURRENT STATUS: North Locally abundant summer resident; casual in winter. 25 April–15 October. Lee Casebere found one at Pigeon River Fish and Wildlife Area 15 February 1974. **Central** Locally uncommon summer resident; casual in winter. 25 April–20 October. **South** Locally uncommon summer resident; casual in winter. 25 April–1 November. Marietta Smith found one 5 December 1975 at Oakland City (Gibson Co.).

§ Sedge Wren
Cistothorus platensis

FORMER STATUS: Butler (1898) listed it as a migrant and summer resident, breeding in suitable localities.

CURRENT STATUS: North Locally common summer resident. 25 April–20 September. **Central** Locally uncommon summer resident. 25 April–

20 September. Nests in Marion, Monroe, Montgomery, and Hamilton counties. **South** Status uncertain, no recent data.

Rock Wren
Salpinctes obsoletus

STATUS: Accidental. One record: a bird seen near Winchester, 18–20 October 1977, by Robert Farlow and Larry Carter, was subsequently observed by many and photographed by Jeff Moore.

Family Mimidae: Mockingbirds and Thrashers
§ **Northern Mockingbird**
Mimus polyglottos

FORMER STATUS: Butler (1898) related: "In the lower Wabash Valley it is a resident, at least north to Terre Haute, but is much more common in summer. Elsewhere in the southern half of the State, it is a rare summer resident, and farther north it is of accidental occurrence."

CURRENT STATUS: **North** Fairly common resident decreasing in abundance further north. **Central** Common resident. **South** Abundant resident.

REMARKS: There has been a considerable increase in status since 1898, generally believed to be coupled with the planting of multiflora rose fence rows.

§ **Gray Catbird**
Dumetella carolinensis

FORMER STATUS: Butler (1898) called it a summer resident.

CURRENT STATUS: **North** Abundant summer resident; casual in winter. 1 May–15 October. One seen in St. Joseph Co., 19 February 1973 (Dufendach *fide* N. Rea). **Central** Abundant summer resident; casual in winter. 25 April–20 October. **South** Abundant summer resident; casual in winter. 20 April–25 October. One was found on the Gibson Co. Christmas count, 31 December 1977, by Charles Mills et al.

§ **Brown Thrasher**
Toxostoma rufum

FORMER STATUS: "Common summer resident, doubtless some years remains in the extreme southern part of the State all winter . . ." (Butler, 1898).

CURRENT STATUS: **North** Common summer resident; casual in winter. 5 April–1 November. One observed in St. Joseph Co., 3 February 1973 (N. Rea). **Central** Common summer resident; very rare in winter. 1 April–5 November. **South** Common summer resident; rare in winter. 25 March–15 November.

Family Turdidae: Thrushes

§ **American Robin**
Turdus migratorius

FORMER STATUS: "The Robin is a common summer resident, abundant during the migrations. It is an irregular winter resident throughout the State, more regular and numerous southward" (Butler, 1898).

CURRENT STATUS: Abundant resident; irregular during the winter ranging in abundance with local food supplies but generally more numerous in the southern third of the State.

Varied Thrush
Ixoreus naevius

STATUS: Accidental. Four records: 9 January 1967 in Wayne Co. (Snow, 1967); 26–29 December 1976 in St. Joseph Co. (J. Buck et al.), the latter record substantiated by photographs; one seen and photographed in Muncie during the winter of 1978 (March) by Charles Wise et al.; and one seen at a feeder near Angola, for one day only in January 1978 by Helen Swenson (*Ind. Audu. Quarterly* 56:176).

§ **Wood Thrush**
Hylocichla mustelina

FORMER STATUS: Butler (1898) called it a common summer resident.

CURRENT STATUS: **North** Common summer resident. 5 May–1 October. **Central** Common summer resident. 25 April–5 October. **South** Common summer resident. 20 April–15 October.

Hermit Thrush
Catharus guttatus

FORMER STATUS: Butler (1898) called it a common migrant and a rare winter resident in the lower Wabash Valley.

CURRENT STATUS: **North** Fairly common migrant; casual in winter. 15 April–10 May; 25 September–1 November. One was seen in Allen Co., 10 February 1974 (J. Haw). **Central** Fairly common migrant; casual in winter. 10 April–5 May; 1 October–10 November. **South** Fairly common migrant; rare in winter. 1 April–30 April; 5 October–20 November.

Swainson's Thrush
Catharus ustulatus

FORMER STATUS: Butler (1898) recorded it as a common migrant and possible summer resident.

CURRENT STATUS: **North** Common migrant. 1 May–1 June; 25 August–10 October. **Central** Common migrant. 25 April–25 May; 1 September–15 October. One was recorded, 3 January 1976, at Muscatatuck Wildlife Refuge. **South** Common migrant; casual in winter. 25 April–20 May; 5 September–20 October.

Gray-cheeked Thrush
Catharus minimus

FORMER STATUS: Butler (1898) related: ". . . generally not a common migrant in Indiana."

CURRENT STATUS: **North** Fairly common migrant. 1 May–1 June; 25 August–10 October. **Central** Fairly common migrant; casual in winter. 25 April–25 May; 1 September–15 October. One recorded on the 1975 Christmas Count at Nashville. **South** Fairly common migrant; casual in winter. 20 April–20 May; 5 September–20 October.

§ Veery
Catharus fuscescens

FORMER STATUS: ". . . chiefly a rare migrant, but occurs occasionally as a summer resident and breeds" (Butler, 1898).

CURRENT STATUS: **North** Uncommon migrant and summer resident except in northeastern Indiana, where it is common. 1 May–5 October. Breeds at Jasper-Pulaski, Indiana Dunes, and several areas in northeastern Indiana. **Central** Uncommon migrant; may breed. Summer records for Marion Co. 25 April–25 May; 1 September–10 October. **South** Uncommon migrant. 20 April–20 May; 5 September–15 October.

§ **Eastern Bluebird**
Sialia sialis

FORMER STATUS: Butler (1898) listed it as a common summer resident.

CURRENT STATUS: **North** Common migrant and summer resident. Very rare in winter. 5 March–1 November. **Central** Common migrant and summer resident. Rare in winter except south-central Indiana where it is usually uncommon. 1 March–15 November. **South** Common migrant and summer resident; uncommon in winter.

REMARKS: Species appears to have decreased in abundance in the last two years probably as a result of the severe winters of 1976–77 and 1977–78. Status of uncommon may now be applicable, at least for the next few years.

Family Sylviidae: Gnatcatchers and Kinglets

§ **Blue-gray Gnatcatcher**
Polioptila caerulea

FORMER STATUS: Butler (1898) listed it as an abundant summer resident, particularly southward.

CURRENT STATUS: **North** Fairly common migrant; uncommon summer resident. 15 April–15 September. One observed in Allen Co., 10 April 1976, was very early (m. ob.). **Central** Common migrant; fairly common summer resident. 10 April–20 September. **South** Common migrant; fairly common summer resident. 5 April–25 September.

Golden-crowned Kinglet
Regulus satrapa

FORMER STATUS: Butler (1898) called it an abundant migrant and an irregular winter resident in the southern half of the State.

CURRENT STATUS: **North** Common migrant; rare in winter. 30 September–5 May. **Central** Common migrant; uncommon in winter. 5 October–1 May. **South** Common migrant; uncommon in winter. 10 October–25 April.

Ruby-crowned Kinglet
Regulus calendula

FORMER STATUS: Butler (1898) listed it as a common migrant and a very rare winter resident in the southern portion of the State.

CURRENT STATUS: **North** Common migrant; very rare in the winter. 1 September–15 May. Jim Haw found one in Allen Co., 22 December 1973. **Central** Common migrant; very rare in the winter. 10 September– 10 May. **South** Common migrant; rare in winter. 15 September–5 May.

Family Motacillidae: Pipits

Water Pipit
Anthus spinoletta

FORMER STATUS: "Abundant migrant" (Butler, 1898).

CURRENT STATUS: **North** Uncommon migrant and very rare in the winter. 25 September–5 May. Edward and Jerome Parrot recorded three in Lagrange Co., 28 December 1974. **Central** Uncommon migrant; very rare in winter. 20 September–1 May. **South** Uncommon migrant; very rare in winter. Data lacking for time span evaluations but probably similar to above.

Sprague's Pipit
Anthus spragueii

STATUS: Accidental. Two records: one in Whitley Co., 27 March 1966 (J. Parrot, George Pacenza, and Steve Rissing), was documented. Nancy Rea and Marie Jones observed 5 in LaPorte Co., 11 April 1973.

Family Bombycillidae: Waxwings

Bohemian Waxwing
Bombycilla garrulus

FORMER STATUS: Butler (1898) called it an irregular winter visitor to Indiana.

CURRENT STATUS: **North** Casual winter visitant. Three recent records: 2 February 1962 at South Bend (Gibson–Vesey) and 17–24 March

1962, White Co., by Burr and Fall (Burr, 1962). One seen near Chesterton 15 March 1978 (K. Brock). **Central** Casual winter visitant. A spring record in 1856 at Indianapolis of 19 collected by J. E. Beasley (Butler, 1898). **South** No data.

§ Cedar Waxwing
Bombycilla cedrorum

FORMER STATUS: Butler (1898) termed it an irregular to abundant resident, depending upon food supply.

CURRENT STATUS: **North** Common spring and abundant fall migrant; fairly common resident. Generally rare during the winter. **Central** Common spring and abundant fall migrant; fairly common resident. Generally rare during the winter. **South** Common spring and abundant fall migrant; uncommon resident. Insufficient data for winter evaluation but probably similar to above.

Family Laniidae: Shrikes

Northern Shrike
Lanius excubitor

FORMER STATUS: "In southern Indiana the Northern Shrike is usually an irregular, rare winter visitor, though occasionally it is found in some numbers. Northward it is a tolerably common winter resident" (Butler, 1898).

CURRENT STATUS: **North** Irregular very rare winter visitant. 15 November–15 March. There are several recent records. It was found in La-Porte Co. (m. ob.) 29 January–12 March 1974, and Delano Arvin observed one in Tippecanoe Co. 2–14 February 1975. **Central** No recent data. **South** Casual winter visitant. One record: Two accidentally captured in a sparrow trap were closely examined and released, 30 December 1972, in Vanderburgh Co. by Virgil and Doris Eicker (documented).

REMARKS: The statement by Butler (1898) that they are "tolerably common" is certainly not true today.

§ **Loggerhead Shrike**
Lanius ludovicianus

FORMER STATUS: "Summer resident, most numerous in central and northern Indiana, although in some localities elsewhere it is common. Resident some winters, at least, in the lower Wabash Valley" (Butler, 1898).

CURRENT STATUS: **North** Very rare resident; recent data lacking. Jim Haw observed one in Wabash Co. 14 December 1974. **Central** Very rare resident. Nested at Geist Reservoir in 1947. **South** Rare resident. Up until about ten years ago it was uncommon. In Vanderburgh, Warrick, and Gibson counties it was sometimes present in fair numbers in winter. Now, for as yet unexplained reasons, it has become quite rare.

REMARKS: Species blue-listed in Indiana; all data should be reported.

Family Sturnidae: Starlings

§ **European Starling**
Sturnus vulgaris

FORMER STATUS: Branham (1958) outlined the spread of this species in Indiana. Reported to have nested in Rush Co. in 1922, they have now increased to the point that this species may well be the most abundant bird in Indiana, and perhaps the United States.

CURRENT STATUS: Abundant resident. A certain segment of the resident population is partially migratory, moving south in winter but being replaced by others from the north.

Family Vireonidae: Vireos

§ **White-eyed Vireo**
Vireo griseus

FORMER STATUS: Butler (1898) related: "It is common in suitable localities in the southern part of the State, generally northward it is more rare, and the northwestern part, particularly about Lake Michigan, it seems to be wanting."

CURRENT STATUS: **North** Rare summer resident. 25 April–10 October. Lee Casebere located three pairs in the Pigeon River area during the

summer of 1976. **Central** Fairly common summer resident. 20 April–
15 October. **South** Common summer resident. 15 April–20 October.

§ **Bell's Vireo**
Vireo bellii

FORMER STATUS: Listed by Butler (1898) as hypothetical.
CURRENT STATUS: **North** Very rare summer resident. Steve Glass found
a pair during the summers of 1974–1975 near Willow Slough, and Arvin
noted them in Tippecanoe Co. during May. Virginia Reuterskiold noted
it in Porter Co. 5 May–1 September. **Central** Uncommon summer resident.
Breeds from Hamilton Co. in the east to the Illinois border, becoming in-
creasingly more common. 1 May–5 September. **South** Uncommon summer resident. Center of abundance appears to be southwestern Indiana
in the vicinity of strip mines. Charles Mills and Marietta Smith have
located singing birds since 1973. 25 April–?
REMARKS: Since the discovery of a pair of these birds at Geist Reservoir (m. ob.) and its subsequent nesting in that area (1946) the bird
has become widespread—particularly in western Indiana.

§ **Yellow-throated Vireo**
Vireo flavifrons

FORMER STATUS: "Common migrant. Summer resident in some numbers
northward, and more rarely southward. Breeds" (Butler, 1898).
CURRENT STATUS: **North** Fairly common migrant and uncommon summer resident. 1 May–15 September. **Central** Fairly common migrant
and uncommon summer resident. 25 April–20 September. **South** Fairly
common migrant; recent summer data lacking but probably a rare summer resident. 20 April–1 October.

Solitary Vireo
Vireo solitarius

FORMER STATUS: Butler (1898) termed it a regular migrant.
CURRENT STATUS: **North** Uncommon migrant. 1 May–25 May; 25
September–20 October. **Central** Uncommon migrant. 25 April–20 May;
1 October–25 October. **South** Rare migrant. Date spans not determined
but probably similar to above.

§ **Red-eyed Vireo**
Vireo olivaceus

FORMER STATUS: "Common" (Butler, 1898).
CURRENT STATUS: **North** Abundant summer resident. 5 May–15 October. **Central** Abundant summer resident. 1 May–20 October. **South** Abundant summer resident. 25 April–25 October.

Philadelphia Vireo
Vireo philadelphicus

FORMER STATUS: ". . . generally a rare migrant, but in the northwestern part of the State, near Lake Michigan, it is sometimes rather common. It is also a rare summer resident" (Butler, 1898).
CURRENT STATUS: **North** Rare migrant. 1 May–1 June; 25 August–10 October. **Central** Rare spring and uncommon fall migrant. 1 May–25 May; 1 September–15 October. Banding data indicates this species more common during the fall. **South** No recent data, probably similar to above.

§ **Warbling Vireo**
Vireo gilvus

FORMER STATUS: Butler (1898) did not classify according to status.
CURRENT STATUS: **North** Abundant summer resident. 25 April–1 October. **Central** Abundant summer resident. 20 April–5 October. **South** Abundant summer resident. 15 April–10 October.

Family Parulidae: Wood Warblers

§ **Black-and-white Warbler**
Mniotilta varia

FORMER STATUS: Common migrant, a few breed (Butler, 1898).
CURRENT STATUS: **North** Common migrant; very rare summer resident. 20 April–25 September. Nests found in Lake, Porter, and Tippecanoe counties. **Central** Common migrant; rare summer resident. Casual in winter. A bird seen, 25 December 1974, at Geist Reservoir (Tompkins, 1975). 15 April–1 October. Nests found in Jackson and Owen counties. Summer records (i.e., mid-June) in several locations. **South**

Common migrant; rare summer resident. 10 April–5 October. Nests found in Clark and Harrison counties.

§ **Prothonotary Warbler**
Protonotaria citrea

FORMER STATUS: A locally common summer resident (Butler, 1898).
CURRENT STATUS: **North** Locally common summer resident; otherwise, a rare migrant. 1 May–10 September. Breeds in LaSalle and Kankakee Fish and Wildlife Areas. **Central** Locally uncommon summer resident; otherwise, a rare migrant. 25 April–15 September. Breeds at South Westway Park (Maywood Bottoms) and formerly at Walnut Grove (Shelby Co.). **South** Locally common summer resident; otherwise, a rare migrant. 20 April–20 September. In the southwest corner of the State, in Knox, Gibson, and Posey counties, they are locally abundant summer residents.

§ **Worm-eating Warbler**
Helmitheros vermivorus

FORMER STATUS: Common summer resident over the southern portion of Indiana (Butler, 1898).
CURRENT STATUS: **North** Very rare migrant or vagrant. 20 April–1 September. Found in Tippecanoe Co. (Arvin) 4–18 May 1975 and in Allen Co. on 19 August and 4 September 1976 (J. Haw–D. Heller). **Central** Very rare migrant and locally rare summer resident. 20 April–10 September. Breeds in Montgomery Co. (A. Bruner) and probably in the south-central Indiana hill country. **South** Very rare migrant. Data lacking but probably breeds in suitable areas. Migration period probably similar to above.

§ **Golden-winged Warbler**
Vermivora chrysoptera

FORMER STATUS: "Throughout the State it is a migrant, and in the northern part of the State where the conditions are favorable—where marshes and bogs in bushy or wooded land are found—it breeds, at places, in some numbers" (Butler, 1898).
CURRENT STATUS: **North** Uncommon migrant and very rare summer resident. 1 May–10 September. Recent breeding data lacking; however, Emma Pitcher noted it with some degree of regularity in Porter Co. during

the summer of 1975. Further east, Lee Casebere has found it once during the summer and considers it very rare. **Central** Uncommon migrant and casual summer resident. 25 April–20 May; 25 August–15 September. Two adults feeding young in Brown Co., 9 July 1978 (Tim Keller). **South** No recent data; apparently a very rare migrant.

REMARKS: Is this species being bred out of existence by interbreeding with *V. pinus?* Much concentrated work must be done before an accurate estimate of its summer status can be given.

§ Blue-winged Warbler
Vermivora pinus

FORMER STATUS: "They are generally common in suitable places in southern Indiana, and locally, farther north, are found in some numbers" (Butler, 1898).

CURRENT STATUS: **North** Fairly common migrant and uncommon summer resident. 1 May–1 September. **Central** Fairly common migrant and uncommon summer resident. 25 April–5 September. **South** Status uncertain but probably similar to above.

Bachman's Warbler
Vermivora bachmanii

FORMER STATUS: A bird was taken at Greensburg in Decatur Co., 2 May 1899 (Butler, 1900).

CURRENT STATUS: No other data.

Tennessee Warbler
Vermivora peregrina

FORMER STATUS: Butler (1898) called it rare in the spring and abundant in the fall.

CURRENT STATUS: **North** Abundant migrant. 10 May–1 June; 25 August–5 October. **Central** Abundant migrant. 5 May–1 June; 25 August–10 October. **South** Common migrant. 1 May–25 May; 1 September–15 October.

Orange-crowned Warbler
Vermivora celata

FORMER STATUS: Very rare migrant (Butler, 1898).

CURRENT STATUS: North Rare spring and uncommon fall migrant; casual during the winter. 5 May–1 June; 5 October–25 October. A bird seen 20–21 December 1975 in Allen Co. (J. Haw et al.). Central Rare spring and uncommon fall migrant, casual during the winter. 1 May–25 May; 5 October–1 November. Has been seen on some area Christmas Counts. South Rare migrant. Recent data lacking but probably similar to above.

Nashville Warbler
Vermivora ruficapilla

FORMER STATUS: Rare migrant (Butler, 1898).

CURRENT STATUS: North Fairly common migrant; casual in winter. 25 April–25 May; 1 September–15 October. One seen (documented) 24 December 1974–12 January 1975 in Tippecanoe Co. (Pablo Ruiz-Ramon). Jim Haw found one in Allen Co. 12 November 1974 (documented). Central Fairly common migrant. 20 April–20 May; 1 September–15 October. South Status uncertain but probably similar to above.

§ Northern Parula Warbler
Parula americana

FORMER STATUS: Butler (1898) cites Ridgeway on its occurrence in the lower Wabash Valley (Knox Co.), and called it a rare summer resident over most of the State.

CURRENT STATUS: North Rare migrant and very rare summer resident. 1 May–10 September. Arvin found it in Tippecanoe Co., 1–25 June 1975, and suspected nesting. The following year (1976) he located a nest during the latter part of May. In northeastern Indiana it is apparently very rare. Central Rare migrant and locally uncommon summer resident. 25 April–10 September. Breeds in Marion, Montgomery, Monroe, Parke, and Owen counties and probably does so in most of south-central Indiana. South Uncommon migrant and summer resident. 20 April–15 September. Charles Mills found an adult feeding two young in the Buckskin Bottoms (Gibson Co.), 15 July 1976.

§ Yellow Warbler
Dendroica petechia

FORMER STATUS: Abundant summer resident (Butler, 1898).

CURRENT STATUS: **North** Fairly common summer resident. 25 April–15 September. **Central** Fairly common summer resident; casual in winter. 20 April–20 September. One feeding on suet at a feeding station 23 December 1975 in Montgomery Co. (Alan Bruner). **South** Fairly common migrant; summer status uncertain. 15 April–25 September.

Magnolia Warbler
Dendroica magnolia

FORMER STATUS: Common migrant (Butler, 1898).
CURRENT STATUS: **North** Common migrant. 5 May–1 June; 25 August–1 October. One was banded 7 June 1975 in Porter Co. by Emma Pitcher; another was found dead on the Lake Michigan Beach in Lake Co. 11 July 1978 by Ray Grow. **Central** Common migrant. 5 May–1 June; 1 September–5 October. **South** Common migrant. 1 May–25 May; 5 September–10 October. A report of two birds on a recent Christmas Count is probably erroneous.

Cape May Warbler
Dendroica tigrina

FORMER STATUS: Butler (1898) related: "In Indiana it appears as a migrant, perhaps more numerous in fall than spring."
CURRENT STATUS: **North** Uncommon migrant. 10 May–25 May; 1 September–1 October. **Central** Uncommon migrant, accidental in winter. 5 May–25 May; 1 September–5 October. One seen 9–13 December 1960 in Morgan Co. by Robert Gregory (*Audu. Field Notes* 1961:334). **South** Uncommon migrant. 5 May–25 May; 1 September–10 October. N. Stocks found two in Vanderburgh Co. 9 May 1974.

Black-throated Blue Warbler
Dendroica caerulescens

FORMER STATUS: Generally a common migrant (Butler, 1898).
CURRENT STATUS: **North** Rare spring and uncommon fall migrant. 10 May–5 June; 1 September–5 October. **Central** Rare spring and uncommon fall migrant. 5 May–30 May; 5 September–10 October. A bird was seen 14 June 1950 in Shelby Co. (*Ind. Audu. Quarterly* 29:39). **South** Rare migrant, recent data lacking but probably similar to above.
REMARKS: Apparently a change in status since Butler's analysis. Eagerly sought by beginning birders, this species is often unrecorded by them for several years, probably due to the rather secretive habits of the bird.

Yellow-rumped Warbler
Dendroica coronata

FORMER STATUS: Abundant migrant and irregular winter visitant (Butler, 1898).
CURRENT STATUS: **North** Abundant migrant; rare in winter. 10 April–20 May; 5 October–20 November. **Central** Abundant migrant; rare in winter. 5 April–15 May; 10 October–25 November. **South** Abundant migrant; uncommon in winter. 1 April–10 May; 15 October–1 December.

Black-throated Green Warbler
Dendroica virens

FORMER STATUS: A very common migrant (Butler, 1898).
CURRENT STATUS: **North** Common migrant. 25 April–1 June; 1 September–15 October. **Central** Common migrant. 20 April–25 May; 1 September–20 October. One found all summer during 1950 at the Shades (Luther, 1976). A pair seen in Monroe Co. 12 June 1976 (Steve Glass). **South** Common migrant. 20 April–20 May; 5 September–25 October.
REMARKS: It is interesting to note that the summer records cited above were in similar habitat (i.e., pine trees). Such areas should be critically watched.

§ Cerulean Warbler
Dendroica cerulea

FORMER STATUS: Common, especially in the lower Wabash Valley (Butler, 1898).
CURRENT STATUS: **North** Fairly common summer resident. 25 April–1 September. **Central** Fairly common summer resident. 20 April–5 September. **South** Insufficient data but probably similar to above.

Blackburnian Warbler
Dendroica fusca

FORMER STATUS: Generally common migrant (Butler, 1898).
CURRENT STATUS: **North** Fairly common migrant. 5 May–1 June; 1 September–1 October. One observed 8 July 1973 in Allen Co. (L. Casebere). **Central** Fairly common migrant. 1 May–25 May; 5 September–5 October. One observed at Pine Hills, Montgomery Co., 5 June 1977 by A. Bruner and the authors, and again, 7–15 June 1978, by

A. Bruner. On one occasion during that period the bird, a male, was observed chasing a female of the same species. **South** Uncommon migrant. 25 April–20 May; 5 September–10 October.

§ **Yellow-throated Warbler**
Dendroica dominica

FORMER STATUS: Butler (1898) called it common in southern Indiana and very rare north.
CURRENT STATUS: **North** Uncommon summer resident. 25 April–1 September. Nests in Tippecanoe Co. (Arvin). **Central** Fairly common summer resident. 20 April–5 September. **South** Common summer resident. 15 April–10 September.

§ **Chestnut-sided Warbler**
Dendroica pensylvanica

FORMER STATUS: "A common migrant most years, but sometimes rather rare. In the extreme northern part of the State it is a summer resident; LaPorte County (Byrkit)" (Butler, 1898).
CURRENT STATUS: **North** Fairly common migrant; very rare summer resident. Ed Hopkins located nests at Willow Slough during the summers of 1974 and 1975. 5 May–20 September. **Central** Fairly common migrant. Summer birds have been seen in Marion (A. Starling), Montgomery (D. Luther), and Wayne counties (W. Buskirk). 1 May–25 May; 25 August–25 September. **South** Fairly common migrant. 25 April–20 May; 1 September–5 October.

Bay-breasted Warbler
Dendroica castanea

FORMER STATUS: Very rare spring migrant; more common in the fall (Butler, 1898).
CURRENT STATUS: **North** Fairly common migrant. 10 May–1 June; 25 August–1 October. **Central** Fairly common migrant. 5 May–1 June; 1 September–5 October. **South** Fairly common migrant. 1 May–25 May; 5 September–15 October.

Blackpoll Warbler
Dendroica striata

FORMER STATUS: "It is an irregular migrant, generally rather rare, but some years common; usually most common in fall" (Butler, 1898).
CURRENT STATUS: **North** Fairly common migrant. 10 May–5 June; 25 August–1 October. **Central** Fairly common migrant. 10 May–1 June; 1 September–10 October. **South** Fairly common migrant. 5 May–25 May; 5 September–15 October.

§ **Pine Warbler**
Dendroica pinus

FORMER STATUS: Rare migrant and summer resident (Butler, 1898).
CURRENT STATUS: **North** Rare migrant; very rare summer resident. No recent breeding data. 15 April–25 September. One found near South Bend 1 June–24 July 1976 (*fide* H. Weber). **Central** Rare migrant; possibly a casual summer resident in the northern portion of the Hoosier National Forest. Steve Glass found a bird 20 March 1976 at Terril Ridge near Monroe Reservoir and heard several 12 June 1976 near that same location. 10 April–1 October. **South** Data uncertain; has been seen during the summer in Clark Co. National Forest.

Kirtland's Warbler
Dendroica kirtlandii

FORMER STATUS: Butler (1898) listed two specimen records for Wabash Co.: 1 May 1893 and 7 May 1895. Unverified observations include: 25 May 1924 (Porter Co.); 21 May 1950 (Randolph Co.) and 14 May 1950 (Hamilton Co.).
CURRENT STATUS: Accidental. A bird heard singing and believed to be this species was recorded at Eagle Creek Park 14 May 1978 (A. Starling et al.). Bird responded to taped calls of that species 15 May 1978 in that locality (T. Keller–M. Brown).

§ **Prairie Warbler**
Dendroica discolor

FORMER STATUS: Rare migrant and summer resident (Butler, 1898).
CURRENT STATUS: **North** Rare migrant and very rare summer resident. 30 April–1 September. **Central** Rare migrant and locally uncommon sum-

mer resident. 25 April–5 September. **South** Uncommon migrant and locally a fairly common summer resident. Center of breeding abundance in the strip-mine areas of Gibson, Pike, and Warrick counties. 20 April–10 September.

Palm Warbler
Dendroica palmarum

FORMER STATUS: "In the western and northwestern parts of the State—the original prairie region—it is very common, often very abundant; much more numerous in spring than in fall. Throughout the southeastern half of our State it is of irregular occurrence, never abundant, and seldom, if ever, really common. From most places it is reported as rare, not common, or tolerably common" (Butler, 1898).

CURRENT STATUS: **North** Fairly common migrant; casual in winter. 20 April–15 May; 15 September–20 October. One seen, 13 December 1975, Wabash Co. (J. Haw). **Central** Fairly common migrant; casual in winter. 15 April–10 May; 20 September–25 October. One seen, 28 December 1975–3 January 1976, Randolph Co. (L. Carter). **South** Fairly common migrant; casual in winter. 10 April–10 May; 25 September–1 November.

§ Ovenbird
Seiurus aurocapillus

FORMER STATUS: Common summer resident (Butler, 1898).

CURRENT STATUS: **North** Common migrant; fairly common summer resident. 25 April–30 September. Peak date in the spring of 1975 for Tippecanoe Co. was 13 May (Arvin). **Central** Common migrant; fairly common summer resident. 20 April–5 October. **South** Common migrant; fairly common summer resident. 20 April–10 October.

Northern Waterthrush
Seiurus noveboracensis

FORMER STATUS: Rare migrant; rare summer resident northward (Butler, 1898).

CURRENT STATUS: **North** Fairly common migrant; possible casual summer resident. Arvin thinks they nest in Tippecanoe Co. and Casebere found one 25 June 1976 in Lagrange Co. 20 April–15 September. **Central** Fairly common migrant. 15 April–20 September. Henry West banded

a "hatching year" bird at Mary Gray Bird Sanctuary 14 June 1975.
South Fairly common migrant. 10 April–25 September.

§ **Louisiana Waterthrush**
Seriurus motacilla

FORMER STATUS: ". . . a summer resident, common in suitable locali-
ties southward, but less common northward" (Butler, 1898).
CURRENT STATUS: **North** Uncommon summer resident. 25 April–10
September. **Central** Uncommon summer resident. 20 April–5 September.
South Insufficient data but probably similar to above.

§ **Kentucky Warbler**
Oporornis formosus

FORMER STATUS: Summer resident over the southern two-thirds of
the state (Butler, 1898).
CURRENT STATUS: **North** Locally rare summer resident. 1 May–1
September. Summer birds at Fox Island (6 singing males–1976) by
J. Haw. Recorded in Steuben and Lagrange counties during the summers
of 1973 and 1974. **Central** Fairly common summer resident. 25 April–
5 September. **South** Fairly common summer resident. 25 April–?

Connecticut Warbler
Oporornis agilis

FORMER STATUS: Very rare migrant (Butler, 1898).
CURRENT STATUS: **North** Rare spring and casual fall migrant. 15 May–
5 June; fall data limited to a few reliable sight records. Alan Bruner found
one at Jasper-Pulaski 3 September 1976. Tim Manolis observed it in
Tippecanoe Co. 29 September 1975. **Central** Rare spring and casual fall
migrant. 10 May–1 June; both the senior author and Henry West have
banded this species during September. **South** Insufficient data, probably
similar to above.
REMARKS: Majority of fall migrants occur on the East Coast. Some
degree of confusion exists in identification, especially with the Nashville
Warbler, which may be responsible for unusually early spring migrants
and fall sightings.

Mourning Warbler
Oporornis philadelphia

FORMER STATUS: Rare migrant (Butler, 1898).
CURRENT STATUS: North Uncommon migrant. 15 May–5 June; 20 August–15 September. Emma Pitcher banded one in Porter Co. 4 July 1975. Central Uncommon migrant. 15 May–1 June; 25 August–20 September. South Insufficient data but probably similar to above.

MacGillivray's Warbler
Oporornis tolmiei

FORMER STATUS: Accidental. One record: one taken in Lake Co. 1 June 1876 (Sharpe, 1885).

§ Common Yellowthroat
Geothlypis trichas

FORMER STATUS: Common summer resident (Butler, 1898).
CURRENT STATUS: North Abundant summer resident. Casual in winter. Jim Haw et al. found one in Lagrange Co. 27 December 1975. 25 April–5 October. Central Abundant summer resident. Casual in winter. 20 April–10 October. South Abundant summer resident. Casual in winter. 15 April–15 October.

§ Yellow-breasted Chat
Icteria virens

FORMER STATUS: ". . . a common and well known summer resident in the southern half of the State, and locally even further north" (Butler, 1898).
CURRENT STATUS: North Uncommon summer resident. 1 May–10 September. Central Fairly common summer resident. 25 April–15 September. South Common summer resident. 20 April–20 September.

§ Hooded Warbler
Wilsonia citrina

FORMER STATUS: Generally a rare summer resident; very rare in northern Indiana (Butler, 1898).
CURRENT STATUS: North Locally uncommon summer resident, otherwise a very rare migrant. Nests in Allen, Lagrange, Porter, and Tippe-

canoe counties. 25 April–? **Central** Locally fairly common summer resident, otherwise a rare migrant. 25 April–10 September. **South** Locally fairly common summer resident, otherwise a rare migrant. 25 April–15 September.

Wilson's Warbler
Wilsonia pusilla

FORMER STATUS: Rather rare spring migrant; more common in the fall (Butler, 1898).
CURRENT STATUS: **North** Uncommon migrant. 10 May–1 June; 1 September–1 October. **Central** Uncommon migrant. 5 May–25 May; 5 September–5 October. **South** Rare migrant. 1 May–25 May; insufficient fall data.

§ Canada Warbler
Wilsonia canadensis

FORMER STATUS: Tolerably common migrant (Butler, 1898).
CURRENT STATUS: **North** Fairly common migrant; casual summer resident. A nest found 16 June 1978 at Pigeon River by Lee Casebere et al. Noted at Pigeon River Fish and Wildlife Area during the summers of 1973–74 (Lee Casebere–M. Weldon), also in Newton Co. in 1973 (Ed Hopkins). 15 May–1 June; 25 August–20 September. **Central** Fairly common migrant. 10 May–1 June; 25 August–25 September. **South** Fairly common migrant. 5 May–25 May; 1 September–1 October.

§ American Redstart
Setophaga ruticilla

FORMER STATUS: Generally common, abundant north (Butler, 1898).
CURRENT STATUS: **North** Common migrant and fairly common summer resident. 5 May–5 October. **Central** Common migrant and uncommon summer resident. 1 May–10 October. **South** Common migrant and rare summer resident. 25 April–15 October.

Family Ploceidae: Weaver Finches

§ House Sparrow
Passer domesticus

FORMER STATUS: Resident throughout State (Butler, 1898).

CURRENT STATUS: Abundant resident. Probably less so than in Butler's day because of the replacement of horse-drawn transportation with motor vehicles. Horses' droppings, which used to be everywhere, contained undigested grain and were therefore a convenient source of food for these birds.

Family Icteridae: Meadowlarks, Blackbirds, and Orioles

§ **Bobolink**
Dolichonyx oryzivorus

FORMER STATUS: Regular but rare migrant; common summer resident in the north (Butler, 1898).
CURRENT STATUS: **North** Common summer resident. 5 May–10 September. **Central** Uncommon summer resident; common migrant. The authors found territorial males at the Atterbury Fish and Wildlife Area during 1976–1977. 1 May–15 September. **South** Common migrant; breeding status unknown. 25 April–20 September.

§ **Eastern Meadowlark**
Sturnella magna

FORMER STATUS: "Abundant summer resident. Resident in the southern portion of the State" (Butler, 1898).
CURRENT STATUS: **North** Common summer resident; very rare in winter. 1 March–30 November. Arvin noted several in Tippecanoe Co., 5 January 1975. **Central** Fairly common summer resident; rare in winter. 25 February–5 December. **South** Fairly common summer resident; during the winter they are often abundant depending upon the severity of the weather. The authors found nearly 100 birds near Newburgh (Warrick Co.) during late December and early January for several consecutive winters in the 1960s.
REMARKS: Most area observers feel that there has been a definite decline in numbers of this species since the 1950s–60s.

§ **Western Meadowlark**
Sturnella neglecta

FORMER STATUS: Butler (1898) listed it as hypothetical.
CURRENT STATUS: **North** Locally uncommon summer resident; winter status largely unknown. 1 March–30 November. **Central** Locally very

rare summer resident. 25 February–5 December. **South** Locally very rare summer resident. Noted in Posey Co., otherwise either casual or completely absent from the area.

Yellow-headed Blackbird
Xanthocephalus xanthocephalus

FORMER STATUS: ". . . is a summer resident in some localities in northwestern Indiana" (Butler, 1898).

CURRENT STATUS: **North** Very rare migrant; possibly a casual summer resident and casual in winter. A female was seen constructing a nest in Newton Co., 17 June 1973 (Ed Hopkins–R. E. Mumford) which was never completed. **Central** Casual migrant. Two recent records include: 10 May 1976, Hamilton Co. (m. ob.); 8 May 1976, Marion Co. (Al and Scott Starling). **South** Casual migrant. No recent records.

§ Red-winged Blackbird
Agelaius phoeniceus

FORMER STATUS: Abundant summer resident and occurring some winters in southern Indiana (Butler, 1898).

CURRENT STATUS: **North** Abundant summer resident; rare in winter. 25 February–30 November. **Central** Abundant summer resident; rare to abundant in winter depending on weather. 20 February–5 December. **South** Abundant summer resident; uncommon to abundant in winter depending on weather. 15 February–10 December.

REMARKS: Species has utilized broader spectrum of habitats since Butler's analysis of 1898.

§ Orchard Oriole
Icterus spurius

FORMER STATUS: Common summer resident, extending range northward (Butler, 1898).

CURRENT STATUS: **North** Uncommon summer resident. 1 May–20 August. Arvin noted young birds during the summer of 1975 in Tippecanoe Co. **Central** Uncommon summer resident. 25 April–25 August. **South** Fairly common summer resident. 25 April–25 August.

§ Northern Oriole
Icterus galbula

FORMER STATUS: Summer resident (Butler, 1898).
CURRENT STATUS: North Common summer resident. 25 April–1 September. Central Common summer resident. 20 April–5 September. Casual in winter. One at feeder in Cambridge City, 9–31 December 1950. South Common summer resident. 20 April–10 September.

Rusty Blackbird
Euphagus carolinus

FORMER STATUS: "Migrant, most places rarely identified, but really common (Butler, 1898).
CURRENT STATUS: North Fairly common migrant; casual in winter. 1 March–20 April; 1 October–1 December. Central Fairly common migrant; normally rare in winter. James and Amy Mason noted 153 in a cowbird roost at the Wabash River Bridge (Vigo Co.) during the winter of 1972. 25 February–15 April; 5 October–5 December. South Fairly common migrant; rare in winter. 20 February–10 April; 10 October–10 December.

§ Brewer's Blackbird
Euphagus cyanocephalus

FORMER STATUS: Listed by Butler (1898) as hypothetical. First nests found in Indiana during 1952 in Lake and Porter counties.
CURRENT STATUS: North Rare summer resident; casual in winter. 1 March–30 November. Ed Hopkins noted one in Tippecanoe Co. 15–25 December 1973. Jim Haw found 2 in Allen Co. 18 November 1975. Central Very rare migrant. 5 March–?; insufficient fall data for date spans. The senior author found 62 in Marion Co. 12 March 1961 (Keller, 1961a) and Al Starling noted them 24 October 1976 at Eagle Creek Park. South No data.

§ Common Grackle
Quiscalus quiscula

FORMER STATUS: Common summer resident (Butler, 1898).
CURRENT STATUS: North Abundant summer resident, normally uncommon during the winter. During the winter of 1975–76 they wintered

in the thousands in Allen Co. (J. Haw). 25 February–30 November.
Central Abundant summer resident, normally uncommon during the
winter. 20 February–5 December. **South** Abundant summer resident; at
times, abundant during the winter. 15 February–10 December.

§ Brown-headed Cowbird
Molothrus ater

FORMER STATUS: "Abundant summer resident. Favorable winters, some
remain in the southern part of the State" (Butler, 1898).

CURRENT STATUS: **North** Abundant summer resident; common in winter at feeders, otherwise rare. **Central–South** Abundant summer resident;
common in winter at feeders, otherwise uncommon.

Family Thraupidae: Tanagers
§ Scarlet Tanager
Piranga olivacea

FORMER STATUS: Common summer resident (Butler, 1898).

CURRENT STATUS: **North** Fairly common summer resident and migrant.
1 May–20 September. Delano Arvin found a nest 18 May 1975 in Tippecanoe Co. **Central** Fairly common migrant; uncommon summer resident.
25 April–25 September. **South** Fairly common migrant; uncommon
summer resident; recent breeding data lacking. 20 April–1 October.

§ Summer Tanager
Piranga rubra

FORMER STATUS: Common summer resident in southern Indiana (Butler, 1898).

CURRENT STATUS: **North** Very rare summer resident and migrant. 5
May–20 September. Found in Noble Co. 5 September 1972 (J. Haw);
Tippecanoe Co. 4 May 1975 (Arvin); and Wabash Co. 9 September
1972 (J. Haw). **Central** Uncommon summer resident and migrant. 1
May– 25 September. **South** Fairly common summer resident and migrant.
25 April–30 September.

Family Fringillidae: Grosbeaks, Finches, Sparrows, and Buntings

§ **Northern Cardinal**
Cardinalis cardinalis

FORMER STATUS: "It is resident throughout the State, being very common in the southern part . . ." (Butler, 1898).
CURRENT STATUS: **North** Common resident. One hundred eighteen were counted on 8 May 1976 in St. Joseph Co. **Central–South** Abundant resident.

§ **Rose-breasted Grosbeak**
Pheucticus ludovicianus

FORMER STATUS: "Throughout northern Indiana this attractive bird is found, in most places, as a summer resident, increasing in numbers as one goes northward. Elsewhere, it is an irregular migrant; some years very common, others, rare or wholly absent" (Butler, 1898).
CURRENT STATUS: **North** Uncommon summer resident and common migrant. 1 May–5 October. **Central** Very rare summer resident and common migrant. 25 April–15 October. Alan Bruner and Larry Peavler found two nests in Montgomery Co. during the summer of 1976. **South** Common migrant. 25 April–20 October.

§ **Black-headed Grosbeak**
Pheucticus melanocephalus

STATUS: One record: one visiting a feeding station in Lake Co., 23 December 1968–20 March 1969, was seen by many (*Audubon Field Notes* 23:488).

§ **Blue Grosbeak**
Guiraca caerulea

FORMER STATUS: "Of rare or accidental occurrence in the southwestern part of the State" (Butler, 1898).
CURRENT STATUS: **North** Casual. A bird seen in Allen Co. during 1938 (J. L. VanCamp *fide* S. Smith); 2 June 1961 in Porter Co. by V. Reuterskiold (Burr, 1961). Two recently observed near Willow Slough during early June 1978 (H. C. West–L. Peavler). There are several records for the Dunes area. **Central** Casual. Reported from Marion, Morgan, Owen,

Johnson and Wayne counties. One seen in early June at Eagle Creek Reservoir by Al Starling and Jo Davidson (1978). One seen at Atterbury Fish and Wildlife Area during spring and summer of 1978 by George Bell and C. Keller. **South** Very rare summer resident. Nest found by Marietta Smith and Charles Mills in Pike Co., 20 June 1975. Birds have been located in this strip-mine region since 1974.

§ Indigo Bunting
Passerina cyanea

FORMER STATUS: Common summer resident (Butler, 1898).
CURRENT STATUS: **North** Abundant summer resident. 1 May–1 October. **Central** Abundant summer resident; casual in winter. 25 April–5 October. One banded in Morgan Co. 18 January 1960. **South** Abundant summer resident. 20 April–10 October.

Lazuli Bunting
Passerina amoena

STATUS: Accidental. One reliable record: one, 8 December 1946–9 February 1947 at a feeding station in Marion Co., was seen by many (*Ind. Audu. Yearbook* 1947:37).

§ Dickcissel
Spiza americana

FORMER STATUS: "In most localities the Dickcissel is an abundant summer resident. However, it is a recent introduction into our fauna. Mr. E. J. Chansler says he can remember when it was rare in Knox County, where its numbers now are perhaps exceeded by no other bird. It appeared in Franklin County some time between 1869 and 1879" (Butler, 1898).
CURRENT STATUS: **North** Irregular uncommon to common summer resident. 5 May–15 September. **Central** Irregular uncommon to common summer resident. Casual in winter. 1 May–20 September. One observed at a feeding station during December 1971 and another in company with House Sparrows in December 1972 (Ruth Erickson–V. Malooley) in Vigo Co. **South** Irregular uncommon to common summer resident. 1 May–25 September.

Evening Grosbeak
Hesperiphona vespertina

FORMER STATUS: "Very irregular winter visitor; sometimes found in numbers" (Butler, 1898).

CURRENT STATUS: North Irregular very rare to abundant winter visitor. 1 November–10 May. Central Irregular very rare to common winter visitor. 5 November–5 May. Three seen 24 September 1975 at Eagle Creek Park, Marion Co. (A. Starling). South Irregular very rare to uncommon winter visitor. 10 November–1 May.

REMARKS: Flight years during 1973, 1975, and 1977.

Purple Finch
Carpodacus purpureus

FORMER STATUS: ". . . a regular migrant in varying numbers, and is irregularly a winter resident . . . in northern Indiana they may possibly be found occasionally to remain through the summer" (Butler, 1898).

CURRENT STATUS: North Irregular uncommon to common migrant and winter visitant. 10 October–15 May. Central Irregular uncommon to common migrant and winter visitant. 15 October–10 May. South Irregular uncommon to fairly common migrant and winter visitant. 20 October–5 May. N. Stocks noted 15–20 birds in Vanderburgh Co. 18 January–9 February 1973.

House Finch
Carpodacus mexicanus

STATUS: At least six records. One reported to have been seen 16 November 1958 at Michigan City by Landing. One male seen by the authors and photographed by Tom Field at the Indianapolis Art Museum, Marion Co. (Keller, 1976). One seen 25 April 1978 near Franklin (Boyd Gill). One reported from Mary Gray Bird Sanctuary, 16 January 1978. (*fide* H. C. West). There are also recent sightings in Monroe and Vanderburgh counties.

REMARKS: Species is spreading east and beginning to nest, apparently competing successfully with the House Sparrow. It seems only a question of time before nesting will occur within the State.

Pine Grosbeak
Pinicola enucleator

FORMER STATUS: "Irregular or accidental winter visitor" (Butler, 1898).
CURRENT STATUS: North Irregular casual winter visitor. 20 November–1 March. Most data for counties bordering Lake Michigan. Was observed at a feeder in Tippecanoe Co. by D. Arvin during early December 1977. Central Irregular casual winter visitor. Reported for Marion Co. during December 1965 (Keller, 1967a). South No data.

Hoary Redpoll
Carduelis hornemanni

STATUS: North Irregular casual winter visitor. One collected by H. L. Stoddard in Porter Co. 23 December 1916 (Stoddard, 1917). Three collected in LaPorte Co. 26 February 1972 by Easterla (Mumford and Keller, 1975). The authors banded three in LaPorte Co. 19 February 1978. Central One seen at feeder near Indianapolis 12 April 1978 by the authors. There are at least two other Marion Co. records for that year. South No data.

Common Redpoll
Carduelis flammea

FORMER STATUS: Irregular winter visitor (Butler, 1898).
CURRENT STATUS: North Irregular rare winter visitor. 15 November–1 March. Robert Krol noted them at his feeder in Lake Co. 6 January–31 March 1974. Central Irregular very rare winter visitor. 20 November–1 March. South A recent report of several birds seen in Gibson Co. during February 1978 (*fide* C. Mills).
REMARKS: During the winter of 1977–78, unprecedented numbers invaded Indiana, with an estimated flock of some 3–4,000 in LaPorte Co.

§ Pine Siskin
Carduelis pinus

FORMER STATUS: "More or less regular winter migrant, and rare winter resident" (Butler, 1898).
CURRENT STATUS: North Irregular rare to abundant migrant and winter visitant. Accidental summer resident. Nests found in Lake and Tippe-

canoe counties during the spring of 1978. 25 September–15 May. Central Irregular rare to abundant migrant and winter visitant. Accidental summer resident. Adult feeding young in Marion Co. during the spring of 1978 (*fide* Al Starling). 1 October–10 May. South Irregular rare to fairly common migrant and winter visitant. 5 October–5 May.

§ American Goldfinch
Carduelis tristis

FORMER STATUS: "Resident; rare some winters, northward" (Butler, 1898).

CURRENT STATUS: North Abundant summer resident; fairly common during the winter at thistle feeders. Central Abundant summer resident; abundant during the winter at thistle feeders. South Abundant summer resident; abundant during the winter at thistle feeders.

REMARKS: The use of thistle feeders has markedly increased the numbers of winter residents.

Red Crossbill
Loxia curvirostra

FORMER STATUS: "A very erratic bird. When found is generally noted as a winter visitor or migrant in flocks; less common in southern Indiana; some winters wholly wanting" (Butler, 1898).

CURRENT STATUS: North Irregular rare to uncommon winter visitor and migrant. 25 September–15 April. There are a few summer records. Central Irregular very rare to rare winter visitor and migrant. 25 September–10 April. A pair constructed a nest and laid one egg before abandoning it in Wayne Co. (Cope *fide* Mumford). South Casual winter visitor (and migrant?). Three seen 31 December 1977 in Gibson Co. by Alan Bruner.

White-winged Crossbill
Loxia leucoptera

FORMER STATUS: "These Crossbills are more rare than the preceding species, but their visits are of the same irregular character" (Butler, 1898). West (1955) summarized the existing data for the State.

CURRENT STATUS: North Irregular very rare winter visitor and migrant. 1 October–1 March. Two recent records: 24 November 1977 at Dunes State Park (K. Brock), and 4 December 1977 in Tippecanoe Co. (Arvin).

Central Irregular very rare winter visitor and migrant. Date spans uncertain. In Clay Co. Litha Smith found a flock of 16–20 birds 9 October 1973. Has been seen at Eagle Creek Park on several occasions recently. As many as 14 observed in Indianapolis during January 1978 (Hood *fide* Tabbert). **South** Reported to have been seen in Vanderburgh Co. during December 1977.

Green-tailed Towhee
Pipilo chlorurus

STATUS: Accidental. One record: 19 April–2 May 1973, St. Joseph Co., South Bend, first seen by Mr. and Mrs. Russell S. Dufendach and thereafter by many observers.

§ Rufous-sided Towhee
Pipilo erythrophthalmus

FORMER STATUS: Common resident in southern Indiana (Butler, 1898).

CURRENT STATUS: **North** Common summer resident; very rare in winter. 1 March–20 November. Dorthy Buck found one 15 January 1976 in LaPorte Co. **Central** Common summer resident; rare in winter. 25 February–25 March. **South** Common summer resident; uncommon in winter.

Lark Bunting
Calamospiza melanocorys

FORMER STATUS: Hypothetical. Based on three records: one male near Indianapolis 30 April 1950 (*Ind. Audu. Yearbook* 28:63–64); one 10 May 1950 near Morristown, Shelby Co. (Mumford and Keller, 1975); and one reported from Michigan City 18 April 1956 by Landing (*Ind. Audu. Quarterly* 40:15–16).

CURRENT STATUS: Accidental. One seen by Ken Brock, Peter Grube, et al. 7 June 1978 near Willow Slough was photographed the following day by Michael Brown and Tim Keller.

§ Savannah Sparrow
Passerculus sandwichensis

FORMER STATUS: Rare resident (Butler, 1898).

CURRENT STATUS: **North** Fairly common migrant; uncommon summer resident; casual in winter. 25 March–1 October. **Central** Fairly common migrant; rare summer resident; casual in winter. May nest as far south as Monroe Co., where Steve Glass found two, 4 June 1976, at the airport. 20 March–5 October. **South** Uncommon migrant; rare in winter. Date spans uncertain but probably similar to above. Two of the authors (C.E.K.–S.K.) observed a flock of 20 in Gibson Co., 31 December 1977. They may prove to be uncommon winter visitants in this area.

§ Grasshopper Sparrow
Ammodramus savannarum

FORMER STATUS: Common summer resident (Butler, 1898).

CURRENT STATUS: **North** Fairly common summer resident. 25 April–15 September. **Central** Fairly common summer resident; casual in winter. 20 April–20 September. One taken in Marion Co. 4 December 1927 (*fide* Mumford). **South** Status unknown except for some very old records which suggest it is similar to the above. There is a large summer population near the Gibson Co. Power Plant (*fide* Charles Mills).

§ Henslow's Sparrow
Ammodramus henslowii

FORMER STATUS: Breeds in northern Indiana; no records for southern Indiana (Butler, 1898).

CURRENT STATUS: **North** Locally uncommon summer resident. Casual in winter. One seen, 22 December 1963 in LaPorte Co. 25 April–1 September. Found in Lagrange Co. by Casebere and Weldon 14 June–25 July 1975 and in Starke Co. by Casebere, 25 June 1975. **Central** Locally uncommon summer resident; casual in winter. One collected in Jackson Co. 24 December 1933. Breeds in Johnson Co. (Atterbury) and at least as far south as Monroe Co. **South** Status unknown.

LeConte's Sparrow
Ammospiza leconteii

FORMER STATUS: Rare migrant (Butler, 1898).

CURRENT STATUS: **North** Very rare migrant. Data sparse but main migratory peaks seem to be during the first week in April and, in the fall, the middle of October. We have seen it at Willow Slough in October and Neil Cutright found one at Dunes State Park 16 October 1976. **Central** Very rare migrant. Alan Bruner has consistently found this species at Lake Waveland in Montgomery Co. during October and Tim Keller banded one there in April 1977 (photographed). **South** Very rare migrant; casual in winter. Three were collected in Posey Co. 1 January 1955 and Charles Mills found 3 in Gibson Co. 22 February 1976. Jackie and Diane Elmore found one 17 October 1976 at Hardy Lake.

Sharp-tailed Sparrow
Ammospiza caudacuta

FORMER STATUS: "Migrant and possibly a summer resident locally in the northwestern part of the State where, only, it has been observed within our limits" (Butler, 1898).

CURRENT STATUS: **North** Very rare migrant; possibly a casual summer resident. One specimen taken 27 May 1922 (Eifrig, 1923). More often seen in the fall when data suggests the peak is mid-October. **Central** Very rare migrant. More often seen in the fall when data suggests the peak is in October. Alan Bruner found as many as seven 4 October 1975 at Lake Waveland. **South** Casual migrant. N. Stocks found two in Warrick Co. 7 October 1973.

REMARKS: Probably more common than these records indicate, but overlooked due to species' secretive habits.

§ Vesper Sparrow
Pooecetes gramineus

FORMER STATUS: Common, winters in southern Indiana (Butler, 1898).

CURRENT STATUS: **North** Fairly common summer resident; very rare in winter. 5 April–15 October. One noted by Jim Williams 22 December 1973 in Allen Co. **Central** Fairly common summer resident; very rare in winter. 1 April–20 October. **South** Uncommon summer resident; very rare in winter. 25 March–1 November.

§ Lark Sparrow
Chondestes grammacus

FORMER STATUS: "In Indiana it is most numerous through the central part of the State. It was rather rare until recently in southern Indiana, and is still scarce in many localities northward. Everywhere it is apparently becoming more numerous" (Butler, 1898).

CURRENT STATUS: **North** Locally very rare summer resident. Date spans uncertain. Has recently been found near Willow Slough in late spring by Tim Keller. **Central** Locally very rare summer resident. Date spans uncertain. A pair was found in Jennings Co. by Steve Glass 26 June 1976. Has been observed in Owen Co. and nests were found in Monroe Co. in 1970 (Frazier, 1971). **South** Locally uncommon summer resident. Date spans uncertain. Charles Mills observed this species in Pike Co. during the last 5 years. Tim Keller observed young during the summer of 1977 in this area.

§ Bachman's Sparrow
Aimophila aestivalis

FORMER STATUS: "Summer resident in the southwestern quarter of the State, usually not common" (Butler, 1898).
CURRENT STATUS: **North** Possibly a casual summer resident. Date spans uncertain. Burr found two in Tippecanoe Co. 25 May 1963 (Burr, 1964). **Central** Very rare local summer resident. Date spans uncertain. Nested at Mary Gray Bird Sanctuary during the early 1950s. Nests were also found in Monroe Co. and the species has been seen in Owen and Marion counties. **South** Possibly a very rare local summer resident. Michael Brown found one in Orange Co. 10 August 1976, and Charles Mills believes the species may occur in the Pike–Gibson Co. area.
REMARKS: The lack of recent data suggests a decline in abundance.

Northern Junco
Junco hyemalis

FORMER STATUS: Butler (1898) intimated that it was common.
CURRENT STATUS: **North** Abundant migrant and winter resident. 25 September–20 April. **Central** Abundant migrant and winter resident. 1 October–10 April. **South** Abundant migrant and winter resident. 5 October–5 April.
REMARKS: Interbreeding of Northern Junco and Oregon-type birds is known to occur. Intermediates are uncommon to rare in all regions.

American Tree Sparrow
Spizella arborea

FORMER STATUS: Common winter visitant (Butler, 1898).
CURRENT STATUS: **North** Common migrant and winter visitant. 20 November–20 April. Veteran observers Lee Casebere and Neil Cutright have recorded this species as late as 14 May 1973 in Steuben Co. (Casebere) and 12 May 1975 in Porter Co. (Cutright). These are very late

records and not the normal terminal dates for this species. **Central** Common migrant and winter visitant. 25 November–15 April. **South** Common migrant and winter visitant. 1 December–5 April.

§ **Chipping Sparrow**
Spizella passerina

FORMER STATUS: Butler (1898) intimated that this species was common.

CURRENT STATUS: **North** Common migrant and summer resident. 20 April–1 November. Jim Haw found one 20 November 1976 in Allen Co. Dorthy Buck found young in the nest 2 September 1973 in LaPorte Co. **Central** Common migrant and summer resident. 15 April–1 November. **South** Common migrant and summer resident. 10 April–5 November.

REMARKS: There are some winter records for this species, particularly for southern Indiana, but wintering has never been satisfactorily proved.

Clay-colored Sparrow
Spizella pallida

FORMER STATUS: "Rare migrant; possibly locally rare summer resident" (Butler, 1898).

CURRENT STATUS: **North** Casual migrant. Date spans uncertain. It was collected in Porter Co. 25 May 1919 (Stoddard, 1921) and Dune Park, Porter Co. 11 May 1924 (Ford, 1956). Other data include: 2 May 1959; 26 October 1958 (Landing); 10 May 1961 (V. Reuterskiold)—all in Porter Co. **Central** Casual migrant. One found in Clay Co. 3 April 1950 (Wright and Marks, 1951). One seen 13 May 1951 by the senior author in Marion Co. **South** No data.

REMARKS: Species probably occurs more frequently than the above few records indicate. Fall birds are very difficult to identify—great care should be exercised in separating them from the more common *S. passerina* to which it bears a close resemblance.

§ **Field Sparrow**
Spizella pusilla

FORMER STATUS: ". . . more numerous than the Chipping Sparrow. . . . Occasionally, at least, it winters in the Wabash Valley, from Knox County, southward" (Butler, 1898).

CURRENT STATUS: **North** Abundant migrant and summer resident; very rare in winter. 1 April–15 November. Robert Krol photographed one at his feeder in Lake Co. 6 January 1974. **Central** Abundant migrant and summer resident; rare in winter. 25 March–30 November. **South** Abundant migrant and summer resident; uncommon to fairly common in the winter.

Harris' Sparrow
Zonotrichia querula

FORMER STATUS: Listed as hypothetical by Butler (1898).

CURRENT STATUS: **North** Very rare migrant; casual in winter. Date spans uncertain. Recent data includes: Allen Co., 27 April 1974 (B. Paxson); Tippecanoe Co., 14 October 1974 (Ed Hopkins); 4–14 February 1973 (V. Inman *fide* N. Rea). **Central** Very rare migrant; casual in winter. The senior author found one 25 December 1950 at Eagle Creek Forest Reserve (now Eagle Creek Park) in Marion Co. Other records include: Brownsburg, 5 March 1949 (*Ind. Audu. Quarterly* 28:48); 13 May 1967 in Montgomery Co. (Luther, 1970); 10 November 1956 in Madison Co. (Fred Miller); 10 October 1978 in Marion Co. (Jo Davidson, Sue Owens, T.K.). **South** Casual migrant and winter resident. One at Hovey Lake 27 December 1953 (*Ind. Audu Quarterly* 32:47). One was found near Hanover by J. D. Webster during the winter of 1975 (Webster, 1976).

White-crowned Sparrow
Zonotrichia leucophrys

FORMER STATUS: "Common migrant; occasional winter resident southward" (Butler, 1898).

CURRENT STATUS: **North** Fairly common migrant; rare in winter. One was reported from 17 July–21 August 1967 in LaPorte Co. 10 September–20 May. **Central** Fairly common migrant and winter resident. 15 September–15 May. **South** Fairly common migrant and winter resident. 20 September–10 May.

White-throated Sparrow
Zonotrichia albicollis

FORMER STATUS: Very abundant migrant; no winter data (Butler, 1898).

CURRENT STATUS: **North** Abundant migrant; very rare in winter. 25 April–25 May; 1 October–15 November. Arvin noted one during the winter of 1974–75 in Tippecanoe Co. and Annette Schaff found one in LaPorte Co. 4 February 1976. **Central** Abundant migrant; rare in winter. 5 October–20 May. **South** Abundant migrant; uncommon in winter. 10 October–15 May.

Fox Sparrow
Passerella iliaca

FORMER STATUS: Common migrant and winter resident in the southern part of the State (Butler, 1898).
CURRENT STATUS: **North** Fairly common migrant; very rare in winter. 15 March–1 May. Interestingly, there are two June reports: 28 June 1975, Porter Co. (breeding bird census) and 12 June 1976, Indiana Dunes, where one was observed "feeding a cowbird." If true, this last record is most unusual; this is considerably south of its normal breeding range. 5 October–1 December. **Central** Fairly common migrant; very rare in winter. 10 March–20 April; 10 October–5 December. **South** Fairly common migrant; rare in winter. 15 October–15 April.

Lincoln's Sparrow
Melospiza lincolnii

FORMER STATUS: Regular but rare migrant (Butler, 1898).
CURRENT STATUS: **North** Uncommon migrant; casual in winter. 1 May–25 May; 15 September–15 October. One seen during December 1946 near South Bend, St. Joseph Co. **Central** Uncommon migrant. 25 April–20 May; 20 September–25 October. **South** Uncommon migrant; casual in winter. 20 April–15 May; 25 September–1 November. There are several sight records during the winter that are open to some question.

§ Swamp Sparrow
Melospiza georgiana

FORMER STATUS: Regular migrant and abundant summer resident (Butler, 1898).
CURRENT STATUS: **North** Common migrant; uncommon summer resident; casual in winter. 1 April–1 November. **Central** Common migrant; rare summer resident; rare in winter. 25 March–10 November. **South** Common migrant; summer status unknown; rare in winter. 20 March–15 November.

§ **Song Sparrow**
Melospiza melodia

FORMER STATUS: Resident, rare in southwestern Indiana (Butler, 1898).

CURRENT STATUS: Abundant resident. Some migrants move into the State in November and return again in March.

Lapland Longspur
Calcarius lapponicus

FORMER STATUS: Irregular winter visitor (Butler, 1898).

CURRENT STATUS: **North** Irregular uncommon to common winter visitant and migrant (occasionally abundant). 15 October–25 March. **Central** Irregular rare to uncommon winter visitant and migrant. 20 October–20 March. **South** Irregular rare to uncommon winter visitant and migrant. 25 October–15 March (abundant, at times, in Gibson Co.–*fide* C. Mills).

Smith's Longspur
Calcarius pictus

FORMER STATUS: "Migrant; sometimes common in the vicinity of Lake Michigan, of unusual occurrence elsewhere; rare" (Butler, 1898).

CURRENT STATUS: **North** Uncommon spring migrant in Newton Co. 30 March–20 April; no fall data. Small flocks of 5–20 birds can be found feeding in freshly plowed fields or among the emerging winter wheat. **Central** Casual during winter. One record: one seen by H. C. West and R. and W. Buskirk in Hamilton Co. 25 December 1961. **South** No data.

Snow Bunting
Plectrophenax nivalis

FORMER STATUS: Irregular winter visitant (Butler, 1898).

CURRENT STATUS: **North** Irregular rare to abundant migrant and winter visitor. 15 October–1 March. Tom and Sallie Potter found a flock of 550 in Tippecanoe Co. 24 January 1976. **Central** Irregular rare to very rare migrant and winter visitor. 20 October–25 February. Alan Bruner found a flock of 20 in Montgomery Co. 9 January 1976. **South** Irregular very rare migrant and winter visitor. 25 October–20 February. Donald Parker recorded a flock of 15 in Harrison Co. 1 February 1976. Has been recorded in southwestern Gibson Co. (*fide* C. Mills).

Hypothetical and Exotic List

Order Pelecaniformes
Family Phalacrocoracidae: Cormorants

Great Cormorant
Phalacrocorax carbo

STATUS: Hypothetical. Henry West's 1958 analysis remains the same except for an additional queried account by Landing (1962) who stated that he observed a bird at Michigan City, 3 November 1956, that was visibly larger than the surrounding Double-crested species.

Order Ciconiiformes
Family Threskiornithidae: Ibises and Spoonbills

White-faced Glossy Ibis
Plegadis chihi

STATUS: Hypothetical. A bird of this species seen 9 May 1977 at Indianapolis Sewage Disposal Plant, Marion Co., by Tim Keller (documented).

Family Phoenicopteridae: Flamingos

American Flamingo
Phoenicopterus ruber

STATUS: Exotic. One found dead at Hardy Lake (Austin), 1 October 1978 by Barnard Palmer-Ball Jr. et al. One leg and several feathers kept. This probably was an escapee from a zoo or private aviary.

197

Order Falconiformes
Family Falconidae: Falcons

Prairie Falcon
Falco mexicanus

STATUS: Hypothetical. Based on a queried account in Ford (1956) of one seen in the Calumet region (Illinois/Indiana). This record probably does not even deserve this status. Another reported to have been seen west of Terre Haute in late December 1931 by Dr. Allyn (Esten, 1933).

Order Galliformes
Family Tetraonidae: Grouse and Ptarmigan

Sharp-tailed Grouse
Pedioecetes phasianellus

STATUS: Hypothetical. Ford (1956) presented data of a bird supposedly seen in Porter Co. in April 1915.

Order Charadriiformes
Family Recurvirostridae: Stilts and Avocets

Black-necked Stilt
Himantopus mexicanus

FORMER STATUS: Listed by both Butler (1898) and Keller (1957) as hypothetical.
CURRENT STATUS: Hypothetical. A recent record for Kentucky.

Family Charadriidae: Plovers

Snowy Plover
Charadrius alexandrinus

STATUS: Hypothetical. In Keller (1957) this bird was listed on the basis of a reply received by him from the Chicago Museum of Natural History which considered the data correct even though the specimen of the bird could not be found. Subsequent investigation of Butler's personal correspondence (unpublished) turned up the following letter written by Colin C. Sanborn to Dr. Butler, dated 30 November 1934: "The Cuban Snowy Plover record was not published because Stoddard thought there might be some doubt about the data. Brandler, who collected the bird in 1887, supplied the data in 1917 and was not too sure of it."

Family Laridae: Gulls and Terns

Gull-billed Tern
Gelochelidon nilotica

STATUS: Hypothetical. Listed by Nelson (1876) as a rare summer visitor in northeastern Illinois–northwestern Indiana. Much of Nelson's data is suspect.

Royal Tern
Sterna maximus

STATUS: Hypothetical. Listed by Kennicott (1854) and Nelson (1876) as occurring in northwestern Indiana.

Family Rynchopidae: Skimmers

Black Skimmer
Rynchops niger

STATUS: Hypothetical. A report of an observation of one bird at Miller, 23 August 1913 (Craigmile, 1935). This same record was cited in Ford (1956) and Smith (1972). It probably does not even deserve the present status.

Order Columbiformes
Family Columbidae: Pigeons and Doves

Ringed Turtle Dove
Streptopelia risoria

STATUS: Exotic. Found near Munster from 12 November 1974–November 1977 at feeding station (R. Krol). One seen at South Bend, 18 April–20 April 1976, by Phillip Wagner et al.

Order Psittaciformes
Family Psittacidae: Parrots

Monk Parakeet
Myiopsitta monachus

STATUS: Exotic. Recorded from Madison, Marion, Montgomery, and Lake counties. Nesting attempted in the first two named counties.

Order Cuculiformes
Family Cuculidae: Cuckoos, Roadrunners, and Anis

Smooth-billed Ani
Crotophaga ani

STATUS: Hypothetical. One seen at Michigan City by Landing and Scott Rea, 27 October and 23 November 1956 (Burr, 1958).

Order Strigiformes
Family Strigidae: Typical Owls

Hawk Owl
Sturnia ulula

FORMER STATUS: Butler (1898) called it an accidental visitor on the basis of a single observation in Franklin Co. during January 1878 by a Mr. E. R. Quick.
CURRENT STATUS: Hypothetical. We do not accept the above record. One seen 7 February 1965 at Michigan City by James Landing (Burr, 1966) does not meet the acceptance criteria.

Order Passeriformes
Family Tyrannidae: Tyrant Flycatchers

Say's Phoebe
Sayornis saya

FORMER STATUS: Butler (1898) listed it as hypothetical because of its occurrence in nearby states. One was reported from Porter Co. 4 April 1937 (Pitelka, 1938).
CURRENT STATUS: Hypothetical.

Family Sittidae: Nuthatches

Brown-headed Nuthatch
Sitta pusilla

STATUS: Hypothetical. Based on a sight record in northern Indiana near Whiting, Lake Co., 6 April 1932 (Smith, 1936).

Family Parulidae: Wood Warblers

Swainson's Warbler
Limnothlypis swainsonii

STATUS: Hypothetical. Butler (1898) cited Ridgway's data that it bred in Knox Co. in 1878. There have been at least four sight records which do not meet the acceptance criteria.

Family Thraupidae: Tanagers

Western Tanager
Piranga ludoviciana

STATUS: Hypothetical. Three records, none of which meet the acceptance criteria: 4 August 1960 (W. Buskirk–B. Fall) and 30 August 1960 (Mrs. W. Morlan), both in Marion Co. (Keller, 1961); and a recent record of 7 May 1977 by Joy Underborn in northwestern Indiana (Heller, 1977).

Family Fringillidae: Grosbeaks, Finches, Sparrows, and Buntings

McCown's Longspur
Calcarius mccownii

STATUS: Hypothetical. One seen by Carmony and Braittain, 2 January 1971 in Tippecanoe Co. (Masons, 1971). The above record does not meet the acceptance criteria.

Literature Cited

Audubon, J. J. (1840–1844) *The birds of America.* Dover Reprint Edition, 1967. 7 vols.

Baczkowski, F. (1955) Whooping Cranes in Porter County 50 years ago. *Indiana Audubon Quarterly* 33:43–44.

Banta, E. (1953) Saw-whet Owl at the sanctuary and report of its status in Indiana. Ibid. 31:62–66.

Barnes, W. B. (1952) Prairie Chicken booming grounds in Indiana. Ibid. 30:7–9.

———— (1971) Sixteen Cattle Egrets in Greene County, Indiana. Ibid. 49:68.

Bartel, K. E. (1948) Scissor-tailed Flycatcher in the Chicago area. *Auk* 65:614.

Baumgartner, F. M. (1931) A list of the birds seen in Marion County. *Proceedings of the Indiana Academy of Science* 40:295–306.

Blatchley, W. B. (1907) The Brown Pelican in Indiana. *Auk* 24:337.

Branham, J. F. (1958) The spread of the Starling in Indiana. *Indiana Audubon Quarterly* 36:92–95.

Brock, K. J. (1977) Purple Sandpiper: A spring record. Ibid. 55:89.

———— (in press) Bird life of the Michigan City Harbor area. Ibid.

Brodkorb, P. (1926) The season: Chicago region. *Bird-Lore* 28:347–348.

Burr, I. W. (1955) Regional report. *Indiana Audubon Quarterly* 33: 50–51.

———— (1956) Ibid. 34:65.

———— (1957*a*) Ibid. 35:28.

———— (1957*b*) Ibid. 35:50.

———— (1958) Ibid. 36:100–105.

———— (1959*a*) Ibid. 37:35.

———— (1959*b*) Ibid. 37:48.

———— (1960*a*) Ibid. 38:2–3.

———— (1960*b*) Ibid. 38:44–45.

———— (1961) Ibid. 39:63–67.

———— (1962) Ibid. 40:55.

———— (1964*a*) Ibid. 42:20–22.

———— (1964*b*) Ibid. 42:35.

———— (1965*a*) Ibid. 43:19.

———— (1965*b*) Ibid. 43:41.

———— (1966*a*) Ibid. 44:47.

———— (1966*b*) Ibid. 44:103.

Butler, A. W. (1890) A catalogue of the birds of Indiana. Appendix to *Transactions of the Indiana Horticultural Society* 15–16, 107.

——— (1898) *Birds of Indiana.* 22nd Annual Report, Indiana Department of Geology and Natural Resources. 515–1187.

——— (1900) Notes on Indiana birds. *Proceedings of the Indiana Academy of Sciences* 8:151.

——— (1906) Some notes on Indiana birds. *Auk* 23:273.

——— (1927) Some interesting Indiana bird records. *Proceedings of the Indiana Academy of Sciences* 36:481–489.

——— (1936) Black Vultures in Indiana. *Indiana Audubon Yearbook* 9:25–27.

——— (1937) Common Tern and Wilson's Phalarope nesting in northern Indiana. *Auk* 54:390.

Carpenter, F. S. (1964) Important observations from the Ohio River region. *Indiana Audubon Quarterly* 42:61.

Chansler, E. J. (1910) Magpie in Knox County, Indiana. *Auk* 27:210.

Cope, J. B. (1951) Pacific Loon in Indiana. *Wilson Bulletin* 63:41.

Cope, J. B., Grow, R., Mumford, R. E., and Nolan, V. (1952) Regional report plan. *Indiana Audubon Quarterly* 30:50–52.

Craigmile, E. A. (1935) Three rare records. *Audubon Annual Bulletin* 24–25:45–46.

DuMont, P. A. and Smith, E. T. (1946) Audubon field notes: Middlewestern region. *Audubon Magazine* 48:Sect. II, 7–8.

Eifrig, C. W. G. (1923) Nelson's Sparrow in Chicago. *Auk* 40:132.

——— (1927) Notes from the Chicago area. Ibid. 44:431–432.

Esten, S. (1933a) Checklist corrections and additions. *Indiana Audubon Yearbook,* 15.

——— (1933b) Barrow's Goldeneyed Duck in Marion County. Ibid. 71.

Ford, E. R. (1956) Birds of the Chicago region. *Chicago Academy of Sciences Special Publication No. 12,* 1–112.

Frazier, H. (1971) Lark Sparrow nests in Monroe County in 1970. *Indiana Audubon Quarterly* 49:92–93.

Grow, R. (1954) Regional report. Ibid. 32:12–15.

Heller, D. (1977) The May 1977 bird count. Ibid. 55:55–84.

Hine, A. (1924) Burrowing Owl in northern Indiana. *Auk* 41:602.

Howell, D. and Thiroff, E. (1976) Scissor-tailed Flycatcher breeding in southwestern Indiana. Ibid. 93:644–645.

Kennicott, R. (1854) Catalogue of animals observed in Cook County, Illinois. *Illinois State Agricultural Society, Transactions for 1853–54* 1:580–589.

Keller, C. E. (1946) Bacon's Swamp notes. *Indiana Audubon Yearbook* 24:42–43.

——— (1957a) The Shorebird families: Charadriidae, Scolopacidae, Recurvirostridae, and Phalaropidae of Indiana. Part 1. *Indiana Audubon Quarterly* 35:30–48.

——— (1957b) The Shorebird families: Charadriidae, Scolopacidae, Recurvirostridae, and Phalaropidae of Indiana. Parts 2–3. Ibid. 35: 54–60.

——— (1958) The Shorebird families: Charadriidae, Scolopacidae, Recurvirostridae, and Phalaropidae of Indiana. Part 4. Ibid. 36:2–39.

——— (1959) Regional report. Ibid. 37:31.

——— (1961a) Ibid. 39:38.

——— (1961b) Ibid. 39:73.

——— (1962) Ibid. 40:42–43.

——— (1966) Status of the Ciconiiformes in Indiana. Ibid. 44:56–86.

——— (1967a) Regional report. Ibid. 45:23.

——— (1967b) Fifth annual May count. Ibid. 45:85.

——— (1972) Shorebird migration at the Indianapolis Sewage Disposal Plant. Ibid. 50:124–135.

Keller, C. E., Keller, S. A., and Keller, T. C. (1976) House Finch in central Indiana: An addition to the avifauna of Indiana. Ibid. 54:108.

Kirkpatrick, C. M. (1942) Western Burrowing Owl in Indiana. *Wilson Bulletin* 54:211–212.

——— (1948) Gannet in eastern Indiana. Ibid. 60:240.

Kleen, V. (1973) Middlewestern prairie region. *American Birds* 27:874–878.

——— (1977) Ibid. 31:182–186.

Landing, J. (1962) Exotic bird records for Michigan City, LaPorte County, Indiana. *Indiana Audubon Quarterly* 40:15–16.

——— (1966) Jaeger migration in northwestern Indiana. Ibid. 44:32–37.

Luther, D. (1970) Harris' Sparrow in Montgomery County. Ibid. 48:136.

——— (1973) A report of an Osprey nest in Parke County. Ibid. 51:23.

——— (1976) Annotated listing of warblers that have nested, or may nest, in the Shades State Park area. Ibid. 54:75–82.

Marks, C. F. and Wright, H. F. (1951) The 1951 spring migration. Ibid. 29:66–71.

Mason, J. and Mason, A. (1971) The 1970 Christmas count. Ibid. 49: 4–14.

——— (1976) The 1975 Christmas bird count. Ibid. 54:20–28.

McKeever, O. D. (1943) The status of the Prairie Chicken in Indiana. *Indiana Audubon Yearbook,* 29–34.

Mengel, R. M. (1965) *The birds of Kentucky.* Ornithological Monographs No. 3, American Ornithologists' Union, 581 pp.

Mumford, R. E. (1953*a*) Regional report. *Indiana Audubon Quarterly* 31:80.

—— (1953*b*) White-rumped Sandpiper in Indiana. *Wilson Bulletin* 65:44–45.

—— (1954) *Waterfowl management in Indiana.* Indiana Department of Conservation. Pittman-Robertson Bulletin #2, 99 pp.

—— (1960) Middlewestern prairie region. *Audubon Field Notes* 14: 38–41.

—— (1961) Ibid. 15:332–334.

—— (1966*a*) A Ross's Goose in Indiana. *Indiana Audubon Quarterly* 44:114.

—— (1966*b*) Some 1965 summer bird records for Indiana. Ibid. 44: 98–100.

—— (1976) Nesting of the Long-eared Owl in Indiana. Ibid. 54: 95–97.

Mumford, R. E. and Keller, C. E. (1975) An annotated checklist of Indiana birds. Ibid. 53:28–63.

Mumford, R. E. and Lehmen, L. E. (1969) Glossy Ibis taken in Indiana. *Wilson Bulletin* 81:463–464.

Mumford, R. E. and Rowe, W. S. (1963) The Lesser Black-backed Gull in Indiana. Ibid. 75:93.

Mumford, R. E. and Weeks, H. P. (1977) Summer records of the Black Rail in Indiana. *Indiana Audubon Quarterly* 55:1–2.

Mumford, R. E. and Whitaker, J. O. (1974) Black Vulture nesting in Crawford County, Indiana. Ibid. 52:67–69.

Nolan, V. (1958) Middlewestern prairie region. *Audubon Field Notes* 12:415–417.

Oswalt, R. and Wilson, L. (1969) The seasonal summary: Spring 1968. *Indiana Audubon Quarterly* 47:18.

—— (1970) The seasonal summary: Fall 1969. Ibid. 48:63–71.

Petersen, P. (1967) Middlewestern prairie region. *Audubon Field Notes* 21:513.

Pitelka, F. A. (1938) Say's Phoebe in northern Indiana. *Auk* 55:280–281.

Price, H. F. (1938) Short-eared Owl nests in Allen County. *Indiana Audubon Yearbook,* 99.

Russell, R. (1973) The extirpation of the Piping Plover as a breeding species in Illinois and Indiana. *The Audubon Bulletin* Summer 1973: 46–48.

Schorger, A. W. (1964) The Trumpeter Swan as a breeding bird in Minnesota, Illinois, and Indiana. *Wilson Bulletin* 76:331–338.

Segal, S. (1954) Additional notes for Michigan City Harbor. *Indiana Audubon Quarterly* 32:9.

———— (1960) Bird tragedy at the Dunes. Ibid. 38:23–25.

Sharpe, R. B. (1885) *Catalogue of the Passeriformes or perching birds in the collection of the British Museum, etc.*, Vol. 10. London.

Smith, D. (1956) The 1955 Christmas count. *Indiana Audubon Quarterly* 34:31–38.

Smith, E. T. (1972) *Chicagoland birds—where and when to find them.* Field Museum of Natural History. 57 pp.

Smith, H. M. (1936) Notes on the birds of the Calumet and Dune regions. Mimeo, 40 pp.

Stoddard, H. L. (1917a) Rare winter visitants in northern Indiana. *Auk* 34:487.

———— (1917b) The Roseate Tern (*Sterna dougalli*) on Lake Michigan. Ibid. 34:86.

———— (1921) Rare birds in the Indiana Sand dunes. Ibid. 38:124.

Tompkins, D. M. (1975) A Black-and-white Warbler winters in Marion County. *Indiana Audubon Quarterly* 53:16–17.

Ward, G. (1957) The Christmas count. Ibid. 35:19–26.

Webster, J. D. (1976) Twenty-ninth winter bird population study. *American Birds* 30:1056–1057.

Weeks, H. P. (1976) Breeding of the Yellow-crowned Night Heron in Indiana. *Indiana Audubon Quarterly* 54:83–86.

West, H. C. (1954) A wintering Sanderling in Lake County, Indiana. Ibid. 32:62.

———— (1955) The status of the White-winged Crossbill in Indiana. Ibid. 33:22–25.

———— (1956) The status of the Grebe family in Indiana. Ibid. 34:42–55.

———— (1958) The order Pelicaniformes in Indiana. Ibid. 36:66–84.

Wilson, L. (1971) Big spring count 1971. Ibid. 49:89–90.

———— (1972) Big May count 1972. Ibid. 50:94.

Woodruff, F. M. (1907) The birds of the Chicago area. Natural History Survey, Bull. No. VI, Chicago Academy of Sciences. 221 pp.

Wright, H. F. (1950) Focusing on fall migrants. *Indiana Audubon Quarterly* 28:14–24.

Wright, H. F. and Marks, C. (1951) Spring flight. Ibid. 29:76.

Appendix: Birding Organizations in Indiana

One of the better ways of increasing your interest and/or knowledge about birds is to join your nearest Audubon Society or birding organization. Most of these are affiliated with the National Audubon Society and joint membership is available; in some cases, a separate membership can be obtained. These include:

Amos W. Butler Audubon Society, 3650 Cold Spring Road, Indianapolis, Indiana 46222.

Dunes–Calumet Audubon Society, P.O. Box 1722, Gary, Indiana 46403.

East Central Audubon Society, 711 University Avenue, Muncie, Indiana 47303.

Evansville Audubon Society, 551 North Boeke Road, Evansville, Indiana 47711.

Illiana Cypress Audubon Society, 703 Church Street, Vincennes, Indiana 47591.

Indiana Audubon Society, 141 South Second Street, Decatur, Indiana 46733. Serves the entire state and maintains the Mary Gray Bird Sanctuary near Connersville. Through its publications, *The Cardinal* and *The Indiana Audubon Quarterly*, it keeps the birder up to date on all the latest sightings.

Northwestern Indiana Bird Club, 1265 Redbud, Chesterton, Indiana 46304.

Sassafras Audubon Society, R.R. #3, Box 36, Nashville, Indiana 47448.

South Bend Audubon Society, P.O. Box 581, Mishawaka, Indiana 46544.

Stockbridge Audubon Society, 1213 West Wayne Street, Fort Wayne, Indiana 46804.

Sycamore Audubon Society, P.O. Box 2514, West Lafayette, Indiana 47906.

Tippecanoe Audubon Society, R.R. #7, Box 73, Warsaw, Indiana 46580.

Wabash Valley Audubon Society, P.O. Box 2161, Terre Haute, Indiana 47802.

Whitewater Valley Audubon Society, 801 Elks Road, Richmond, Indiana 47374.

Index

Bold-face numbers next to a species' name refer to its appearance in the Finding Guide.